African Bargainin

This book provides a detailed account of the political economy around investment deal negotiations between African governments and private Chinese investors.

The book draws on evidence from experiments and hundreds of interviews with policy makers and Chinese investors across Nigeria, South Africa, Kenya, Ethiopia and Tanzania. It shows that governments of authoritarian or one-party dominant states, which are among the top-receivers of Chinese investments, are able to easily and successfully act collectively to impose human capital and technology transfer requirements. The book argues that, rather than treating African countries as "price-takers" in the face of increasing Chinese influence in the continent, we should instead recognize the significant bargaining leverage that many African governments have to influence deal conditions, especially with smaller private Chinese companies. It demonstrates that several African governments can instead act "as price-setters" and that the success of the rising Chinese presence in Africa, and whether this leads to positive or negative development outcomes, fundamentally depends on the development strategies that individual African governments decide on.

In the context of an often-polarized debate, the original research presented in this book has important implications for the future economic development strategies of African countries. As such, it will be of interest to researchers working on Chinese and African investment, politics, institutions, business, economics, and international relations.

Christina Seyfried completed her PhD at Yale University, USA.

African Governance

24. Managing Violent Religious Extremism in Fragile States
Building Institutional Capacity in Nigeria and Kenya
Abosede Omowumi Babatunde, Mahfouz A. Adedimeji, Shittu Raji, Jacinta Mwende Maweu and John Mwangi Githigaro

25. Colonial Legacies and the Rule of Law in Africa
Comparing Ghana, Kenya, Nigeria, South Africa, and Zimbabwe
Salmon A. Shomade

26. Governance and Inclusive Growth in the Africa Great Lakes Region
Progress, Problems, and Prospects
Paul Mulindwa

27. Contemporary Governance Challenges in the Horn of Africa
Edited by Charles Manga Fombad, Assefa Fiseha and Nico Steytler

28. Multidisciplinary Perspectives on Zimbabwe's Liberation Struggle
Revolutionaries and Sellouts
Edited by Munyaradzi Nyakudya, Joseph Mujere and Wesley Mwatwara

29. Nigeria's Fourth Republic, 1999–2021
A Militarized Democracy
Michael Nwankpa

30. African Bargaining Power with China
Foreign Investment and Rising Influence
Christina Seyfried

For more information about this series, please visit: https://www.routledge.com/Routledge-Contemporary-Africa/book-series/AFRGOV

African Bargaining Power with China

Foreign Investment and Rising Influence

Christina Seyfried

Routledge
Taylor & Francis Group

LONDON AND NEW YORK

First published 2023
by Routledge
4 Park Square, Milton Park, Abingdon, Oxon OX14 4RN

and by Routledge
605 Third Avenue, New York, NY 10158

Routledge is an imprint of the Taylor & Francis Group, an informa business

© 2023 Christina Seyfried

The right of Christina Seyfried to be identified as author of this work has been asserted in accordance with sections 77 and 78 of the Copyright, Designs and Patents Act 1988.

All rights reserved. No part of this book may be reprinted or reproduced or utilized in any form or by any electronic, mechanical, or other means, now known or hereafter invented, including photocopying and recording, or in any information storage or retrieval system, without permission in writing from the publishers.

Trademark notice: Product or corporate names may be trademarks or registered trademarks, and are used only for identification and explanation without intent to infringe.

British Library Cataloguing-in-Publication Data
A catalogue record for this book is available from the British Library

Library of Congress Cataloging-in-Publication Data
Names: Seyfried, Christina, author.
Title: African bargaining power with China : foreign investment and rising influence / Christina Seyfried.
Description: Abingdon, Oxon ; New York, NY : Routledge, 2023. | Series: African governance | Includes bibliographical references and index. | 9781032312491 (hbk) | ISBN 9781032312507 (pbk) | ISBN 9781003308768 (ebk)
Subjects: LCSH: Investments, Chinese--Africa. | Economic development projects--Africa.
Classification: LCC HG5822 .S45 2023 (print) | LCC HG5822 (ebook) | DDC 332.67/3096--dc23/eng/20220923
LC record available at https://lccn.loc.gov/2022027839
LC ebook record available at https://lccn.loc.gov/2022027840

ISBN: 978-1-032-31249-1 (hbk)
ISBN: 978-1-032-31250-7 (pbk)
ISBN: 978-1-003-30876-8 (ebk)

DOI: 10.4324/9781003308768

Typeset in Bembo
by SPi Technologies India Pvt Ltd (Straive)

Contents

List of Figures		vi
List of Tables		viii
1	African Bargaining Power: An Introduction	1
2	A New Theory on African Bargaining Power	27
3	An Empirical Assessment of the Relationship between Bargaining Power and Deal Quality	39
4	Bargaining Power and Deal Quality: Experimental Evidence from Nigeria	75
5	Perceptions of Bargaining Power	120
6	Information and Historical Frames around Bargaining Power	134
7	Information-Sharing Incentives around Bargaining Power	160
8	African Bargaining Power, Foreign Investment and Development: A Conclusion	186
	Appendix: Survey Material	201
	References	218
	Index	228

Figures

1.1	Comparison of US and Chinese Investment Stocks Over Time	3
1.2	Deal Quality Index	10
A1.1	GDP Per Capita in Africa vs. China	24
A1.2	Chinese FDI vs. US FDI to Africa, Flow	24
A1.3	Small and Medium Private Chinese Investment in Africa (number of projects)	25
3.1	Chinese Investment Stocks in Africa, 2017	45
3.2	Distribution of Small and Medium Private Chinese Enterprises in Africa	49
3.3	Actual and Predicted Chinese FDI Stocks for Countries with Aggressive Deals	50
3.4	Actual and Predicted Chinese FDI Stocks for Countries with Medium Investor-Friendly Deals	50
3.5	Actual and Predicted Chinese FDI Stocks for Countries with Very Investor-Friendly Deals	51
A3.1	The Top Investor Economies in Africa 2011 and 2016 (Billions of Dollars)	53
A3.2	US: Investment Stocks in Africa, 2012	53
A3.3	Chinese FDI vs. US FDI to Africa: Flow and Stocks	54
A3.4	Chinese Investment Stocks in Africa, 2015	55
A3.5	Distribution of Small and Medium Private Chinese Enterprises in Africa	56
A3.6	The 30 Low-Income Countries with the Most Debt to China	57
4.1	Investment Deal [Template]	83
4.2	Comparison between Question 1 (Government Responses) and Question 4 (Company Responses): Likelihood to Sign the Deal	90
4.3	Interaction Effects (ACIEs) between Ownership and Type of Respondent	91
4.4	Interaction Effects (ACIEs) between Employment and Type of Respondent	91
A4.1	Question 1 (Government Perceptions): Perceived Likelihood of Both Parties Signing the Deal (0–3)	101

A4.2	Question 2 (Government Perceptions): Will the Government Sign the Deal? (Y/N)	102
A4.3	Question 3 (Government Perceptions): Will The Company Sign the Deal? (Y/N)	103
A4.4	Question 4 (Company Responses): Likelihood to Sign the Deal (0–3)	104
A4.5	Differential Effect of Attribute on Chinese Respondents' Reports of Whether Company Would Sign	105
A4.6	Heterogeneous Effects by Type "Perceived Bargaining Power" (0 = low perceived bargaining power, 1= high perceived bargaining power)	106
A4.7	Heterogenous Effects by Type "Corrupt" (0 = not corrupt, 1 = corrupt)	107
A4.8	Heterogenous Effects by Type "Liberal Ideology" (0 = no liberal ideology, 1 = liberal ideology)	108
A4.9	Government Respondents – Heterogenous Effects Pre- vs. Post-Covid-19 Induced Lockdown (Question 1)	109
A4.10	Company Respondents – Heterogenous Effects Pre- vs. Post-Covid-19 Induced Lockdown (Question 4)	110
A4.11	Subgroup Results by Remaining Government Background Variables	111
A4.12	Subgroup Results by Company Background Variables	115
S1.1	Distribution of Chinese ODI Projects by Country and Sector	209

Tables

1.1	Actual and Perceived Bargaining Power	16
1.2	Number of Interviews Per Country	21
1.3	Position of Government Interviews Per Country	22
3.1	Correlations between Chinese Investment Stocks and Deal Quality	47
3.2	Correlation between Debt and Deal Quality	47
A3.1	Scoring	59
A3.2	Deal Quality Index and Sub-Indices	60
A3.3	Resource-Seeking Motivations of Chinese Investment	62
A3.4	Resource- and Market-Seeking Motivations of Foreign Investment	63
A3.5	Resource-, Market- and Efficiency-Seeking Motivations of Foreign Investment	63
A3.6	Economic and Political Motivations of Foreign Investment	64
A3.7	Resource-Seeking Motivations of Chinese Investment (Hot-Deck)	65
A3.8	Resource- and Market-Seeking Motivations of Foreign Investment (Hot-Deck)	66
A3.9	Resource-, Market- and Efficiency-Seeking Motivations of Foreign Investment (Hot-Deck)	66
A3.10	Economic and Political Motivations of Foreign Investment (Hot-Deck)	67
A3.11	Private Chinese FDI Stocks Rankings – Five Different Approaches	68
A3.12	Chinese FDI Stocks and Ease of Doing Business Index	71
A3.13	Chinese FDI Stocks and Global Competitiveness Index: Pillar 6.2 – Foreign Competition	71
A3.14	Correlation between Chinese Activity and Global Competitiveness Index: Pillar 6.2 – Foreign Competition	72
A3.15	Chinese FDI Stocks and Deal Quality Index	72
A3.16	Chinese FDI Stocks and Deal Quality Sub-Index 1: Converting and Transferring Currency	72
A3.17	Chinese FDI Stocks and Deal Quality Sub-Index 2: Starting a Foreign Business Across Sectors	73
A3.18	Chinese FDI Stocks and Deal Quality Sub-Index 3: Employing Skilled Expatriates	73

A3.19	Chinese FDI Stocks and Deal Quality Sub-Index 4: Arbitrating and Mediating Disputes	73
A3.20	Chinese FDI Stocks and Deal Quality Sub-Index 5: Taxes, Tariffs and Property Ownership	74
A3.21	Correlation between Bargaining Power and Deal Quality Index	74
4.1	Summary of Predictions of Each Mechanism	81
4.2	Set of Respondents and Total Number of Ratings	86
5.1	Background Characteristics	122
5.2	Actual and Perceived Bargaining Power – Case Selection	125

1 African Bargaining Power
An Introduction

1.1 Introduction

Imagine that four development experts sit at a round table and discuss how African countries could not only attract larger amounts of foreign investments, but also request more local benefits from investors for their economies. The first one to speak is a dependency theorist:

> The problem is that African countries are weaker members of a capitalist world order and are being structurally exploited by the West. No investments, skills or technology will come unless the stronger members of the Global North deliberately start to share them.

The second expert, a neoclassical economist, interrupts: "Investments, skills, and technology transfers will eventually flow in, but they can't be forced now. Countries need to continue to deregulate, privatize, and liberalize. They must make their countries more attractive to investors."

The third one, a poverty trap specialist, speaks up:

> No, the key issue really is that many countries in the African region have such weak institutions that even with reforms, no investor will want to come. And because there is no capital coming in, they can also not build stronger institutions. So, all that can really help us to break that cycle is foreign aid.

Finally, the fourth one – an experimentalist – concludes:

> That also means we first need to get rid of poverty that exists due to market imperfections and government failure. So, let's focus on identifying causes of poverty at the micro-level, estimate the effects of different policies, then evaluate their cost effectiveness and take it from there.

What the four experts have in common is that they all essentially portray the majority of African countries as price takers. Many are too poor to attract the significant amounts of foreign capital needed for growth, and resource endowments are also too similar to build competitive advantages. There are also simply too many endemic economic and political issues at the micro- and macro-level that need to be solved first in order to appeal to investors that are interested in high returns and political stability. So, many African governments ultimately have to agree to whatever deals potential trade and investment partners ask for if the region's goal is to attract foreign capital and develop.

This sentiment is also visible in the questions that scholars have asked about the relationship between Africa and China. For example, is China solely interested in oil and other natural resources? Will China trap African countries in debt? Is China only bringing in Chinese workers and exploiting the region? Or will Chinese companies in fact introduce manufacturing and develop Africa? This somewhat one-sided perspective of China's strategy implies that the African region is a rather passive unit that can essentially only be a price taker of global economic and political power dynamics. Many African countries can then, seemingly only through the goodwill of an external player, either stay behind or prosper.

Surprisingly then, we observe that some African countries with relatively low bargaining power – with bargaining power defined here by economic and political structural variables that are less replaceable by exit options for the investor – ask private Chinese investors to contribute more toward developing local content, and that Chinese investors tend to, in fact, accept these stricter deals (Figure 1.1).

For example, in 2008, Zimbabwean President Robert Mugabe signed the Indigenization and Economic Empowerment Act into law. The act required 51 percent control by locals in the major sectors of the economy and was first adopted in 2006 for the hydrocarbons sector and later expanded to all sectors. Similarly, against a massive outcry from Western and especially French investors, the Algerian government adopted 51 percent local ownership in all companies in its 2007 investment law reforms. These laws were blamed for Zimbabwe's and Algeria's inability to attract foreign investment. Indeed, Figure 1.1 shows that US investments significantly decreased in both countries after they had strengthened local participation requirements on foreign investments. Yet, interestingly, Chinese investment stocks in Zimbabwe have in fact dramatically increased since 2010, so after the regulations were set in place.

These developments are also visible in other countries around different types of policy shocks. For instance, the Ethiopian government developed its famous comprehensive industrial policy in 2002/03 and introduced local content requirements in manufacturing industries and limits on the employment of expatriates, where companies applying for investment permits must provide a time schedule for the replacement of foreign employees by Ethiopian employees in addition to training programs. As Figure 1.1 shows, US investment stocks in Ethiopia dropped while Chinese investment stocks heavily increased after 2002.

In Angola, US FDI stocks grew until 2011, when the government was about to enact a new foreign exchange law in 2012, requiring the petroleum industry to channel all payments through the local banking system, and later, in 2015, a new investment law that would raise taxes on early repatriation of profits and dividends for foreign companies and create disadvantages for foreign investors relative to domestic investors by imposing local partnership requirements for foreign investment in several key sectors (US Department of State Investment Climate Statements 2017). Chinese investment stocks, meanwhile, steadily increased.

In Madagascar, US investment stocks only picked up when the government introduced the Investment Law 2007-036, allowing foreign investors to hold up to 100 percent of shares of stock in the company in which they carry out their activities, except for in the telecommunication sector, where shares of the foreign companies could not exceed 66 percent. At the same time, Chinese investments have been growing at a fast rate in Madagascar since 2003.

Finally, in Tanzania, US investment stocks never picked up and have been stagnating since 2016, when the government began to encourage the hiring of Tanzanian citizens over foreigners, and to protect local industries. In particular, Tanzania enforces limits on expats, where companies are required to present a transition plan for training locals. In addition, the country has also increased tariffs

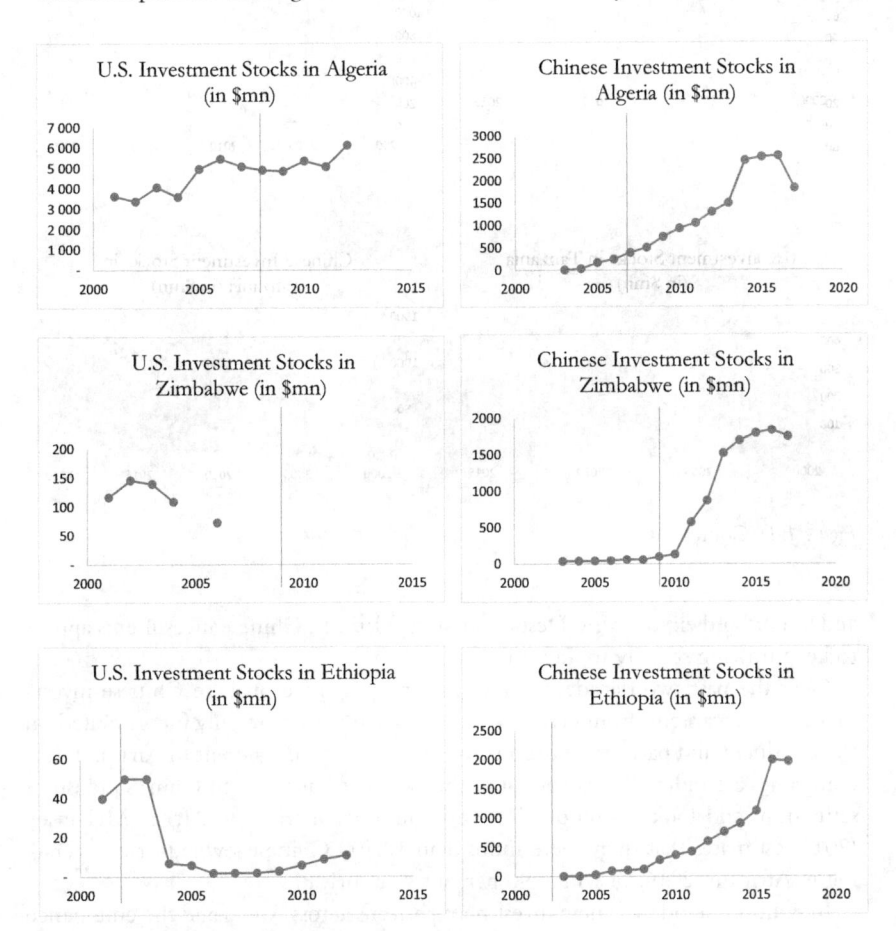

Figure 1.1 Comparison of US and Chinese Investment Stocks Over Time.

UNCTAD US Investment Statistics, CARI Investment Data. Please note that UNCTAD data on US Investments was only available until 2012, while CARI data on Chinese investments was available until 2017.

(Continued)

4 African Bargaining Power

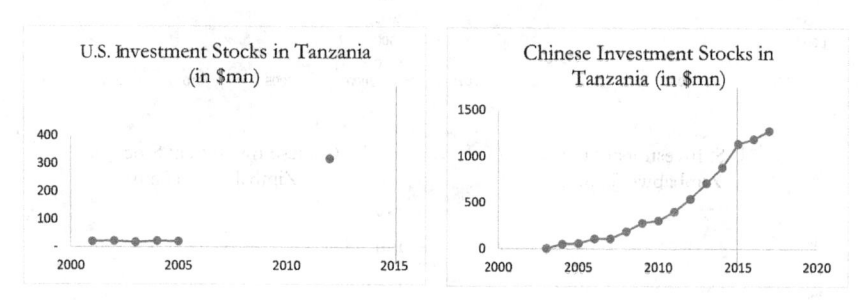

Figure 1.1 (Continued).

and import and export bans. Despite these regulations, Chinese investments appear to keep flowing steadily to Tanzania.

Over the past two decades, a rapidly increasing share of these Chinese investments in Africa stems from private Chinese investors that are only incorporated on the continent and part of the third wave[1] of Chinese engagement in Africa. These companies are indirectly driven out of their own country due to China's industrial saturation, and look for production and consumer markets in Africa. McKinsey (2017) estimates that there were more than 10,000 Chinese-owned firms operating in Africa in 2016, of which 90 percent were private.

In light of the odd Chinese investment patterns across Africa and the emergence of Chinese private players that account for a rapidly increasing share of total Chinese investments, this book asks: How much bargaining power do African economies have today with this new type of investor? What explains variation in government strategies around private Chinese capital? And finally, could some

African governments be asking more from private Chinese investors than canonical development theories suggest?

The central argument of this book is as follows: The top recipients of private Chinese investments, seemingly paradoxically, have significant bargaining power due to changes in the global economic and political environments. While African governments often face a lack of exit options due to a scarcity of different investors to choose from, the theory developed here shows that Chinese investors have placed more value on creating a new investment pie (however small) with an additional African country rather than investing the same amount in a country with existing investment stocks. The political benefits for China of entering new markets, therefore, outweigh the costs. I show that private Chinese capital first moves with politically motivated Chinese investments but, once on the ground, stays rather immobile. As a result, even African countries with small structural endowments have received a minimum amount of private Chinese capital – and countries with larger endowments have received substantially larger amounts – around which there is surprisingly substantial space to ask for local ownership and employment requirements.

I further argue that commonly cited variables such as corruption are insufficient direct causal explanations of the variation that we observe across government strategies. Instead, this book shows that before such factors come into play, some African governments are more aware of their bargaining power with private Chinese investors than others.

The argument is based on statistical analysis of investment data; the findings from 218 interviews that I conducted with government officials and Chinese companies across five country case studies over the course of 15 months; as well as on two complementary conjoint experiments that I designed and implemented with the Nigerian government and Chinese companies in Lagos and Ogun State in the spring and summer of 2020. The results of the research demonstrate that there are three components that determine governments' perceptions of bargaining power: first, the extent to which countries have been exposed to local participation policies before; second, the extent to which the Weak Bargaining Power Narrative has penetrated their countries; and third, the extent to which countries are able to collect information about the number of Chinese investments flowing into their economies. If conceptualized as a game, I demonstrate that the first two questions concern information that political actors receive about the game, while the third one is about incentives to share or not to share information with other political actors within the game.

Overall, this book shows that, perhaps counterintuitively, governments in competitive democracies (e.g. Nigeria and Kenya) have lower perceptions of bargaining power because parties' short-term ruling horizons as well as stronger historical relationships to the West have led negotiators to receive inaccurate information about their bargaining power with private Chinese players. In addition, the de-centralized nature of these competitive democracies – with de-centralization defined by weak parties and/or de facto weak centralized institutions – has also incentivized different domestic actors to compete for foreign investments across federal ministries and between federal and sub-national levels rather than to share information on investment inflows and work on a common strategy. The ruling government is then unable to collect accurate information on investment inflows, which in turn influences their perceptions on bargaining power to be lower than their actual bargaining power.

In contrast, governments in one-party dominant systems or authoritarian regimes with long-term ruling horizons (e.g. Ethiopia or Tanzania) have higher perceptions of bargaining power because parties' long-term ruling horizons as well as closer relationships to the East led negotiators to receive more information on Chinese investment patterns and to test stricter local content policies. Additionally, the centralized nature of these regimes – with centralization defined by strong parties and/or de facto strong centralized institutions – has enabled ruling powers to control the system and gather information on Chinese investment inflows that, in turn, influenced perceptions on bargaining power to match their actual bargaining power.

Finally, South Africa is a hybrid case with a one-party dominant system and de facto centralism but closer relations to the West, where the government has learned from experience that companies interacting with the government will follow its B-BBEE (Broad-Based Black Economic Empowerment) regulations, but also where Western economic thought has led the government to deem their bargaining leverage with private Chinese players that do not interact with the government to be low.

The main contribution of this piece is the finding that several African governments can, in fact, act as price setters around local participation with private Chinese investors, and that perceptions of bargaining power fundamentally matter for investment deal outcomes. Questions such as: "Will China exploit or develop Africa?" are therefore misguided. Instead, this book illustrates that whatever China-Africa story will be told in the future fundamentally also depends on what stories individual African governments choose to write – as they do have substantial space here to be narrators.

1.2 Defining Private Chinese Direct Investments in Africa

In this book, the term "foreign direct investment", also for the purposes of readability simply called "investment" or "FDI", is used to denote any capital movements in which an entity from one country directly controls the enterprise in another country in which the investment is made.[2] I purposely focus only on Chinese investments – as opposed to Chinese loans and trade – in Africa. China-Africa studies often analyze Chinese loans, grants, and investments together under the umbrella terms "Chinese development finance", "financial support" or "aid",[3] or focus predominantly on trade or loans.[4] This is because China as a non-OECD (Organization for Economic Cooperation and Development) member is not bound to report its official aid. Chinese engagement in Africa is consequently often more opaque than Western nations. This has led the media and data collection initiatives to sometimes conflate and confound different forms of Chinese engagement in Africa. In addition, the Chinese government itself promotes holistic cooperation with Africa. For example, at the triennial Forums on China-Africa

Cooperation (FOCAC), China has consistently offered grant, loans and investment packages that suggest the existence of one bundled development strategy. Finally, China is Africa's largest trading partner and is already competing with the World Bank in loan volume in the African region.[5] At the same time, Chinese investments are still a relatively small part of China's overall engagement in Africa. A whole strand of literature is therefore concerned with Chinese and Western infrastructure loans to Africa, perhaps most famously with infrastructure deals, and the origins and implications of deal conditions in Chinese contracting work around these infrastructure projects (e.g. Soulé 2019). In contrast, academic literature focused on Chinese investment in Africa is at best "thin" (Bräutigam et al. 2015, p. 2).

A growing body of literature distinguishes between different forms of Chinese foreign direct investment. Kaplinsky and Morris (2009) suggest four ideal types of overlapping Chinese investors in sub-Saharan Africa: central government state-owned enterprises (SOEs), provincial government SOEs, private sector incorporated in China, and private sector incorporated in sub-Saharan Africa only. My interviews with all sub-types confirm He and Zhu (2018)'s findings that Chinese companies in Africa are heterogeneous in their motivations and behavior: SOEs are generally operating under the strong control of Chinese central or provincial governments, and are driven by economic incentives, but also by the diplomatic relationship between the respective African country and China. As a result, they do not necessarily prioritize profit maximization and tend to be allowed to operate at razor-thin margins. In contrast, big private companies that are incorporated in China (e.g. Huawei) tend to be mostly driven by economic incentives, and aim to compete with Western companies in Africa. Still, due to their size and profile, they cannot completely eschew the Chinese government's directives.

Finally, there is a last and rapidly growing subset that this book focuses on: private Chinese companies incorporated in the African region only, exclusively driven by economic incentives and able to keep a low profile (Feng and Pilling 2019, Sun 2017). They are generally located in the manufacturing and service sectors, and typically enter African markets through one of two channels: Chinese workers would travel to Africa through a Chinese SOE and later venture off to start their own companies in search of larger profits. Otherwise, private entrepreneurs in China would contact their friends in existing private Chinese companies that have already settled in an African country and ask them where to invest. This decision-making process is surprisingly quite independent of the political strategy of the Chinese government. McKinsey (2017) estimates that there were more than 10,000 Chinese-owned firms operating in Africa in 2016, of which 90 percent were private.

Despite the growing presence of this new player on the continent, we have surprisingly very little grasp on African governments' responses to these new companies. In order to fill this gap, this study includes all capital flows of these Chinese private entities that invest across all sectors, in all forms, including the opening of a subsidiary or associate company in an African country, acquiring a controlling interest in an existing African company, or establishing a merger or joint venture with an African company. Understanding what relationships governments engage in with these relatively new players on the continent and how these relationships could be optimized for the African side is the core task of this book.

1.3 The Outcome Variable – Deal Quality

I define the quality of investment deals by the degree to which they address the transfer of economic rent from foreign investment to domestic factors of production and consumption (following Globerman and Shapiro (1999) who only focus on production). In particular, I consider all policies that address domestic revenue mobilization and developing local content such as ownership, employment, taxes, license fees or property rights, among other variables.[6]

That countries once deemed "price takers" did ultimately write their own development strategies is visible from other examples, like, most famously, China itself. From today's perspective, it may seem a bit difficult to believe that before China started its market reforms in 1978, its economy actually performed worse than those of countries of the African region. China's GDP/capita was less than one-third of the average in sub-Saharan African countries. In fact, in 1980, only Guinea-Bissau and Uganda's GDP/capita were lower than China's. Like many countries in the African region, China had high birth and death rates, low primary school enrolment, and very little infrastructure. Yet, fast forward 40 years, and the picture has changed dramatically: China is now the world's second largest economy and the world's fastest-growing consumer market. In 2018, per capita income in the African region ($1,589.2) was only about a sixth of that in China ($9,770.8), with only Equatorial Guinea, Mauritius and the Seychelles' economies performing better than China's.[7]

Surely, in the late 1970s, development experts also knocked on China's doors and offered their advice? Neoliberal economists tout China's market-oriented reforms post-1978 and the establishment of property rights that attracted foreign investment as responsible for its long-term growth (Zitelmann 2019). State-centered scholars stress the autonomy of the Chinese government and its strong involvement in the economy that welcomed foreign investors to certain sectors as the key to development (Yao 2010, Oi 1992). Finally, a third approach combines the neoliberal and the developmental model to argue that an appropriate mix of the two led to China's growth (Montinola et al. 1995).

China certainly worked hard on providing a conducive environment for growth. But there is something that these debates on China's enabling policy environment overlook: While China did listen to some advice from development experts, the government also maintained a set of equity caps, joint ventures restrictions, and Chinese national leadership requirements that, in fact, imposed significant costs on investors and that have been exceptional across countries' FDI regimes.[8] Yet, despite these costs, China has been boasting the largest amount of FDI inflows of all developing countries since 1996 (UNCTAD 2012). Why was China able to impose such restrictions without losing out on valuable foreign capital? Investors must have been willing to take on the costs of domestic revenue mobilization and developing local content in exchange for China's cheap labor in the manufacturing sector and, more recently, for a large consumer market. Simply put, China possessed bargaining power with Western investors.

And China actively used this power to grow at a pace that has been unparalleled in the world. In fact, China's economy emerged so fast that it had amassed large amounts of foreign reserves by 2000 and decided to invest the money abroad, including in the African region. And its involvement on the continent over the past two decades has certainly been impressive: In 2018 alone, China and Africa traded a grand volume of US $185 billion. Between 2003 and 2018, Chinese FDI stocks in Africa increased from US $0.49 billion to US $46 billion, and from 2000 to 2018, China extended US $148 billion in loans to Africa.[9] These financial contributions have certainly been driven by geopolitical considerations, but also reflect China's growing demand for resources (e.g. oil, gas, copper or uranium) and export markets, as well as a push for Chinese infant corporations to expand overseas. With a significant slow-down in US involvement in Africa over the past years,[10] China is already Africa's most important trading partner, and set overall to become the continent's most important economic partner in the near future.

How have different African governments met foreign investors – including private Chinese ones – with their foreign direct investment regulations, and how varied have these approaches been over time? Starting with Soskice and Hall (2001), the Varieties of Capitalism literature has been primarily designed with a view to developed economies, with very limited applicability to the African context. A few studies have attempted to identify the extent to which varieties of capitalism imported from colonial powers have fashioned today's African economies (Vogel 2011). Indeed, during the Cold War, different ideologies including Marxism, socialism and capitalism spread through the African continent and impacted growth trajectories. This was documented for example by Crawford (1982), who studied ideological importance for the performance of African states in economic growth, distribution, self-reliance, human dignity, participation, and societal capacity. Bates (1981)'s work on inefficient state intervention in the agricultural sector in tropical Africa then led to increasingly louder calls to "deregulate, privatize, and liberalize". With the end of the Cold War that further symbolized a victory of democracy and market capitalism, structural adjustment programs finally spread through the African region in the 1980s and 1990s. Overall, a general impression may have therefore emerged that the way capitalism has been practiced in post-Cold War Africa has been rather homogenous across individual countries.

Interestingly, however, and against the prevalent advice from Western development experts, some African countries did in fact develop regimes that meet foreign investors more aggressively than others, especially since the start of the 21st century. For example, the Ethiopian government formulated an Industrial Policy Strategy (IPS) in 2002, and as part of its Investment Proclamation, asked for local content requirements in the manufacturing industries and imposed limits in the employment of foreign staffers (excluding managerial positions), where foreign companies had to provide a succession plan for foreign employees by Ethiopian nationals in addition to training programs. While Tanzania started to borrow from the IMF in the mid-1980s and the first market-oriented investment code was introduced in June 1990, its foreign investment policy framework has remained relatively strict and become increasingly aggressive on raising revenue, on hiring of Tanzanians and on protecting and growing local industries since the election of

10 *African Bargaining Power*

President John Magufuli in 2015. Moreover, South Africa's Broad-Based Black Economic Empowerment (B-BBEE) regulations around black ownership and employment are yet another example that emerged out of a need to rectify the racial inequalities that the apartheid era had produced up until the 1990s, and that are still strictly enforced with domestic and foreign companies today. These cases suggest that developing countries can also pick "varieties of capitalism" as part of their overall development strategy.

Figure 1.2 summarizes the scores from the "Deal Quality Index 2020" Index that I developed based on US Department of State Investment Climate Statements on 44 African countries and that focuses specifically on local ownership and employment regulations. The benefit of this index is that it captures both formal and informal policy regulations. Higher scores indicate more aggressive policies,

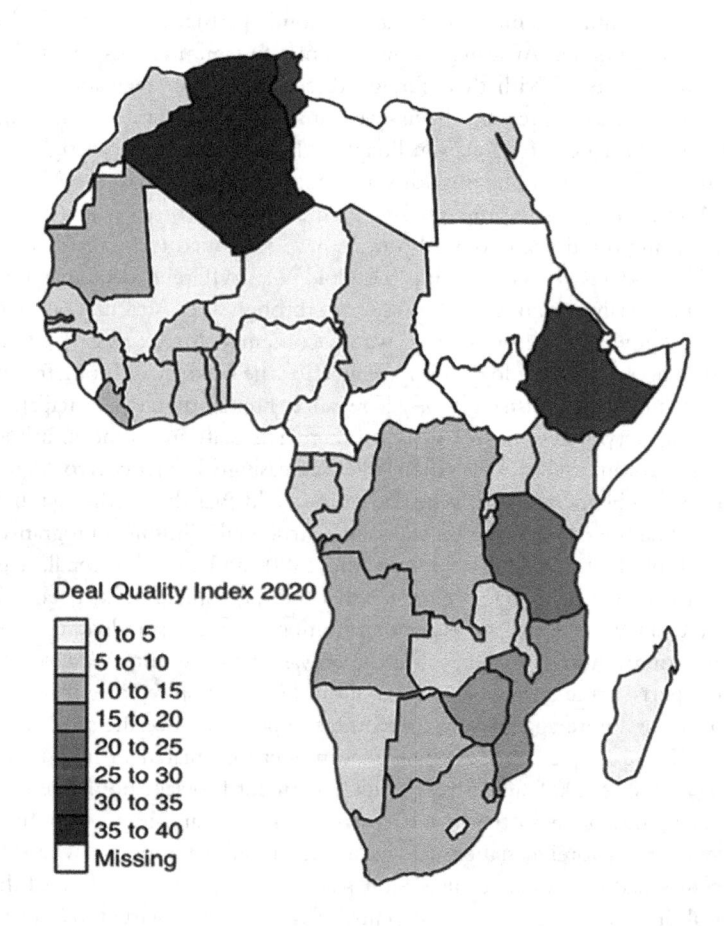

Figure 1.2 Deal Quality Index.

Index developed by author, based on local ownership and employment policies outlined in the US Department of State Investment Climate Statements 2019/20. The index accounts for both formal and informal regulations, as indicated in the statements. Higher scores reflect stricter local ownership and employment regulations while lower scores describe more investor-friendly policies.

and lower scores indicate more investor-friendly policies. As Figure 1.2 shows, how African governments strategize around foreign investment varies quite substantially. Why is that the case? Below, I discuss several theories that attempt to answer the question.

1.4 Existing Explanations For Variation in Deal Quality

Why are private foreign investors interested in developing economies? Neoclassical growth theory assumes that developing countries should grow at a faster rate than developed ones. As Gerschenkron (1962) famously noted, this is because developing countries have an "advantage of backwardness" – they can import technology, industry and institutions at low risk and costs; have low capital-labor ratios, which should increase the return on investment holding everything else constant; and can sell products on the domestic and global market. This translates into both cheap production and access to new markets. (Boddewyn and Brewer 1994).

On the other hand, governments have incentives to provide at least a minimum level of economic growth and employment to their population as means of gaining "consent from the governed" (Lipset 1983, Dahl 1971, Locke 1689). Given their low stocks of technology and capital, however, developing countries are often unable to kickstart "catch-up" growth without external sources of capital (Sachs et al. 2004). Foreign investment is therefore an attractive solution to supplement domestic savings; to access new export markets; and to induce technology and human capital development that arise from technological transfers and trainings. (UNCTAD 1995, Stopford and Strange 1991).

Bargaining power is often loosely defined as parties' relative abilities to exert influence over each other in a particular situation. However, bargaining literature diverges on what exactly determines this relative ability. As a consequence, scholars often conflate structural factors, bargaining techniques and resulting policies meant to attract investment into an overall term that is hard to define or measure.[11]

Responding to this inconsistency, I make an important distinction between *bargaining power* and *deal quality*. Bargaining power is based on economic and political factor endowments that stand out as relatively rare and are therefore less replaceable by exit options for the investor. In contrast, the outcome variable deal quality describes the resulting formal policies and informal agreements. Deal quality should, in theory be a reflection of countries' relative bargaining power. Yet, this is not always the case due to the political economy around deal negotiations that comprises the core of this book's analysis.

I define bargaining power as the relative structural attractiveness of a market to the investor. This attractiveness is purely based on countries' economic factor endowments as well as political structural variables that are importantly not controllable by the state, relatively sticky over time and less replaceable by exit options on the investor side. This value will be higher when countries can offer larger stocks of productive labor, technology, infrastructure, natural resources, and large consumer markets as well as when they display politically favorable background conditions.

I assume that the stronger the bargaining power of the African government, the more likely that investors will want to sign a deal and be willing to carry costs, including of domestic revenue and participation restrictions, if required by the government. As outlined in the introduction, that firms will be more willing to carry these costs in exchange for higher prospective returns is also reasonable given empirical examples from East Asia, and as described in the introduction, in particular from China itself.

As the roundtable discussion in the introduction of the chapter meant to demonstrate, the dominant academic discourse on foreign investment in Africa suggests that most African governments should have very limited bargaining power to exert influence over the conditions of deals with foreign investors. A brief historical overview shows that foreign investment in Africa is indeed a relatively recent phenomenon, has been largely driven by former colonial powers and remains scarce. Under colonialism, investments were primarily made to extract natural resources and labor from African colonies as well as to build and maintain local institutions that facilitate this export. A first global wave of foreign direct investment into colonies emerged at the start of the 20th century, slowed down during the First World War and continued thereafter with a focus on colonial trade (Buelens and Marysse 2006). After political independence, several African leaders – beginning in Kenya, Zimbabwe, Tanzania, Zambia, and Nigeria in the early 1960s – sought to become independent from the West through rapid industrial development following the advice of several dependency theorists to invest in local production of goods (Wallerstein 1974, Rodney 1972, Prebisch 1949,Singer 1949). But the suggested economic recipe of import substitution policies without a clear export strategy failed, and many countries were therefore left in even poorer conditions and dependence on the West (Bruton 1998). Most investment flows to Africa at the time originated from former colonial powers, the Soviet Union and China, and were politically motivated in order to keep alliances (to the US or the Soviet Union; and after the Sino-Soviet split also to the Non-Aligned Movement) during the Cold War.

As a response to the oil and debt crises, multiple economic depressions, and stagflation in the 1970s in several developing economies across the world, the World Bank and the International Monetary Fund (IMF) intervened to implement structural adjustment programs, which included stabilization (e.g. balance of payment and budget deficit reductions) and long-term adjustment policies (e.g. liberalization and privatization). Countries were required to implement these policies in order to obtain new loans or to lower interest rates on existing ones. As part of the trend of economic liberalization across national economies in the 1980s, development countries also gradually removed restrictions on inward foreign FDI such as screening or performance requirements, ownership restrictions and licensing agreements featuring technology transfer (UNCTAD 2000). Yet, these measures did still not lead to a significant increase in Western investment in Africa.

At the turn of the millennium, Sachs (2004) famously called for a shift from private to public investment and aid because the African region was still not competitive enough to attract significant amounts of private capital or from various sources. This was because several African economies were caught in a "poverty trap" (consisting of capital traps, saving traps and demographic traps) that has led to an equilibrium of both weak institutions and weak economic growth. Several scholars later criticized Sachs' call for aid and argued that there had been weak evidence for a positive causal relation between aid and development, and that negative effects of aid for governance and dependence overall outweighed its benefits (Deaton 2013, Moyo 2009, Easterly 2006). It remains the case, however, that compared to other developing regions, Africa has received the least amount of foreign investment inflows since the 1990s.

In the early 2010s, a new wave of economic thought, "experimental economics" (most famously Banerjee and Duflo 2011), emerged as a response to the aid versus investment debate between Jeffrey Sachs and William Easterly. Rather than tackle poverty with grand, national, one-size-fits-all policies, randomized impact evaluation should help us to better identify economic and political obstacles at the micro-level and create situation-specific policy solutions to slowly reduce poverty and kickstart growth. But even then, the assumption has generally been that there are endemic issues that need to be overcome first in order to become more attractive to foreign capital, and to set countries on a path of longer-term development.

Overall, all theories highlight high entry barriers to foreign investors and lead to two outcomes that disadvantage the African side. First, many countries in the African region still face a lack of significant foreign investment flows pouring in from various sources. As a result, there is often no or little competition on the investor side, which overall raises the cost of being selective as governments. Second, African economies compete in an environment with plenty of countries that offer similar "added values"; investors' costs of replacing one country with another one that offers a better deal are consequently low. Overall, these two factors describe what I call here the Weak Bargaining Power Narrative – they force governments to act as deal takers and lead to a race to the bottom, with countries with the most open economies having the best chances of attracting foreign investors. In other words, when the ability to offer unique goods, fiscal incentives, or political stability to attract FDI to host countries is limited, but when investors are already hesitant to enter, the only way of luring them is then the removal of demands and policy restrictions.

Given that political leaders have limited bargaining power to impose restrictions on foreign investors, why would some countries, especially poorer ones like Ethiopia or smaller ones like Tanzania, still choose to impose stricter regulations at the cost of becoming even more unattractive to foreign investors as illustrated in Figure 1.1? Some governments might simply not view FDI as an important source of growth, prioritize nationalist policies, overestimate their bargaining power, or need to be accountable to domestic interest groups. The global spread of capitalism starting in the late 1980s has led to heightened awareness among governments that foreign investment is essential for achieving positive development outcomes. Yet, as Rodrik (2006) writes, "the policies spawned by the Washington Consensus have not produced the desired results" (p. 973) across developing countries. As a result, some governments might still be suspicious of the benefits of FDI. Relatedly, countries may prioritize nationalist policies over externally imposed advice or overestimate their own bargaining power. For example, against the advice of the Western organizations and businesses, Robert Mugabe passed an

Indigenization and Economic Empowerment law in 2007, coming into effect in 2008, which transferred 51 percent control of all firms to black Zimbabweans. Only in 2019, the finance minister Mthuli Ncube announced that the law would be lifted under mounting pressure from the crashing economy to attract more foreign investment.

In addition, political accountability may matter. Governments may face a trade-off between attracting foreign investment and ensuring that locals benefit from the new capital because they want to be re-elected. Some African governments have certainly used IMF conditions "to push through their preferred policies, which otherwise would not be approved", thereby essentially using the IMF as a "scapegoat" (Vreeland 1999, p. 1). At the same time, for example South Africa with significant structural inequality inherited from apartheid may still face domestic political pressure to keep their B-BBEE policies privileging black individuals in the labor market although it may hurt the country's attractiveness to investors. This suggests that rather than following the advice of the World Bank to liberalize and privatize in order to become more competitive, some countries may still choose for political reasons to engage in non-cooperative bargaining relationships with foreign investors over entry (following the models proposed by Grosse 1996, Grosse and Behrman 1992, Kobrin 1987, Vernon 1977, 1971).

The Weak Bargaining Power Narrative hinges on a few assumptions about investors, type of growth models, and the benefits and costs that are associated with entering and operating in developing markets but that may not hold anymore for all investors on the African continent today. The first assumption that the Weak Bargaining Power Narrative makes is that foreign investors are homogenous in their preferences, specifically in the types of markets they are looking to enter, and that African countries have such low bargaining power that if they imposed any restrictions on foreign investors, the costs to investors would always outweigh the benefits. But with the emergence of South-South cooperation, an increasing number of investors originate from environments that have very different economic and political realities to the West. How does this affect their motivations, preferences and cost-benefit rationale when seeking to invest abroad? Put differently, and as Figure 1.1 suggests, what if for a subset of investors, the benefits actually outweigh the costs in more African countries than previously assumed?

Relatedly, the second assumption is that foreign investors are hesitant to enter African economies because their stocks of human capital and technology are low and cannot be accumulated short-term (as assumed by exogenous growth models). Yet, as outlined earlier, developing countries have an advantage of "catch-up growth" (Gerschenkron 1962). As a result, it is not clear that we always deal with investors who choose a narrative of "We are going to invest in country X *although* there is nothing there" or rather follow a strategy of "We are going to enter country X *because* there is nothing there (yet)" in the hope of large future returns. Perhaps the most famous example that the Weak Bargaining Power Narrative has failed to explain is the rise of China itself, where – as mentioned in the introduction – foreign investors poured in starting in the 1980s despite low stocks of human capital and technology, and significant policy barriers to entry.

These considerations raise important challenges to scholars who argue that countries with so called unfavorable background characteristics should always get rid of policy restrictions for foreign investors. Below, I challenge this assumption and offer a new explanation – the Power of Weak Economies Theory. The theory aims to explain the empirical observations around Chinese investments in the African region observed in Figure 1.1 that do not match theoretical predictions of the Weak Bargaining Power Narrative.

1.5 Toward A New Perspective – The Power of Weak Economies in Africa

The central argument of this book is as follows: First, due to significant global political and economic changes, several African economies have more bargaining power with private Chinese players than existing literature is suggesting. Africa is often called "the world's last region to industrialize" (Sun 2017), and there is certainly still a significant amount of money to make from structural transformation, with particularly high profitability for first-comers. In addition, over the past two decades, the African region has also gained significant value as a marketplace for Chinese companies that are leaving China out of overcapacity concerns. This is similar to China's attractiveness to Western investors starting in the 1970s that has only recently been tailing off due to an increase in China's labor prices.

The second part of the book then aims to contribute to the understanding of the root causes of development by examining how five African governments (Nigeria, Kenya, Ethiopia, Tanzania, and South Africa), that are among the top receivers of Chinese investment, strategize around private Chinese capital. I, thereby, for the first time describe and analyze the political economy around national foreign investment policies and investment deal negotiations to better understand the role of power relationships in the resulting quality of deals.

Under the assumption that some African governments do have bargaining power with China, why would they still choose to negotiate weaker deals? Several reasons stand out in the literature. First, capitalism might simply be "locked in" as the African region's economic ideology (Jalata 2016, Sender and Smith 1986), which has reduced the general policy space of African governments. This suggests that countries and foreign companies engage in two-tier bargaining, where international organizations or foreign governments dominate tier 1 through bilateral investment treaties or international agreements on foreign investment that prescribe FDI-friendly policies (Ramamurti 2001).

A second explanation is that some governments may be corrupt or do not feel accountability pressure to stay in power. They will therefore accept weak investment deals for an exchange of personal money (Abotsi 2015, Hanson 2009). Indeed, it is not immediately clear why the political or economic elite would be interested in local technology and human capital development. The issue should be less pronounced in democracies because democratically elected leaders face re-elections. Yet, when democratic elites are able to seek rent from the nationalized oil and gas industry, they are still less dependent on taxes, can pay off voters and may have to be little accountable. This theory suggests that elites and interest groups may be able to capture benefits from investment deals with Chinese players while having few incentives to ask for more benefits for their population.

A third and final explanation is that countries with strong bargaining power, like South Africa, may be receiving so much total foreign investment that the relative amount of Chinese investment in the country is small compared to Western inflows. In that case, the stakes of reaping additional benefits from Chinese investors may be sufficiently low to preclude additional effort to be more strategic. In such cases, countries might simply not bother to invest in learning strategies to maximize their interests (Green and Shapiro 1994).

The existing explanations assume that governments have perfect knowledge of their bargaining power. But what if that is not always the case? Especially in light of the dominant discourse that the African region is in fact a price taker, one has to ask how African governments themselves perceive their bargaining power with foreign investors. I posit that perceptions of bargaining power fundamentally matter for the resulting deal quality that we observe across the African continent. I propose the following new typology (Table 1.1) on the relationship between bargaining power, perceived bargaining power, and deal quality. Countries either have weak, medium, strong, or very strong bargaining power depending on their relative structural economic and political attractiveness to private Chinese investors. Countries' bargaining power will be higher when their structural economic and political endowments are less replaceable by exit options for Chinese investors, such as when countries have a comparative advantage in large stocks of productive labor, technology, infrastructure, natural resources and large consumer markets as well as display politically favorable background conditions.

It is important to note that I classify relatively larger economies among the 15 top receivers[12] of Chinese investments to have either "strong" or "very strong bargaining power". Countries like South Africa or Nigeria, who receive more

Table 1.1 Actual and Perceived Bargaining Power

	Weak Perceived Bargaining Power	Medium Perceived Bargaining Power	Strong Perceived Bargaining Power	Very Strong Perceived Bargaining Power
Weak Bargaining Power	e.g. Gabon	—	—	—
Medium Bargaining Power	e.g. Mauritius	e.g. Ghana	—	—
Strong Bargaining Power	e.g. Kenya	e.g. Congo, Democratic Republic	e.g. Ethiopia, Tanzania, Zimbabwe, Algeria	—
Very Strong Bargaining Power	e.g. Nigeria, Egypt	e.g. South Africa	—	—

absolute Chinese investments and whose share of Chinese investments of total GDP is lower (1.87 percent and 0.65 percent, respectively) should have even higher bargaining power than countries like Ethiopia, Tanzania and Kenya that receive relatively less Chinese investment and where the share of Chinese investments of total GDP is higher (3.14 percent and 2.44 percent and 2.23 percent respectively).[13] This is because it is not only important how much investments matter to both the African and the Chinese side, but also the difference of which player they are more important to (Hirschman 1958). If the number of Chinese investments relative to total GDP is small, it matters less for economic development, and African countries should have even more bargaining leverage with China.

This book argues that private Chinese investors are more likely to agree to strong deals if a country's added value is high and they are less replaceable by exit options. Whether governments negotiate strong or weak deals with private Chinese investors then depends on their perceived bargaining power. With all else equal, governments that do not think they could ask for local value-adding requirements will be less likely to do so than governments that view such requirements as part of their policy options. Overall, this typology also suggests that, in many cases, private Chinese investors would agree to stronger deals if African partners asked for them.

At the same time, this book is not meant to show that updating African governments about their true bargaining power will necessarily lead to better deals. After learning about their true power, they could, for example, still choose to be corrupt, or not invest resources in negotiation capacity for different reasons. Yet, the book is meant to challenge the assumption that African governments always have perfect knowledge of their bargaining power, and that more commonly cited variables such as corruption or ideology are the direct driving forces of weak deals.

This book focuses on Nigeria, South Africa, Ethiopia, Kenya, and Tanzania, which are all among the top 15[14] receivers of private Chinese investments and have strong or very strong bargaining power. I selected these specific countries because they provide variation in both independent and dependent variables and, therefore, lend themselves as suitable cases for making claims about the larger universe of receivers of Chinese investments in Africa. While China has invested in 51 out of 54 countries, the top15 receivers of Chinese investments still account for 77.5[15] percent of total investments. Despite the magnitude of investment deals negotiated in these countries, the literature has little grasp on Chinese investments in Africa,[16] let alone on the negotiation processes around investment deals that are often signed behind closed doors. Understanding how African leaders from top-receiving nations think about negotiating with Chinese investors is, therefore, especially important to capture and describe for the first-time governments' logic around a substantial amount of investment deal negotiations on the African continent. In addition, this book argues that smaller countries with fewer natural resources also possess bargaining power with China due to political alliances that overlap with China's economic decision-making. I address implications of the theory for smaller receivers of Chinese investments in Chapter 3 and in the conclusion.

Overall, perhaps counterintuitively, competitive democracies (e.g. Nigeria and Kenya) have lower perceptions of bargaining power because parties' short-term ruling horizons as well as stronger historical relationships to the West have led negotiators to receive inaccurate information about their bargaining power with private Chinese players. In addition, the de-centralized nature of these competitive democracies – with de-centralization defined by weak parties and/or de facto weak centralized institutions – has also incentivized different domestic actors to compete for foreign investments across federal ministries and between federal and sub-national levels, rather than to share information on investment inflows and work on a common strategy. The ruling government is then unable to collect accurate information on private Chinese investment inflows, which, in turn, influences their perceptions of bargaining power to be lower than their actual bargaining power.

In contrast, one-party dominant systems or authoritarian regimes with long-term ruling horizons (e.g. Ethiopia or Tanzania) have higher perceptions of bargaining power with private Chinese investors because parties' long-term ruling horizons as well as closer relationships to the East led negotiators to receive more information on private Chinese investment patterns and to test stricter local content policies. Additionally, the centralized nature of these one-party dominant systems or authoritarian regimes – with centralization defined by strong parties and/or de facto strong centralized institutions – has enabled ruling powers to control the system, manage the bureaucracy and gather information on Chinese investment inflows that in turn influenced perceptions of bargaining power to match their actual bargaining power.

I classify South Africa as a hybrid case with a one-party dominant system and de facto centralism but closer relations to the West, where the government has learned from experience that companies interacting with the government will follow its B-BBEE regulations but also where Western economic thought has led the government to deem their bargaining leverage with private Chinese players that do not interact with the government to be low.

1.6 Challenges to Conventional Wisdom

The main contribution of this piece is the finding that several African governments can in fact act as price setters around local participation with private Chinese investors, and that perceptions of bargaining power – that are shaped through both historical frames and incentives to share information with other political actors – fundamentally matter for investment deal outcomes. With the crisis of the West, which started with the financial crash in 2008, China stepped in to "fill the void" that the West had left behind in Africa, and has been increasing its presence until today. Since then, China-Africa studies have asked many questions around the Chinese strategy in Africa. For example, is China only interested in oil and other natural resources? Is China directly supporting authoritarian regimes in countries such as Sudan and Zimbabwe? Is China hurting efforts to promote democracy and human rights? Or even, is China making corruption worse? This one-sided perspective in the literature may have given the impression that the African region is one passive unit that is essentially a price taker of global economic and political power dynamics. After all, the whole strand of literature is called "China-Africa studies", not "Africa-China studies" although the phenomenon is taking place on the African continent.

This book strongly questions this perspective and shows that questions such as: "Will China develop or exploit Africa?" are the wrong ones to ask. I provide evidence that whether the rising Chinese presence in Africa leads to positive or negative development outcomes fundamentally depends on the development strategies that individual African governments decide on. And adding to the Varieties of Capitalism literature, the evidence presented here suggests that developing countries can also pick "varieties of capitalism" as part of their overall development strategy. As a result, the book calls for a shift in the China-Africa literature to pose less absolute questions that assume that only one China-Africa story exists on the continent, and instead to study different China-Africa stories that may vary depending on the host countries' strategies. The book therefore joins efforts by Corkin (2016), Gadzala (2015) or De Oliveira and Soares (2007) to highlight African agency in China-Africa relations, with a novel angle on private Chinese investment, which has been growing significantly as a share of total Chinese investment on the African continent, as opposed to public sector engagement.

Further, the findings of this study contribute to the literature on political regimes, centralization and party politics, and democracy and economic development. A key question in China-Africa studies is whether China is actively trying to support and strengthen authoritarian regimes (Broich 2017, Dreher and Fuchs 2011). But my findings suggest that the influence may be more indirect, where African authoritarian or one-party dominant states are, on average, more aggressive in negotiating investment deals around local participation than multi-party democracies, which may or may not be reinforcing their performance legitimacy and political rule.

In addition, across the African continent calls for de-centralization and power-sharing have become louder in the international discourse since the 1990s, as they are supposed to present a pathway out of poverty and conflict in Africa (Fombad and Steytler 2019, Crawford and Hartmann 2008). Yet, systems without a strong central government appear to be struggling with competition across ministries and sub-regional units. Political actors will then be less likely to share vital information on Chinese investment inflows that in turn influence the perceived bargaining power of the central government. Strong parties or strong centralized institutions therefore may be necessary pre-conditions for negotiating as a unified central government that has complete information about the amount of Chinese investment flowing into the economy.

Finally, and relatedly, literature on party politics suggests that inter-party competition should lead to better policy outcomes. A single dominant party could be acting like a monopoly in a market, which was found overall to lead to less efficient growth policy outcomes, for example, in some US states (Besley et al. 2008). At the same time, party strength also matters for economic outcomes: Party organization affects incentives and the capabilities of politicians, which then influences what policies are selected, and finally leads to different domestic groups responding to these policies and influences economic performance (Bizzarro et al. 2018). In addition, and as Simmons (2016) argues, "well-institutionalized" ruling parties matter for technological progress because these parties have sufficient long-term horizons to accept the deferred returns around promoting innovation and technology adoption. Taking inter-party competition and party strength together, in countries like South Korea, where both the left and the right party blocks are strong enough to run the political system, manage the bureaucracy and speak with one voice, economic growth will follow.

Further, Rosenbluth and Shapiro (2018) show that competition between two strong parties should allow for politics that aim "for the political middle" (p. 12). Applied to the African region, competition between two strong parties would then also lead to stronger deals around local participation since the majority of voters (perhaps unlike the minority elite) would vote for more local benefits from investment deals. Yet, I show that in countries such as Nigeria or Kenya, parties are weak, fractioned and clientelist. This form of party competition has led to rivalrous relationships and re-staffing of government offices. Both factors have limited political actors' learning about bargaining power through their relationship with the West and China, as well as disincentivized these actors to share information regarding Chinese investment inflows with each other. In this type of environment, one strong party with a history of local participation policy experimentation and relatively closer ties to the East may therefore be more effective at negotiating aggressive investment deals than two or more weak ones.

1.7 Research Design

I aim to show first, that the top receivers of Chinese FDI in the African region possess substantial bargaining power with private Chinese companies, and second, that some governments currently underestimate this bargaining power because they base their estimate on inaccurate or incomplete information. The first task is therefore to highlight sources of African bargaining power and to track patterns of Chinese investments that underline this power. The second task is then to dissect the political economy of deal negotiations and test different causal drivers of weak and strong deals.

Reports and newspaper articles on Chinese investments in Africa often use one term to describe the landscape of Chinese investments in Africa: "opaque". Since China is not an OECD member, the government is not mandated to report official aid, trade, and investment figures. As a result, many investment deals are signed behind closed doors with little information for the public to grasp. To make matters worse, the growing number of private Chinese players is not nearly fully captured by the existing databases.

In order to solve this concern, this project relies on 15 months of field work in Nigeria, South Africa, Ethiopia, Kenya, and Tanzania that I completed over two semesters and three summers between the years 2018 to 2020. I employed a combination of techniques. I first used regression analysis of Chinese investment data from the Johns-Hopkins University China-Africa Research Initiative and complemented it with literature and interview evidence to better understand private Chinese investment behavior on the African continent. I also used four different measures of "deal quality" (two self-designed) to make larger claims about the correlations between bargaining power and deal quality. I then designed and implemented two complementary conjoint experiments that presented hypothetical investment deals to the government and private Chinese companies in Nigeria in the spring of 2020. The deals were meant to mimic real investment deal scenarios and included a list of policy attributes that addressed domestic revenue mobilization and local content development. The experiments help us to understand for the first time the rationale behind deal-signing behavior expressed by both the government and the investor sides.

Finally, I conducted 218 semi-structured interviews with government officials and Chinese company managers over 15 months of fieldwork across five case studies – Nigeria, South Africa, Kenya, Tanzania, and Ethiopia – to be able to distinguish between correlations, root causes, and causal mechanisms that explain the relationship between bargaining power and deal quality in investment negotiations. The cases were selected because they provided variation in both dependent and independent variables. Chapter 5 outlines the case selection in detail. In total, I interviewed 131 government officials and 87 Chinese managers (Tables 1.2 and 1.3) across the five selected cases.

The final potential challenge in conducting the research was my own positionality as the principal investigator, a white Austrian woman, aiming to study Chinese investments in Africa. Most (84 percent) of the actors I interviewed were male, and all of them were either black or Chinese. It proved surprisingly easy to gain access to government offices and Chinese companies, who were willing to talk to me about their experiences, perceptions, and opinions. Yet, they may still have not fully trusted me enough to share their honest opinions. I therefore hired fully Nigerian and Chinese survey teams to conduct the experiments with the government and Chinese companies to account for co-ethnic trust and foreigner bias.

Table 1.2 Number of Interviews Per Country

	Nigeria	Kenya	South Africa	Ethiopia	Tanzania	TOTAL
#Government Interviews	45	23	23	21	19	131
#Company Interviews	38	15	5	13	16	87
TOTAL	83	38	28	34	35	218

Table 1.3 Position of Government Interviews Per Country

	Nigeria	Kenya	South Africa	Ethiopia	Tanzania	TOTAL
Minister or General of Federal Government Agency/Parastatal	3	1	1	0	0	5
Deputy Minister or Deputy General of Federal Government Agency/Parastatal	1	0	0	1	0	2
Senior Staff (e.g. senior economist, investment promotion commissioner, senior foreign affairs officer)	28	13	19	18	16	94
Sub-regional Leader (e.g. governor/county leader)	1	0	0	0	0	1
Mid-level Staff (e.g. deputy economist, trade bureau officer etc.)	5	4				9
Members of Parliament	1	3	0	0	1	5
Opposition Leaders	2				1	3
Village Chiefs	1	0	0	0	0	1
Others (senior business individuals, villagers etc.)	3	2	3	2	1	11
TOTAL	45	23	23	21	19	131

1.8 Overview of the Book

The first part of the book (Chapters 1–2) sets up the theoretical argument about the bargaining space of African governments. The second part (Chapters 3–4) aims to demonstrate that several African governments do, in fact, possess bargaining power with private Chinese players on the continent by providing a cross-national statistical analysis and two complementary experiments conducted in Nigeria. The third part (Chapters 5–7) then homes in on the reasons why some governments underestimate their bargaining power. The last part (Chapter 8) finally addresses policy implications.

The second chapter details the logic of the theory, and why its validity is inherently an empirical question that holds in the case of Chinese investments in Africa. It summarizes the premise, assumptions, and logic behind the first central hypothesis of the book, that several African governments do have bargaining power with private Chinese investors, and the second central hypothesis, that perceptions on bargaining power fundamentally matter for deal outcomes. The rest of the book then empirically tests the validity of both hypotheses.

The third chapter aims to identify reasons for diverging patterns of Western and Chinese investments in Africa. The chapter develops two "deal quality indices" and shows that Chinese investments are widespread across the continent, and uncorrelated with deal quality. The analysis suggests that there is indeed space for counties to negotiate more aggressively with Chinese investors, and with private investors in particular. Explaining why bargaining power and deal quality do not always correlate then guides the analysis in the rest of the book.

The fourth chapter uses the case of Nigeria to examine whether African countries in fact have bargaining leverage with Chinese investors, and highlights the importance of perceptions of bargaining power in deal negotiations with Chinese investors against competing hypotheses that attempt to explain weak deal conditions.

The fifth chapter outlines the rationale of the case selection and perceptions of bargaining power in five countries, Nigeria, South Africa, Kenya, Tanzania, and Ethiopia. Together, they account for 35 percent of total Chinese investment stocks.[17] Understanding how and why African leaders from top-receiving nations decide to negotiate with Chinese investors is therefore especially important to capture and describe for the first-time governments' logic around a substantial amount of investment deal negotiations on the African continent.

Chapters 4 and 5 establish that a gap exists between perceptions and actual bargaining power in some African countries while Chapters 6 and 7 then dive into why the gap exists and persists. Chapter 6 homes in on the historical relationships between the selected countries and the West as well as with China. It highlights that cases that had authoritarian or one-state dominant systems with a socialist past have learned over time that Chinese investors are staying under stricter local participation regulations. In contrast, such regulations were seemingly always out of any feasible policy range for countries with closer relations to the West and competitive multi-party systems that – with every new ruling government in power – led to information-erasing, constant new learning and re-defining of a relationship to the West and East.

Chapter 7 then shows that centralized political systems – that either emerge from strong parties or strong de facto centralized institutions – encourage political actors to share information on Chinese investment flows, while de-centralized systems with high levels of political competition and clientelism tend to disincentivize politicians at various sub-levels to share information on Chinese investment flows "up" to the central government. Overall, out of the cases studied, it is, therefore, governments of authoritarian or one-party dominant systems with a longer ruling party like Ethiopia or Tanzania who are very confident in their bargaining power with private Chinese investors, while governments in competitive democracies like Nigeria or Kenya lack the same confidence.

Chapter 8 summarizes the argument, highlights main contributions to existing literature, offers concrete policy advice on how to design "policy menus" that allow for maximum buy in from both Western and Chinese investors, provides a discussion on future prospects of African economic and political development, addresses the theory's applicability to smaller receivers of Chinese FDI, describes future research areas and finally, it concludes.

Appendix

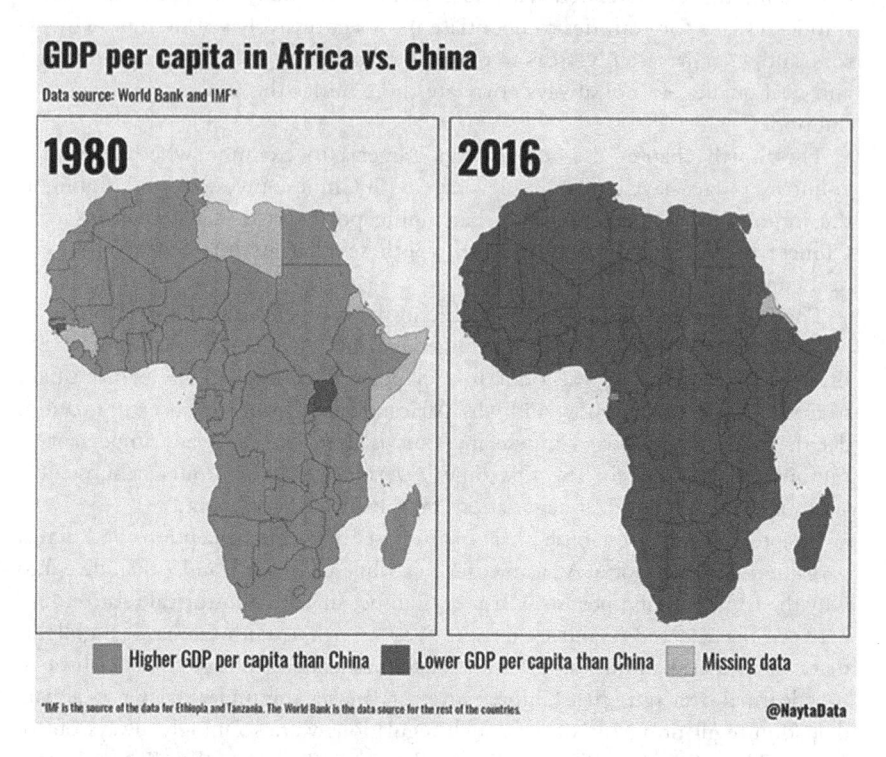

Figure A1.1 GDP Per Capita in Africa vs. China.

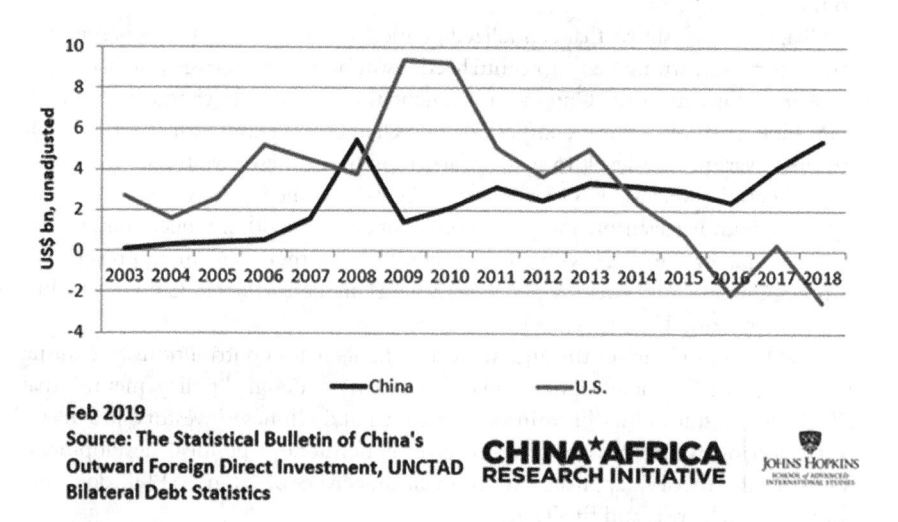

Figure A1.2 Chinese FDI vs. US FDI to Africa, Flow.

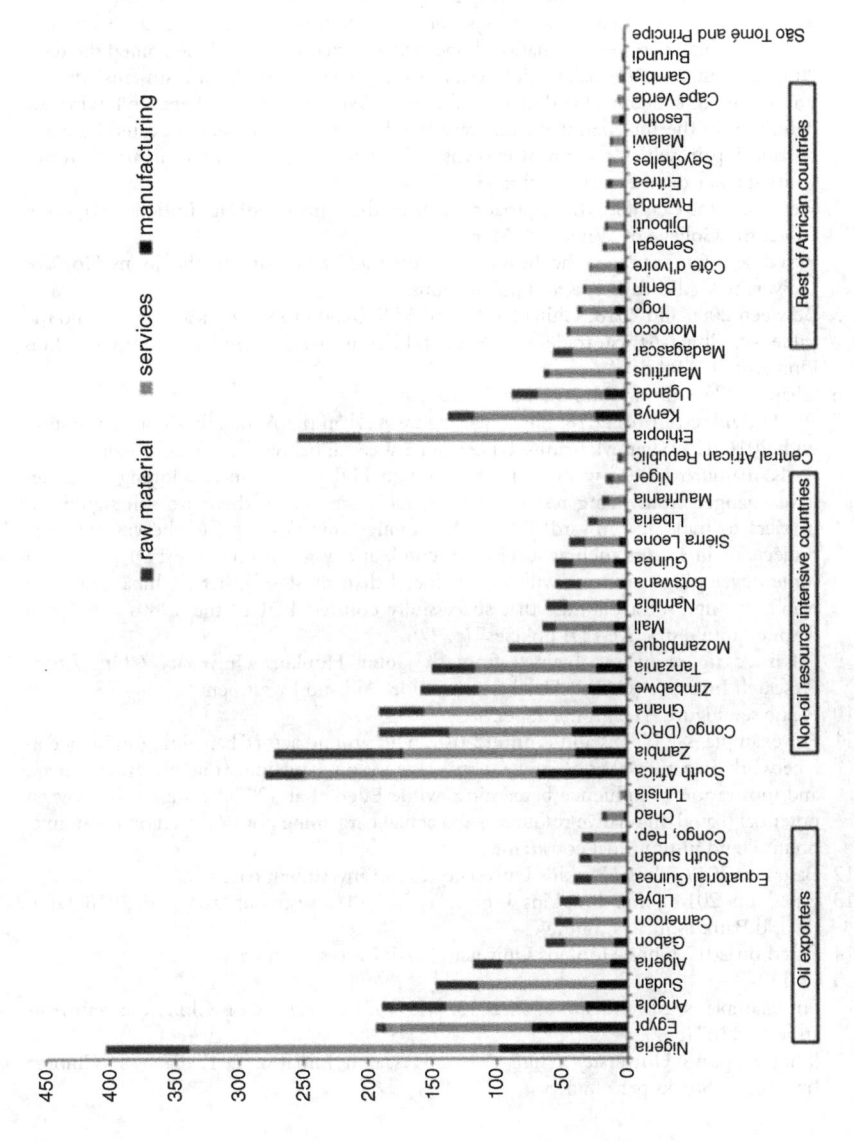

Figure A1.3 Small and Medium Private Chinese Investment in Africa (number of projects).

Notes

1. The first phase followed the Bandung Conference of Non-Aligned Nations in 1955 when China provided political aid and assistance until the end of the Cold war. The second phase started in the mid-1990s, when China's trade with Africa increased, and large and predominantly state-owned enterprises arrived in Africa as investors and contractors in infrastructure projects (Kaplinsky and Morris 2009).
2. This definition is based on a famous body of literature that emerged from Hymer's (1960) seminal work on international operations of firms, in which he coined the term "direct investment" to make a distinction from "foreign portfolio investments" that do not require direct control and that are also excluded in the analysis here. Following the definition of the International Monetary Fund, a direct investment is treated here as a relationship in which the investor owns at least 10 percent of the ordinary shares or voting power of an enterprise abroad.
3. Please see, for example, the approach taken by the China AidData Initiative Research Lab at the College of William & Mary.
4. Please see, for example, the heavy focus on trade and loans in the Johns-Hopkins University CARI databases and publications.
5. Between 2000 and 2018, China has loaned $148 billion to the African region, and the value of China-Africa trade was $192 billion in 2019 (based on Johns-Hopkins University CARI data).
6. Chapter 2 lists all variables used in detail.
7. World Bank estimates 2018; please see Figure A1.1 in the Appendix for an illustration with 2016 data when Mauritius' GDP/capita was still below China's GDP/capita.
8. As Ramamurti (2001) writes: "First, although FDI policies in developing countries have changed from being restrictive to being more liberal, there are still significant barriers to trade and inward FDI in developing countries, e.g., in the case of large projects or in sectors such as services. Second, at any given time, the FDI policies of some developing countries will be less liberal than those of others, China being the prime example of a country that successfully courted FDI in the 1980s and 1990s despite quite restrictive FDI policies" (p. 27).
9. All listed figures were obtained from the Johns-Hopkins University China-Africa Research Initiative (CARI) Database on Trade, Aid and Investment.
10. Please see Figure A1.2 in the appendix.
11. For example, see Nebus and Rufin (2010), who ground actors' bargaining influence in a network on actors' basis of power, network position, bargaining outcome preferences, and motivation to influence bargaining, while Eden et al. (2004) distinguish between potential (based on relative resources) and actual bargaining power (based on economic, political and institutional constraints).
12. Based on 2017 Johns-Hopkins University CARI investment data.
13. Based on 2018 Johns-Hopkins University CARI investment data and 2018 GDP (World Bank estimates) figures.
14. Based on 2017 Johns-Hopkins University CARI investment data.
15. Ibid.
16. For example, see Bräutigam et al. 2015, who called literature on Chinese investments at best "thin" (p. 2).
17. Johns-Hopkins University China-Africa Research Initiative 2017 data on Chinese Investment Stocks per country.

2 A New Theory on African Bargaining Power

2.1 Introduction

When thinking about African development, it is worthwhile to look back at how China – in the mid-1970s poorer than most African countries at the time – was able to overcome the poverty trap that Sachs (2004) describes as the key impediment for African development today. Operating in China's political environment was extremely difficult, especially in the beginning. China had just emerged out of a period of immense conflict, was agricultural and even poorer than the African region. Its human capital and technology stocks were low, and its institutions were weak. But as Ang (2016) puts it in her response to Sachs' poverty trap theory, institutional and economic development in China were in fact co-evolutionary: China harnessed its weak institutions to achieve growth, which in turn developed stronger institutions that were then used to maintain growth. This implies that in the beginning of China's "reform and opening up", weak institutions forced foreign investors to rely on personal relationships and trust to mitigate expropriation risks. On top of that, since its economic opening in 1978, China has been implementing a strict Foreign Investment Catalogue, which outlines industry sectors that are open to foreign investment but subject to equity caps, joint ventures restrictions and Chinese national leadership requirements. Up to today, foreign investors have complained about China's strict policies, and this has also been one of the reasons for the ongoing trade war with the United States.

Why then were investors still willing to buy into this? Steven Chapman, group vice president at Cummins, a multinational engine producer, summarized in a lecture[1] at the School of Management at Yale University in 2018 why the company entered the Chinese economy and built a Joint-Venture soon after its opening in 1978: "The Joint-Venture requirements were initially forced. But it was the only way for us to get market share, so it was the right financial incentive." This implies that the benefits from entering the Chinese market simply outweighed the costs imposed by the Chinese government on the firm. And Cummins was not alone with its plan to expand to China – the country has been boasting the largest amount of FDI inflows of all developing countries since 1996.

Why was China able to impose such restrictions without losing out on valuable foreign capital? Simply put, China possessed bargaining power. Only because China's economy was the poorest in the world, its cheap labor, potential to

DOI: 10.4324/9781003308768-2

industrialize and enormous future consumer market also rendered China the most alluring investment destination at the time. And China actively used this power to "force" investors to contribute to building local human capital and technology, which led to economic growth at a pace that has been unparalleled in the world.

This implies that, in order to harness weak institutions and set countries on the development path that Ang describes, governments need a minimum level of bargaining power with foreign investors. In the late 20th century, China, compared with the rest of the world, possessed significant bargaining power with the West because it was poor and the cheapest country to outsource production to from the West.

But due to China's steep learning curve, China has now itself been transitioning towards a consumer economy that is looking for steady resources of raw material and cheap labor. And the African region has many pockets where industrialization has been underexplored. These motivations influence the two central impediments of African regions to attract investment – there is now less of an undersupply of investors as well as less need for intra-continental competition for Chinese capital among African countries. Both factors translate into substantive bargaining power regarding local participation requirements with private Chinese players that this chapter describes in detail.

2.2 A New Theory on African Bargaining Power

The premise of the argument advanced here is that governments of developing countries need the support of investors to induce economic growth; and in return, investors need labor and/or land for their capital to become productive. Foreign investors and governments together can increase overall output. To what extent each actor benefits from the relationship is dependent on government policies. Respective levels of bargaining power between governments and foreign investors are consequently relevant when assessing the impact of foreign investment on countries' growth and development.

The first assumption is that economic growth is the result of endogenous forces. Exogenous growth models assume that output is determined by exogenously given forces, for example the savings rate (Harrod–Domar model), the stock of technology (Solow model) or both stock of technology and human capital (Mankiw, Romer and Weil Model). The last model is often used to explain why developing countries do not receive enough foreign investment – it is because their human capital and technology stocks, exogenously given, are low. At the same time, starting with Romer's (1986) seminal work, development literature began to acknowledge that endogenous forces, including investments in human capital and technology (e.g. Lucas 1988, Ortigueira and Santos 1997, Rebelo 1991), do matter for growth. As a result, I also assume that investments in human capital, innovation and knowledge contribute to growth.

The second assumption is that policies matter for technology spillovers and human capital development. Neoclassical models tend to assume that foreign investments add to local development organically through market forces (Blomström et al. 2001, Lim 2001). However, the composition of the workforce, management and ownership certainly matter for who captures the benefits and development outcomes, and it is not always clear from empirical evidence how local human capital and technology can in fact grow in developing countries without a coherent government strategy to leverage this capital and the potential resources it entails (Chen et al. 2016, Osabutey 2013).

The host countries' added value is land and labor, and the foreign investor contributes capital. However, while desirable for increasing output, it is not immediately clear who would pay for developing local technology and human capital. Host countries could invest in education and training but they often have restricted financial means so that their policy space around education is limited. Foreign investors, on the other hand, lack incentives to build local human capital if cheaper options are available. The main motivations for foreigners investing in emerging markets are market access, cheap unskilled labor, and natural resources. At the same time, in environments with low stocks of human capital and technology, it may often be less costly to import skilled labor than to train them locally.

Perhaps a classic example is the light manufacturing businesses in East Asia that moved from country to country starting in the late 1980s up to today, depending on wherever labor was the cheapest. While workers benefited in the short-term from employment, even the factory buildings were often flexible enough to be folded up and taken to the next country.[2] China was therefore extremely aggressive in requiring Joint-Venture agreements, local employment, and training to ensure that foreign companies helped to build local capacity before moving elsewhere.

The third assumption is that governments have credible commitment issues with foreign investors; and that foreign investors want to minimize renegotiation risks, which can both be solved by creating mutual dependencies, for example, through local participation. As governments, how can you provide enough commitment to foreign investors so that they would enter, but not so much that they would have a free hand to do as they please? And as investors, how do you negotiate deals to minimize the renegotiation risk, that is, so that the government does not later decide to open up negotiations again once capital has already been moved to the country? By creating mutual dependencies, for instance, through ownership or employment requirements, both issues can be mediated. For example, establishing a Joint-Venture between a local and a foreign firm with 50:50 ownership creates more mutual dependencies than a 40:60 division, where the partner with 60 percent ownership maintains the upper hand. Another example is that of a foreign company that focuses on engine production and of local truckers that are responsible for distribution, where both sides need and depend on each other.

The fourth and final assumption is that companies' willingness to enter such mutual dependencies, for instance, through local participation, depends on whether overall benefits outweigh overall costs on both sides. Governments should have at least minimum incentives to push for local participation. At the same time, developing countries operate in a competitive environment with other countries offering for example, similar raw material or comparably cheap labor. As a result, governments have to weigh their options when designing policies that are meant to maximize foreign company buy-in. In particular, a central question becomes:

Under what conditions do foreign investors agree to contribute to human capital and technology transfers if they want to enter and stay in a specific market?

2.2.1 Bargaining Power – A Question of Relative Benefits and Costs

Based on Nalebuff and Brandenburger's (forthcoming) transformative work on the illusion of power in negotiation, I assume that governments and foreign investors are in a perfectly symmetric bargaining position over the output that they can create together, minus the sum of the outputs that each actor can create individually. A toy example illustrates this: If A can by herself create output of the size 1, and B can by herself create output of the size 2 [both values reflecting each player's Best Alternatives to a Negotiated Agreement (BATNA)], and if A and B can together create output of size 9, they have equal bargaining power over the pie of size 6 [pie = total value with deal – (A's BATNA + B's BATNA); 6 = 9 – 2 – 1]. This is because, as the authors state, A needs B just as much as B needs A to create the extra 6 – if one person quits, the whole pie is lost.

The Weak Bargaining Power Narrative suggests that developing countries are poor and need to request external assistance. This seems to imply that capital is more valuable than land or labor. However, it is not clear from empirical evidence why that would be the case: Only when countries are agricultural and have a relatively low GDP/capita, labor is cheap and the pie from industrialization-led growth is large. Capital and labor should therefore have the same value in the relationship.

A second concern about Nalebuff and Brandenburger's example is that, as traditional bargaining theory suggests, actors may have different BATNAs that should then in theory influence respective bargaining leverage. If one negotiator lacks alternatives to the current negotiation, then she will be likely to want to stay with the negotiation. As a result, her bargaining power should be smaller than the one of her opponents if he has more attractive alternatives to choose from (Fisher and Ury 1981).

Applied to the toy example above, if player B can choose to create a pie with player A or to create the same pie with player C, but player A only has player B who offers to create a pie together, then player B should have more bargaining leverage because of her exit options. Yet, by Nalebuff and Brandenburger's definition of the pie [pie = total value with deal – (A's BATNA + B's BATNA)], it becomes clear that while individual BATNAs influence the size of the pie itself, both actors still maintain equal power over that pie. In other words, while the size of the pie itself increases or decreases with different BATNAs, once its size is determined, it should still be divided equally. How big the total pie is and whether both actors deem that pie large enough to, in fact, want to work together, is then an inherently empirical question of exit options for both players.

As discussed in the previous section, African governments often face a lack of such exit options due to scarcity of different investors to choose from. This implies that if an investor expresses their interest, governments can either create a pie with that one investor, or create no pie at all (equal to size 0). Based on this logic, the Weak Bargaining Power Narrative suggests that African governments, therefore, must act as deal takers and grant most of the benefits to the investors as that is still better than or equal to having no deal at all.

At the same time, even when a host government's reservation value is 0, this does not imply that they should accept their reservation value. Even if governments cannot create any pie without the investor, what is created under cooperation minus what the investor can create by herself could still be divided equally. Under the assumption that the host governments' reservation value is in fact 0, what fundamentally matters for the creation and the division of the pie is then only the total value with the deal and the BATNA of the foreign investor [pie = total value with deal − (0 + B's BATNA)].

If the investor's BATNA is smaller than their share of the pie they can create with a particular government, she has an incentive to stay and start to negotiate. If the BATNA is equal to their share of the pie, she is indifferent. Finally, if the BATNA is larger than their share of the pie, the investor will choose to look for other markets. For example, Nigeria offers a market of around 200 million people, which can hardly be matched by any other country on the continent (e.g. the next most populous African countries, the Democratic Republic of the Congo, Egypt, or Ethiopia, all offer markets half the size). When a Chinese actor expresses high interest in the Nigerian market, Nigeria's bargaining power – due to a lack of comparable exit options to the Chinese investor – should therefore be high, even if Nigeria does not find another actor who is as interested as the Chinese player.

In addition, even African countries with small structural endowments have received a minimum amount of Chinese capital. These data suggest that Chinese investors may have placed more value on creating a new investment pie (however small) with an additional African country rather than investing the same amount in a country with existing investment stocks. The benefits of entering a new market may therefore outweigh the costs. I offer a more detailed discussion below on why the BATNA of private Chinese companies in particular often appears to be smaller than the pie that they can create with different African countries.

2.2.2 Determining the BATNA of Private Chinese Investors

2.2.2.1 Benefits

This book argues that the motivations of private Chinese actors to venture into the African region are distinct in nature from Western ones. At the core, Western and Chinese investors face different domestic economic and political realities in their home countries that influence the type of engagement they seek in Africa. Concretely, three "China-idiosyncratic" push factors have provided clear financial incentives for private Chinese companies to move to Africa.

First, while most countries only indirectly support outward foreign investment, the Chinese government has been actively encouraging Chinese companies to invest overseas through its "Going Out" strategy, launched in 1999. This is for several reasons: China's economy, while slowing down, is still growing at a rate of 6.6 percent[3] per year and the country is in need of raw material to fuel the growth. In addition, the Chinese government would also like companies to gain international experience so they can better compete in China's domestic market with foreign players. Finally, the strategy complements China's efforts to rebalance its economic growth and make the shift toward higher value-added economic activity. As a result, the Chinese government is extending low-interest loans to Chinese entrepreneurs who venture abroad to open businesses.

Second, labor costs in China's coastal factory belt started to rise in 2005, which has incentivized industries to migrate like geese to places with cheaper production, as part of global networks and value chains (Akamatsu 1935, 1937, 1962). Studies show that over the past decade, Chinese investments have indeed significantly increased in Africa's manufacturing sector (Bräutigam 2009, Sun 2017). As the Chinese founder of Goodwill Ceramics stated, "Chinese labor is so expensive now, so you have to walk out the door [*zouchuqu*]." (Chen et al. 2018) In addition, some countries in the African region have other cost advantages: For example, some regions (e.g. Kogi State, Nigeria) have seen a massive influx of Chinese companies in environmentally sensitive sectors such as ceramics due to China's increasing environmental regulations.

Finally, the African region is not only seen as a place for production but increasingly also as a lucrative marketplace. As China's economy has recently been slowing down, overcapacity concerns have generally incentivized companies to enter markets in less competitive environments abroad. Large private Chinese players such as Huawei, Opay, or Transsion but also single entrepreneurs have therefore flooded African markets in search for market-creating opportunities (Bräutigam et al. 2018).

Overall, there are clear economic incentives for private Chinese companies to migrate to the African region. But what costs are they facing once they are on the ground?

2.2.2.2 Costs

As Bräutigam (2009) shares from one of her interviews:

> Umar Sani Marshal, a Nigerian industrialist, said that his northern city of Kano was being rejuvenated by growing Chinese investment in plastics manufacturing: 'Most of the plastic goods that are going to the market were imported before, but now when you look at it, the Chinese are discovering that they can have raw material at a cheap rate, they can have a good environment, they can have cheap labor' he said. 'The highest number of private employers in Kano are the Chinese and they have been expanding day by day.'
> (p. 189)

What is particular interesting about this story is that Kano is located in northern Nigeria and has struggled to attract Western investment as it is one of the more dangerous places in the country due to the presence of Boko Haram. Yet, there is plenty of Chinese activity in the region. My interview evidence with private Chinese companies in the South of Nigeria on their attitudes towards kidnappings is similarly telling: I visited a village in Oyo State, where a Chinese manager of a foam factory shared with me: "Last week, a Chinese man in a different village was kidnapped" and that "many Chinese now have policemen that go with them."[4] But when I asked whether they would consider leaving the region because of the safety issues, the manager said: "No… I have heard of the ones kidnapped, they often pack their bags and go on the next plane back to China [laughs]… but most Chinese stay."[5] Asked why they would stay, she said: "This just happens, it's part of life, we just go back to work."[6] While political risks (e.g. expropriation or violent conflict) often discourage Western foreign investment, these and other stories suggest that private Chinese investors seem to have higher market exit thresholds in "high-risk" environments.

In addition, corrupt practices appear to be a more acceptable way for small Chinese companies to facilitate business transactions, and not an absolute barrier: While US and European investors must stick to strict acts that prevent them from engaging in corrupt practices abroad, the Chinese government appears to be de facto unable to track the behavior of smaller Chinese companies abroad, despite President Xi Jingping's recent efforts to extend his domestic anti–corruption campaign to the Belt and Road initiative. As one Chinese manager shared with me in Oyo State: "Yes we pay officers, they come sometimes to get some money, but we also pay in China, it isn't different. It's common practice for business."[7] That Western companies were engaging in less corrupt behavior compared to Chinese ones was also confirmed by several government officials across multiple African countries. But even if Chinese companies have higher exit thresholds around political risks and corruption, why would private Chinese companies be operating in almost all African markets, and not still choose the most economically profitable and politically stable ones?

First, for political reasons, the Chinese government is interested in creating an investment pie with as many (African) countries as possible. China's value of having an investment presence in more countries is therefore higher than having an investment presence in only a few countries that offer them the best investment terms. Chinese SOEs consequently do not only select countries based on economic profitability or ease of doing business. Since many private entrepreneurs originally move to Africa through these SOEs, they do not initially decide what country would be best to invest to, and only later venture off to open their own companies that are purely profit-driven in the same country. Their decision to enter a particular country is therefore first indirectly politically driven and only later based on economic variables. Most managers (76 percent) that I interviewed came directly to the African destination country through referral by a Chinese friend who had already been operating in the same country and recommended it. Yet, they could almost all tell me stories of Chinese managers that had entered the country through an SOE and then simply decided to stay.

Second, and closely related to the first motivation, once Chinese companies have set up their operations, they are relatively immobile and geared towards a longer-term commitment to that particular African country. McKinsey (2017) suggests that among surveyed Chinese firms, 44 percent have made capital-intense investments in Africa that include factories or purchasing manufacturing equipment. In addition, 19 percent invested in capital-light sectors such as shop fittings, and technology in retail and service businesses, reflecting an interest in the local market. Asked whether they felt optimistic about the future in Africa, 74 percent said "yes", and "many of the firms said they had plans for expansion, particularly in new products and industries" (McKinsey 2017, p. 35). Certainly, capital is more mobile than labor. Yet, with labor costs rising globally, there are fewer "exit options" to move industries elsewhere. Chinese manufacturing has consequently been penetrating several African markets that have been under-industrialized. Of all the Chinese managers that I interviewed, only 7 percent had been operating in another African country before. One interviewee in Lagos shared with me that Chinese businesses in Lagos knew that corruption levels in Ethiopia were much lower. But in his words,

> Nigeria is the best place to be in Africa… you see, the government has come after me for taxes, since Buhari came to power, they targeted my company because they know we are making a lot of money…. But how we say here, 'we manage.' It's overall still worth it.[8]

Across the five countries I visited, only 16 percent of Chinese managers reported that they had considered moving to another African country, and only 6 percent said that they had thought about it "more intensively".

My interviews with Chinese companies in Nigeria, Kenya, South Africa, Ethiopia, and Tanzania also largely confirm McKinsey's findings: Asked about how long they envisioned to stay in their particular African countries, most Chinese managers indicated that they are working with longer time horizons of at least 10–15 years, even if they were not profitable yet today. Their capital investments often included building a factory or renting out an office, buying raw material, hiring local insurance companies, paying bribes, and getting police protection. As one interviewee in Ogun State, Nigeria, who produces bottles, shared with me:

> We just started, so we are making losses but it is all a longer investment… Nigeria is the China in the 1970s. I want to be here when money grows, I think this is the best place to be in the world right now.[9]

This sentiment was echoed[10] by many other Chinese managers I interviewed across the five countries.

Third, and relatedly, operating in countries that are less politically stable also allows Chinese companies to be first movers as relative latecomers on the continent, and to therefore operate in markets with little competition. Compared to Western companies, Chinese companies importantly are not only concentrated in urban areas but have penetrated rural Africa as well. They have set up electricity businesses or small manufacturing parks, which suggests a high tolerance for modest living standards and risk in exchange for profits. They are like Tecno, a mobile phone manufacturer based in Hong Kong, that exclusively focuses on selling phones in Africa. Tecno is now one of the top three mobile phone sellers in the region. The company started the production of "Made in Ethiopia" phones already in 2011 although Western investors have been shying away from Ethiopia until today due to high political risks. Similarly, as mentioned earlier, the vast majority of interviewees (74 percent) indicated that they entered the African region to produce for or serve the African economies, not to export beyond the African continent. New markets therefore appear to be especially attractive, even if they are less safe compared to areas that have already been frequented by other Western companies. These examples also help to explain why there is a Chinese investment presence even in Kano in the north of Nigeria.

Finally, some Chinese firms, particularly small private firms, may also not have the funds or resources available to obtain sufficient information. Since they may not be as familiar with the business environment in some African countries, investment decisions may, therefore, be made with insufficient attention to the actual associated risks (He and Zhu 2018). To shield themselves against risks once they are on the ground, most respondents told me that they would hire security guards to protect their facilities, use police escorts to travel around, and consult local insurance companies. Some managers said that they would also stay in company clusters while others reported the opposite, that they try to stay isolated from other Chinese companies, integrate themselves, and keep a low profile. Asked whether they thought that the country they were operating in was dangerous, Chinese managers almost unanimously said yes. They also shared stories of Chinese employees who had been kidnapped just a week before the interview, and how they had increased police escorts for whenever they go outside. Asked if that was a reason for them to leave the country, however, two managers said that they had heard of the actually kidnapped individuals leaving the country, but no single manager said that they would personally leave. I also asked about insurance, and interestingly, most companies I asked either had no insurance or were insured with local insurance providers.

Overall, these distinct motivations suggest that the Chinese governments' diplomatic relationships open doors to the African region through SOEs for private Chinese companies, which later choose to simply stay in the country rather than to find another African country that provides a more investor-friendly environment. Based on these considerations, the benefits of private Chinese companies in Africa often appear larger than the benefits of Western companies; and their costs appear smaller than those of Western companies. As a result, there are more African countries in which the benefits outweigh the costs for Chinese investors than for Western ones.

This has a direct influence on the salience of intra-continental competition for Chinese capital as well as the importance of exit options for African governments to Chinese capital. In particular, if all countries are allocated an investment pie that has a certain size depending on economic and political importance of the country, local participation becomes only one out of many considerations. As long as what the Chinese government can create by itself politically and economically is smaller than what it can create by adding another diplomatic partner country, private Chinese investors will enter that country. So, once African countries are allocated that pie, they possess bargaining leverage to ask for more local participation from private Chinese players.

2.3 The Importance of Perceptions of Bargaining Power

Given that African countries possess bargaining power with private Chinese investors, why do their policy approaches towards foreign and Chinese investment vary? Existing explanations make an important assumption, namely that when African governments negotiate with foreign investors, governments usually have perfect knowledge of their bargaining power. Yet, it is in fact not clear how perceptions of bargaining power are formed, and how African governments assess their power in investment negotiations with China and the West. The second central hypothesis advanced here, therefore, offers a new explanation to the observed variation in government strategies regarding foreign investment in Africa. Depending on the political economy around deal negotiations, some African governments may significantly underestimate their actual bargaining power with private Chinese investors. When governments are unaware of their countries' actual added values, they are also less likely to ask for the same share of the pie that they would request under perfect information about this added value.

What determines how countries perceive their bargaining power? Based on my research, there are two aspects that are central to answering this question: If the negotiation process can be understood as a game, first, what information and historical frames do political actors start the game with? And second, what information do political actors share within the game?

The first question ("What information and historical frames do political actors start the game with?") can be divided into two sub-themes: What is the extent to which countries have been exposed to local participation policies before? Countries that have traditionally used local participation policies have information on how private Chinese investors respond to these policies, while other countries lack that direct information. Second, to what extent has the Weak Bargaining Power Narrative penetrated their countries? The more governments have engaged with this narrative, the more internalized misperceived views on bargaining power will be. The second question ("What information do political actors share within the game?") asks about the extent to which information is being shared "up" to the central government that helps them to accurately count all inflows, so they are able to make better judgements on their actual bargaining power with private China.

Overall, I show that perhaps counterintuitively, one-party dominant systems or authoritarian regimes with long-term ruling horizons (e.g. Ethiopia or Tanzania) have higher perceptions of bargaining power with private Chinese investors than competitive democracies (Nigeria and Kenya). South Africa is classified as a hybrid case with a centralized government but closer ties to the West, resulting in accurate perceptions of bargaining power on government-company interactions, but underestimated bargaining power around private Chinese companies that do not interact with the government.

The logic for each of the three mechanisms is as follows: First, several authoritarian regimes and one-party dominant systems in the African region have emerged from a tradition of socialist/communist movements after independence with a focus on Pan-Africanism and a narrative on anti-colonialism and liberation. The original aim across African independence movements was to cut ties to the West and become economically independent through import-substitution industrialization. These efforts famously failed across Africa due to an inward-focused approach rather than an export-driven strategy. Some countries later orientated themselves towards the West and adopted structural adjustment programs that included liberalization of their economies to create an investor-friendly environment. In contrast, others were more selective in their adoption of Washington Consensus elements and applied more hybrid models that took into account local participation.

The assumption is that countries in the latter category simply placed more strategic interest on an inward-focused strategy and cared less about attracting foreign investment relative to local production and distribution. Yet, beginning in the 1990s, traditionally socialist regimes did in fact also concern themselves more with attracting foreign investment and have maintained that concern until today. How have authoritarian regimes or one-party dominant systems helped governments to learn that they can take a different approach with Chinese investors compared to Western ones? One party dominant system or authoritarian states have had longer ruling horizons that have helped them to experiment with different types of investors. They were, therefore, able to test the boundaries of what attributes to include in negotiations, and what deals were in fact impossible to strike. In contrast, countries with democratic backgrounds that were supported by the West and took the advice to open up their economies in the 1990s and then had different parties in power missed the same long-term learning opportunity. They therefore experimented less with policies that they perceived to be out of the feasible policy range.

Second, a stronger historical economic and political relationship to the West has naturally led some African countries to internalize the signaling that they cannot increase local participation requirements. I show that governments studied here generally know that in weak institutional settings, there is both room for case-by-case negotiations with deal conditions that can differ between investor types. Yet, the Western narrative has permeated ideological, educational, and intellectual spheres in Nigeria and Kenya as well as to some extent in South Africa. These developments have perpetuated a Western-centric focus despite China's growing presence in their countries. This includes where political actors received their education, and the books they have read; development models they have encountered and are aspiring to follow; and to what extent they ascribe to Western "policy fitness" indices, including the "Ease of Doing Business Index" by the World Bank. Since some governments have so much internalized the Weak Bargaining Power Narrative, they also believe that private Chinese players would not enter, or exit their markets under stricter policy regulations. As a result, these governments have come up with relatively few strategies on how to position stricter demands in formal FDI policies and in informal case-by-case deal negotiations with all types of foreign investors.

Third, countries with centralized systems, with centralization defined by strong parties and/or de facto strong centralized institutions – are able to accurately collect information on Chinese investment inflows while a de-centralized system – defined by weak parties or weak de facto centralized institutions – hinders free information flows. Competition among regions may only be beneficial when the central government is still able to track how much investment is flowing into the economy, and what national policy restrictions are feasible to implement given the overall amount of FDI flows. In other cases, if there are a lot of actors competing for investment, and they generally have incentives not to cooperate and share information, this can lead to a race-to-the-bottom in deal quality when in fact, the country would have the bargaining power to impose stricter regulations. The same logic holds true for federal government ministries and agencies. If there are incentives in place for central government offices to employ a collaborative approach in attracting investment, they are also more likely to share how much investment comes in through their collaborative effort. In contrast, if government bodies have incentives to employ a Machiavellian approach, then they are less likely to share investment-related activities with other government bodies, who are competing in the same environment.

2.4 Conclusion

Some observers of China-Africa relations are optimistic about China's intentions in the African region, hoping that Chinese investors are interested in industrialization, which will automatically lead to local technology and human capital development. In contrast, others warn against China's exploitative quest in the African region, where Chinese companies simply bring in Chinese workers or provide little training to unskilled local labor, with consequently small prospects for sustainable skill transfers. The theory outlined in this chapter provides a third perspective – that the fate of African development can also be decided by African players themselves. This is because private Chinese investors, whose presence is rapidly growing on the continent, are more willing to give in to local content demands relative to Western investors. In order to test this novel theory, the rest of the book employs a variety of empirical techniques across five country cases that are outlined in the subsequent chapters.

Notes

1 As part of Professor Ian Shapiro and Professor Mushfiq Mobarak's course: "State and Society".
2 Anecdote about Nike factory provided by Professor Shapiro in his course "Business and Government After Communism" in the Fall of 2018.
3 World Bank estimates 2018.
4 VA1.
5 Ibid.
6 VA1.
7 O3.
8 L18.
9 O8.
10 e.g. J7, DS36, AA25, 27, N24.

3 An Empirical Assessment of the Relationship between Bargaining Power and Deal Quality

3.1 Introduction

This project focuses on explaining the relationship between countries' bargaining power and the quality of deals with private Chinese investors across the African continent. A major challenge to studying African bargaining power or deal quality is that it is difficult to define and empirically measure both terms. Bargaining power is often loosely defined as the relative ability of parties in a situation to exert influence over each other. However, bargaining literature diverges on what exactly determines this relative ability. As a consequence, studies often conflate structural factors, bargaining techniques, and resulting policies meant to attract investment into an overall term that is hard to disentangle.

As a response to the shortcoming described above, I make an important distinction between *bargaining power* and *deal quality*. I define *bargaining power* as the relative structural attractiveness of a particular economy to the investor. This attractiveness is purely based on countries' economic factor endowments (e.g. natural resource endowments, size of the industrial sector, market size) as well as macroeconomic and political variables (e.g. inflation, regime type, or political stability) that are importantly not controllable by the state in the short-term, relatively sticky over time and less replaceable by exit options for the investor. In contrast to these structural variables, policies and deals can be adjusted as a response to countries' relative structural attractiveness. As a result, they are captured by the *deal quality* variable that should in theory be a direct reflection of countries' bargaining power.

This project is concerned with private Chinese investment in Africa but unfortunately, there is, to date, very limited data available on this relatively new player. For large parts of the statistical analysis below, I use 2003–2017 Chinese investment data from the Johns-Hopkins University China-Africa Research Initiative (CARI) as its methodology is the most sophisticated among Chinese investment data collection efforts[1] and widely used by academia and media.[2] Unfortunately, this database, like all other major ones, does not distinguish between private and state-owned enterprises, and certainly underreports the number of private Chinese players. Yet, since the share of private Chinese companies has recently significantly increased in the African region (e.g. Sun 2017), understanding how patterns of overall Chinese investments have changed over time can give us first

DOI: 10.4324/9781003308768-3

important clues on the preferences of this new private type of Chinese investor. Certainly, the statistical results still only provide us with a first approximation, and I complement the regression analysis with: data from McKinsey and Chen et al. (2018) on private Chinese investments in Africa; interviews that I conducted across five countries; and evidence from the literature to more qualitatively describe African bargaining power with private Chinese investors.

Based on the definitions that I developed in the introduction, this chapter first proposes different measures for deal quality across the African continent. I then conduct a regression analysis to determine the benefits and costs of Chinese investments in Africa for Chinese, US, and total investment and describe the distinct patterns and nature of (private) Chinese investments across the continent. It finally shows that countries' bargaining power with private Chinese investors is indeed largely determined by their structural economic endowments but, importantly, independent of the different measures of deal quality that I proposed. Explaining how the political economy around investment negotiations influences the relationship between these two variables is then the core of the analysis of the subsequent chapters.

3.2 Measuring the Outcome – Deal Quality

The ambiguity of the difference between structural factors and policies, pointed out in the introduction, is also directly visible in existing efforts that aim to assess countries' relative attractiveness to foreign investment. The Ease of Doing Business (EDB) Index by the World Bank Group was launched in 2003 and measures countries' business regulations across 11 sub-indices for local companies across 190 countries. The index is based on an expert survey and covers a wide span of topics such as "starting a business", "registering property" or "trading across borders". One of its shortcomings for this project's analysis is that the index measures both government strategies in the form of policies as well as structural capacity that is less about strategy. For example, the sub-index "Starting a Business" assesses both the number of procedures required to start a business (deliberate government policy) and the time required to start a business (structural capacity). In addition, the EDB Index also only assesses the regulatory framework for domestic firms. As a result, it fails to capture strategic differences that governments may decide to take around imposing regulations specifically on foreign investors.

Like the EDB Index, the Global Competitiveness Index (GCI) by the World Economic Forum conflates both intentional policies and capacity in its expert survey that aims to assess countries' overall attractiveness over 12 pillars: institutions, infrastructure, macroeconomic environment, health and primary education, higher education and training, goods market efficiency, labor market efficiency, financial market development, technological readiness, market size, business sophistication, and innovation. Pillar 6, on goods market efficiency, includes Section 2: Foreign Competition that offers an index for: prevalence of non-tariff barriers, trade tariffs, prevalence of foreign ownership, business impact of rules of FDI, burden of customs procedures, and imports of goods and services (% of GDP).

Unfortunately, the outcome variables are only measured as respondents' opinions[3] and may not reflect the actual state.

In light of the existing indicators' shortcomings for this project, I develop two additional indices that solely measure government policies around foreign investments as opposed to structural factors. The third measure of deal quality is called "FDI Regulations Index 2012", and based on data from the International Finance Corporation (IFC)'s "FDI Regulations" initiative executed in 2012 complemented with variables that I found relevant to add based on my interview findings with foreign investors and government officials across the five case studies. The 2012 index measures countries' policies around Converting and Transferring Currency, Starting a Foreign Investment Across Sectors, Employing Skilled Expatriates, Arbitrating and Mediating Disputes, and Tariffs, Taxes and Property Ownership. Since US and Chinese investment stocks were only available from 2000–2012 and 2003–2017 respectively, I use the FDI Regulations 2012 Index to determine US and Chinese policy sensitivity for the year 2012. The fourth measure of deal quality is the "Deal Quality Index 2020" Index that I developed based on US Department of State Investment Climate Statements on 44 African countries and that focuses specifically on local ownership and employment regulations. I use this index to show the current FDI policy landscape as well as correlate it with 2018 Chinese investment stocks (the last available year at the time of publication).

3.3 Measuring Bargaining Power

Academics, international organizations, and thinktanks often base their advice to African governments on an analysis of these overall FDI flows into the African region without distinguishing FDI by origin. This is because Western investments still account for by far the largest share of foreign investments in Africa (UNCTAD 2020). And even though FDI flows to the African region have risen, these flows are still small by global standards (3 percent of total global FDI inflows in 2019, UNCTAD 2020). Advisors have consequently often urged governments for very investor-friendly policies if they want to attract more investments.[4] The argument is that because there is so little investment flowing into the region, any barriers to entry should be removed. Since Chinese investments account for a fast growing but still very small share of these overall investments, then naturally, African governments should have even less bargaining leverage with Chinese investors and treat them the same as Western investors.

But what if Chinese investment patterns are different not in volume (yet) but in allocation? Depending on their home economy, investors from the West and China may be interested in fundamentally different markets that complement their expectations from home (Calvo et al. 1993). Their diverging rationales then also determine how African governments should respond to these different players.

For the regression analysis, I consider resource-seeking, market-seeking, and efficiency-seeking variables as well as variables concerning governance that have been suggested by literature (please see Table A3.2 in the Appendix) to influence companies' decisions to invest in the African region. For resource-seeking motives, I consider[5]:

- *Imports*: Imports of goods and services (BoP, current US$), World Bank Open Data
- *Natural resource rents*: Total natural resources rents (% of GDP), World Bank Open Data
- *Agricultural land*: Agricultural land (% of land area), World Bank Open Data
- *Manufacturing*: Manufacturing, value added (% of GDP), World Bank Open Data
- *Electricity*: Access to electricity (% of population), World Bank Open Data

It is important to note here that investors could be looking for different "types" of resources, either natural resources (e.g. natural resource rents or agricultural land) or labor for manufacturing or services (e.g. manufacturing (value added), electricity, or imports).

For market-seeking motives, I used:

- *Population*: Population, total, World Bank Open Data
- *GDP*: GDP (Current US$), World Bank Open Data
- *Exports*: Exports of goods and services (BoP, current US$), World Bank Open Data

For efficiency-seeking variables, I used:

Inflation: Inflation, consumer prices (% annual), World Bank Open Data

For governance, I considered the following variables:

- *Regime type*: polity2 variable, a 21-point index, where the highest value corresponds to a fully institutionalized democracy, Polity IV Project
- *Corruption*: 0–100, with 100 being very clean, Corruption Perception Index, Transparency International
- *Rule of law*: index, measures perceptions of the extent to which agents have confidence in and abide by the rules of society, and in particular the quality of contract enforcement, property rights, the police, and the courts, as well as the likelihood of crime and violence. Estimates range from −2.5 to 2.5, World Bank Governance Indicators
- *Political stability and absence of violence and terrorism*: index, measures perceptions of the likelihood of political instability and/or politically-motivated violence, including terrorism. Estimates range from −2.5 to 2.5, World Bank Governance Indicators

Finally, I use the following outcome variables:

- Chinese foreign direct investment stocks 2003–2017: Johns-Hopkins University China-Africa Initiative

- US foreign direct investment stocks 2001–2012 (unfortunately, no later years are available), UNCTAD Investment Statistics
- Total FDI inward stock 2003–2017: World Bank Open Data

Resource-Seeking Motivations

A panel data regression using country- and year-fixed effects with standardized variables shows that, most importantly, Chinese investments have increasingly shifted from raw material to manufacturing (Table A3.3 in the Appendix.) While the "natural resource rents" coefficient was positive and statistically significant (0.08) for Chinese investments between 2003–2007, the coefficients become negative and remains statistically significant (-0.35 and -0.17, respectively) for the periods 2008–2017 and 2003–2017.

Meanwhile, after controlling for natural resource rents, the "manufacturing" coefficient is negative and statistically significant (-0.29 and -0.57, respectively) between 2008–2017 and 2003–2017 and remains large, negative, and significant (-0.41) between 2003–2017 after controlling for other resource-seeking motivations. The "access to electricity" coefficient is positive (0.79 and 0.97 respectively) and significant with controls between 2008–2017 and 2003–2017. These results support the Flying Geese Theory, that Chinese investors have increasingly become attracted to African countries that are not industrialized yet (therefore having the negative coefficient on manufacturing) but with robust access to electricity to start manufacturing. Finally, agricultural land seems to matter less as a pull-factor for Chinese investment: The coefficient decreases over time and has no statistical significance throughout the regressions.

Market-Seeking Motivations:

After accounting for resource-seeking factors, what are the market-seeking motives of Chinese and other investors? (Table A3.4 in the Appendix.) In addition to countries with fewer natural resources and less manufacturing, Chinese FDI is mostly attracted to economies with large imports and populations, confirming its market-seeking motivations. After introducing inflation as an efficiency-seeking variable (Table A3.5 in the Appendix), the coefficient on GDP becomes statistically significant and negative while the coefficient on inflation is not statistically significant. This points toward efficiency-seeking factors playing less of an overall role.

Governance Indicators:

Finally, how do governance indicators attract or deter Chinese and other foreign investments (Table A3.6 in the Appendix)? After controlling for resource- and market-seeking motives, only the rule of law and corruption coefficients remain statistically significant (with the corruption coefficient turning negative) for Chinese FDI stocks.

Since the OLS regression analysis may be prone to multicollinearity, I also employed the LASSO (Least Absolute Shrinkage and Selection Operator) method with cluster dependent errors on the same regression that I used to produce Tables A3.3–A3.6 in the Appendix for Chinese investment stocks.

The LASSO performs both variable selection and regularization in order to enhance the prediction accuracy and interpretability of the statistical model it produces. The analysis reveals three variables, lagged imports (coefficient: 0.031), population (coefficient: 1.53) and lagged GDP (coefficient: 0.57), to be predictive of Chinese FDI stocks per country.

Comparison to US and total investment:

Similar results hold for US and total foreign investment, which have decreasingly been attracted to countries with high natural resource rents (Table A3.5 in the Appendix). US investments seem to be more drawn to places with less electricity, and higher imports and GDP. Total FDI, meanwhile, is more attracted to places with higher imports and larger populations (and fewer exports and higher inflation although both coefficients are small).

Regime type, rule of law, corruption and political stability, and absence of terrorism and violence all appear to be important for US FDI stocks, with more democratic and less corrupt countries being able to attract more US investors. Total FDI is larger in countries with less political stability and absence of terrorism and violence.

Overall, the regressions reveal that it is countries with high GDP, potential for manufacturing, access to energy, large imports and populations, rule of law, and corruption that Chinese investors are attracted to. Figure 3.1 summarizes that, unsurprisingly, South Africa, the DRC, Zambia, Nigeria, Angola, or Ethiopia rank among the top recipients of Chinese investment. Their bargaining power should therefore be higher than that of smaller recipients of Chinese capital.

Based on the theory, if countries possess enough appeal – bargaining power – through their relevant structural endowments identified above, Chinese companies should be entering their countries regardless of how friendly or aggressive investment policies are. As a result, Chinese investment stocks and policy restrictiveness should be uncorrelated. In contrast, if countries' bargaining power was weak and their structural endowments were not sufficient pull-factors by themselves, Chinese investments would respond to policy attractiveness. We would then also see both variables correlated. The next section aims to test both claims.

3.4 Overall Assessment of Bargaining Power and Deal Quality

Several studies point out that foreign investment in Africa is sensitive to trade openness, investment climate, proactive and reform-oriented policies, and FDI-related policy liberalization (Asiedu 2005, Bende-Nabende 2002), to an increase in corporate tax rates in host countries (Fedderke and Romm 2006), or to limitations of ownership, restriction of repatriation of capital, inefficient financial systems, and economic and political instabilities (Yasin 2005), and that the importance of these factors has even increased over the past years (Chen et al. 2018). This seems to be consistent with the Weak Bargaining Power Narrative – that only providing an enabling policy environment will attract more foreign investment to environments that are otherwise too difficult and costly for investors to enter.

Relationship of Bargaining Power & Deal Quality 45

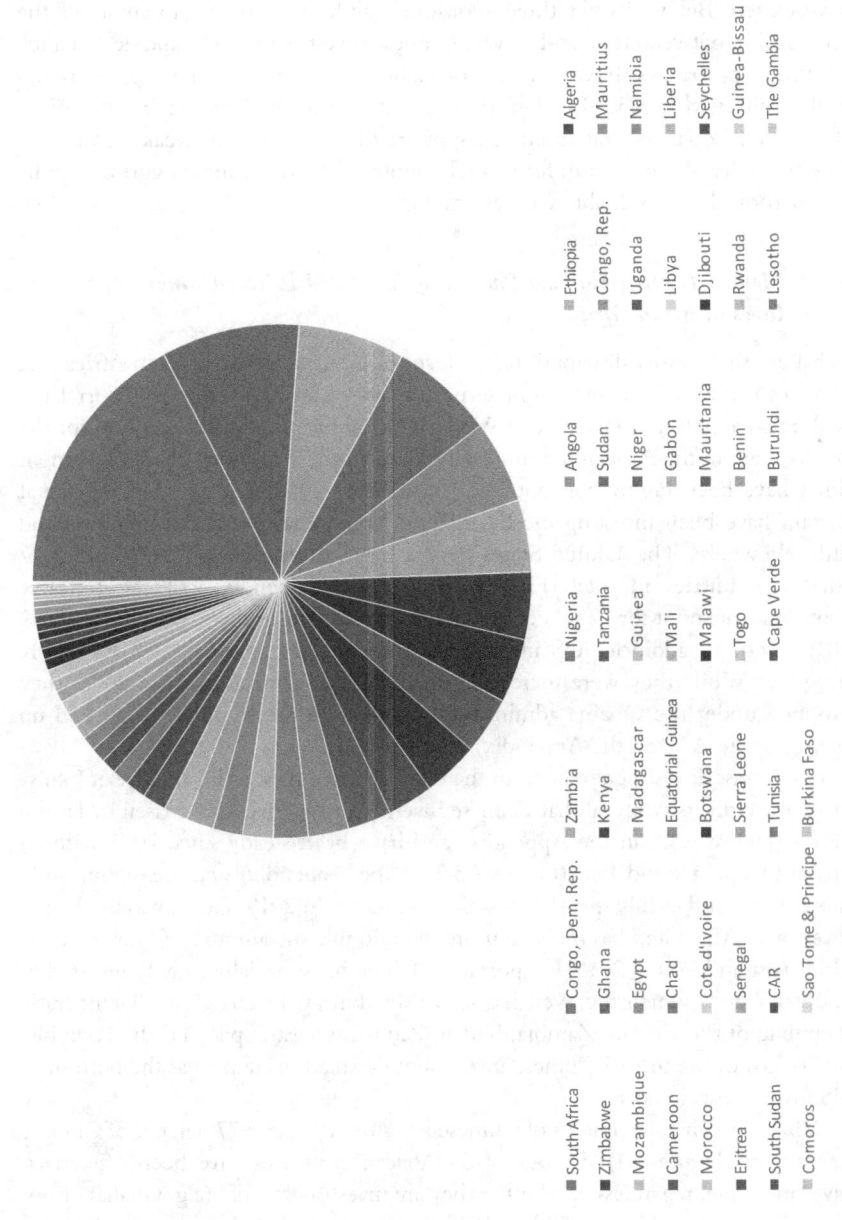

Figure 3.1 Chinese Investment Stocks in Africa, 2017.

At the same time, Figure 1.1 in Chapter 1 reveals something odd with this claim – that some African countries such as Zimbabwe, Angola or Ethiopia have started to implement stricter foreign investment policies, but that – seemingly unconcerned – Chinese investors keep increasing their presence while US ones have exited. Below, I offer three additional methods to more closely assess the relationship between total and private Chinese investment stocks and deal quality. All three approaches show that the correlation between investment patterns and deal quality is very low. Together, they provide strong evidence against the Weak Bargaining Power Narrative and in support of the Power of Weak Economies Theory – that there is room for several countries to ask for more aggressive policies without losing valuable Chinese capital.

3.4.1 Method 1: Distributional Patterns of Total and Private Chinese Investments in Africa

What are the distinct distributional patterns of Chinese investments in Africa that may point toward a general Chinese push to invest in Africa that is uncorrelated with relative policy attractiveness? While Western investment still accounts for the largest share in the African region (Figure A3.1 in the Appendix) these investment flows have been highly concentrated (UNCTAD 2012 data). France and Great Britain have been investing mostly in their larger former African colonies, and little elsewhere. The United States have a more diverse investment profile (27 African countries in total; Figure A3.2 in the Appendix) but the top five economies account for 77 percent of all US investments in the region (UNCTAD 2012 data). In addition, US investment flows in the region have been highly irregular: While they were increasing up until the financial crisis in 2008, they dropped under the Obama administration and have not significantly picked up again (Figure A3.3 in the Appendix).

In contrast, investment data from the China-Africa Research Initiative at Johns-Hopkins University reveal that Chinese investments in Africa have risen by far the fastest (Figure A3.1 in the Appendix) and have been steady since 2003 with an upward sloping trend line (Figure A3.3 in the Appendix) and are significantly more wide- and evenly spread across the continent. In 2019, China was the largest investor in Africa and has invested more than double the amount of France or the US (Ernst and Young 2019). Importantly, China has especially heavily invested in countries from which the West has so far shied away. In 2012,[6] six (Democratic Republic of the Congo, Zambia, Sudan, Zimbabwe, Ethiopia, and the Republic of Congo) of the top 15 Chinese investment destinations ranked at the bottom of US investments in Africa.[7]

While the top 15 recipients of Chinese investment receive 77 percent of Chinese investment (Figure 3.1), 51 out of 54 African countries have been offered an investment pie, regardless of whether they are investor-friendly (e.g. Ghana) or not (e.g. Liberia). In addition, Table 3.1 shows that the correlation between Chinese investment stocks (2018) and deal quality 2020 is very low (0.24). This points toward a general investment push across the continent in which more countries are receiving Chinese capital independent of their policy choices.

Table 3.1 Correlations between Chinese Investment Stocks and Deal Quality

Country	Chinese Investment Stocks in $M, 2018	Ranking	Deal Quality Index 2020
Aggressive Deals			
Ethiopia	2568	4	33
Algeria	2063	7	38
Zimbabwe	1766	9	16
Mozambique	1410	11	15
Tanzania	1303	13	20
Average	1822	9	24
Medium-Investor Friendly Deals			
South Africa	6532	1	10
Congo, Dem. Rep.	4444	2	11
Angola	2299	6	10
Average	4425	3	10
Very Friendly Deals			
Zambia	3523	3	5
Nigeria	2453	5	4
Ghana	1797	8	6
Kenya	1756	10	8
Egypt	1079	14	8
Mauritius	998	15	5
Madagascar	803	16	0
Average	1773	10	5

But even if Chinese investment stocks appear uncorrelated with deal quality, the amount of debt that countries hold with China could still be influencing deal quality as countries may be forced to provide political and economic concessions, thereby resulting in limited bargaining leverage for countries with most debt to China. However, empirical evidence suggests that this is not the case. Table 3.2 shows that Angola and Ethiopia are the highest debtors with China but also have strict foreign investment policies that private Chinese investors do not appear to shy away from. Overall, the correlation between debt ranking and deal quality is very low for the largest debtors to China (0.05), which again supports the Power

Table 3.2 Correlation between Debt and Deal Quality

Ranking:	Countries With The Most Debt to China 2018	Deal Quality Index 2020
1	Angola	27.43
2	Ethiopia	32.50
3	Kenya	8.08
4	Cameroon	0.00
5	Zambia	13.16
6	Nigeria	11.74
7	Congo	24.80
8	Mozambique	38.46
9	Cote d'Ivoire	23.28
10	Uganda	13.16
Correlation:		0.05

of Weak Economies Theory. While total Chinese investment appears to be directed by the Chinese government to spread across Africa, private Chinese actors could still be sensitive to policy restrictiveness. So, how are private Chinese players distributed across the African continent? Chen et al. (2018) utilize the Chinese Ministry of Commerce (MOFCOM) database on small and medium private firms investing in Africa. Figure 3.2 shows the distribution of small and medium private Chinese enterprises on the continent.

Unsurprisingly, the top three hosts are Nigeria (oil rich country), South Africa (non-oil resource intensive country) and Ethiopia (non-resource rich country) but their investment policies vastly differ, indicating that all three countries provide attractive production and consumption markets irrespective of their policy choices. In addition, it is again striking that while the "investment pies" that each of the 49 countries are receiving are different in size, the sectoral distribution is still very similar, especially for the top 20 recipients. In other words, independent of their policy environment, countries all appear to receive investments in raw material, services, and manufacturing that are proportionally related.

3.4.2 Method 2: LASSO Predictions

While investment patterns across Africa suggest that Chinese companies enter countries irrespective of deal quality, it could still be the case that countries that changed their aggressive policies to investor-friendly ones would suddenly be able to receive higher amounts of Chinese investment. As a second test, I therefore split the Deal Quality Index 2012 into three baskets and used the LASSO method with cluster-dependent errors to determine structural drivers of Chinese investments for countries that offer very investor-friendly deals. The LASSO is a regression analysis method that performs both variable selection and regularization in order to create simple, sparse build models out of many variables. The method reveals one single variable, "GDP lagged" (coefficient: 0.61).

I then use this coefficient to predict Chinese FDI investment stocks for countries currently offering medium-friendly and aggressive policies (Figures 3.3 and 3.4) for if they suddenly offered investor-friendly deals. If FDI regulations mattered for attracting Chinese investors, the predicted Chinese investment stocks under friendly policies would be higher than the actual investment stocks that we observe for medium-friendly and aggressive countries. Yet, as Figures 3.2 and 3.3 show, this does not appear to be the case everywhere – actual Chinese FDI stocks are, in fact, in several cases larger than the predicted stocks, especially for the top receivers of Chinese investments such as South Africa, Nigeria or Tanzania. In other words, if GDP is actually the dominant deciding factor for Chinese investors to enter markets and if countries with medium-friendly or aggressive FDI policies suddenly decided to implement more investor-friendly policies, the results suggest that they would not necessarily be able to attract more Chinese investment.

Similar to the analysis above, I also used the LASSO method to determine structural determinants of Chinese investments for countries that currently offer medium investor-friendly or aggressive policies. The LASSO method reveals two variables, lagged imports (coefficient: 0.01) and lagged GDP (coefficient: 1.35).

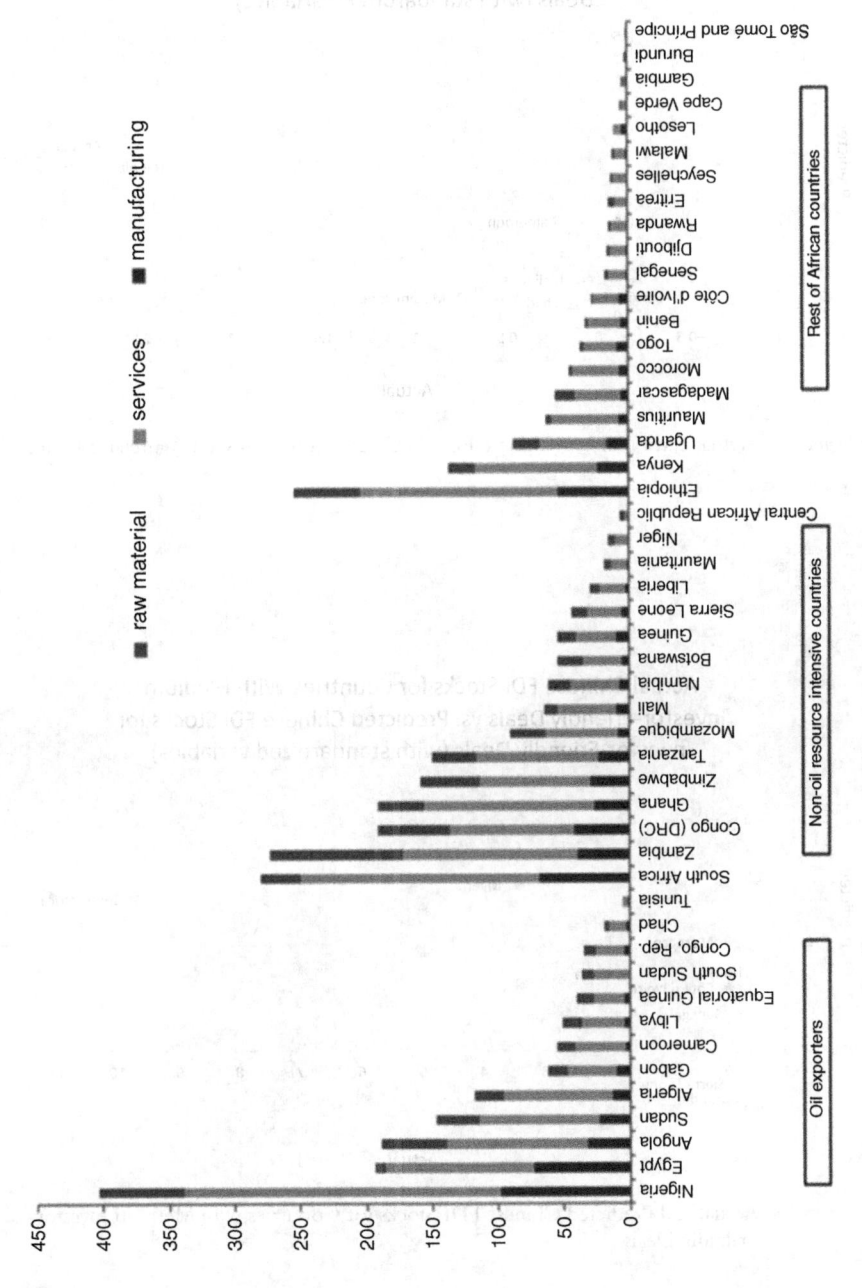

Figure 3.2 Distribution of Small and Medium Private Chinese Enterprises in Africa.

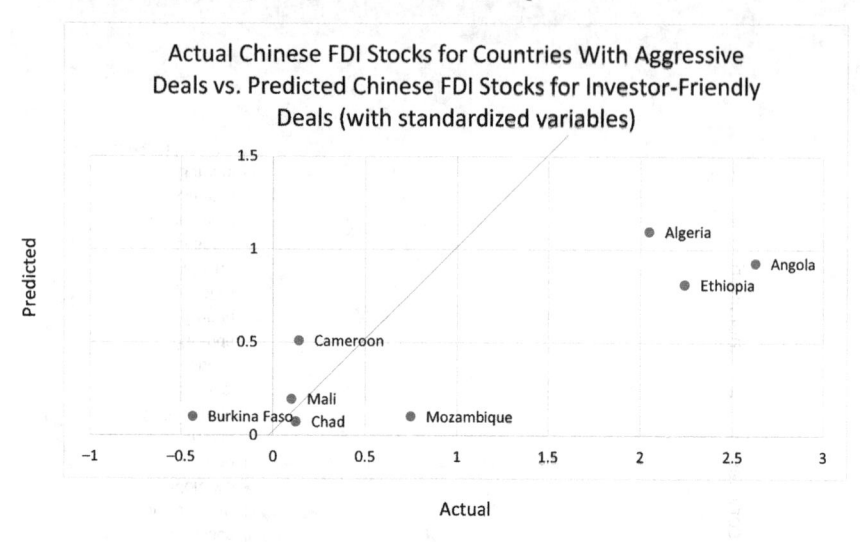

50 *Relationship of Bargaining Power & Deal Quality*

Figure 3.3 Actual and Predicted Chinese FDI Stocks for Countries with Aggressive Deals.

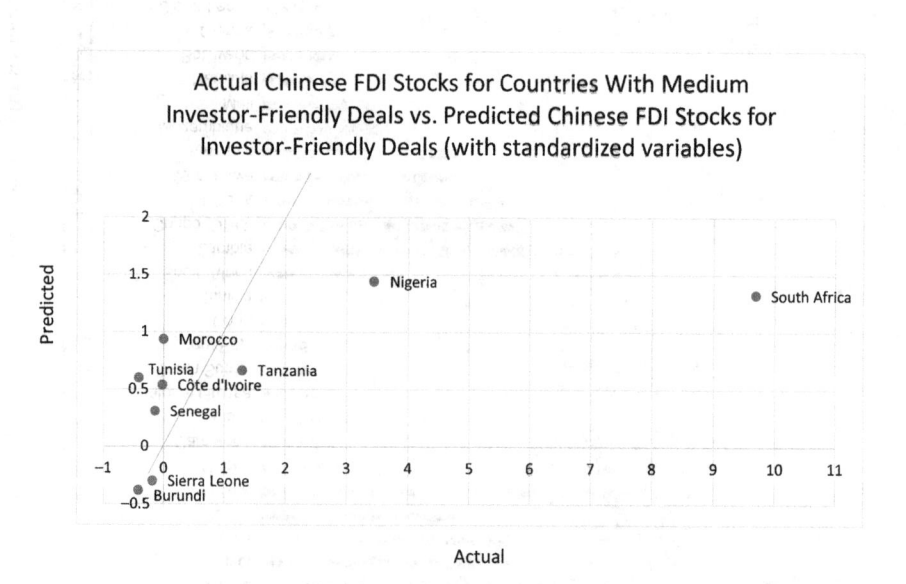

Figure 3.4 Actual and Predicted Chinese FDI Stocks for Countries with Medium Investor-Friendly Deals.

Actual Chinese FDI Stocks for Countries With Very Investor-Friendly Deals vs. Predicted Chinese FDI Stocks for More Aggressive Deals (with standardized variables)

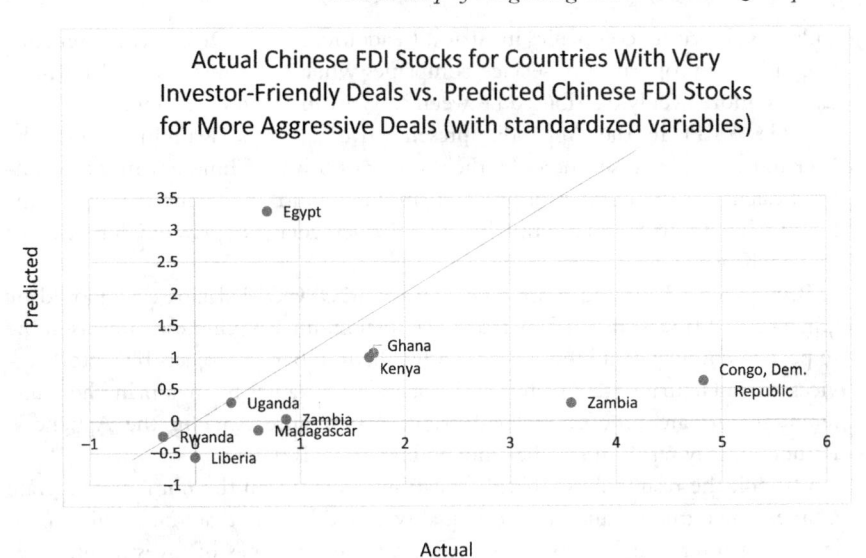

Figure 3.5 Actual and Predicted Chinese FDI Stocks for Countries with Very Investor-Friendly Deals.

I then again use the coefficients on these variables to predict Chinese FDI investment stocks for countries offering very investor-friendly deals if they offered stricter regulations (Figure 3.5). If FDI regulations mattered for attracting Chinese investors, the predicted Chinese investment stocks under stricter regulations would be lower than the actual investment stocks that we observe for very investor-friendly countries. While observed stocks are indeed on average higher than predicted ones, most of them are within one standard-deviation change per standard deviation increase in the predictor variable.

3.4.3 Method 3: Correlations between Private Chinese Investment Stocks and Deal Quality

Methods 1 and 2 have heavily focused on total Chinese investment stocks. As a third approach I therefore calculated correlations for different measures of deal quality (EDB, GCI, and Deal Quality Index 2012[8]) and private Chinese investment. To measure these private investments, I employ both Chen et al. (2018) and McKinsey data. Both sources are likely underreporting the number of private Chinese companies across the African region. Yet, the rankings still seem to moderately overlap (please see Table A3.11 in the Appendix).

The differences observed between the MOFCOM and McKinsey rankings most likely arise due to different measuring methods: the MOFCOM database captures small and medium private Chinese companies while the McKinsey data addresses all private companies in Africa. In addition, the MOFCOM dataset contains a heavy proportion of service companies while companies in the McKinsey data are more evenly distributed between services and manufacturing.

Table A3.11 in the Appendix presents five rankings: Ranking 1 lists the McKinsey country case studies by the number of private Chinese firms per country. I calculated the number of private firms per country by taking the total number of Chinese firms and multiplying it by the percentage of private Chinese firms that McKinsey lists for each country.

Rankings 2, 3, 4, and 5 are based on the MOFCOM database employed by Chen et al. 2018. Ranking 2 measures the total number of Chinese projects in the respective country. Ranking 3, 4 and 5 list the number of projects by sector (services, manufacturing, raw material). I obtained the values by measuring how different sectors are proportionally distributed in Figure A3.5 in the Appendix. Rounding may result in numbers not adding up to 100%.

Overall, the results show that the relationship between the number of private Chinese investments and the deal quality is weak, and that the coefficient is larger but interestingly also not significant for other types of investment. After introducing controls, none of the deal quality indices serve as strong predictors of Chinese, US, or total investment stocks (Tables A3.12, A3.13 and A3.15). The same holds for all five Deal Quality 2012 sub-indices and foreign investment stocks (Tables A3.16–A3.20), except for Sub-Index 3 and Sub-Index 5: The coefficient on the Sub-Index 3: Employing Skilled Expatriates is negative and statistically significant for Chinese FDI stocks, suggesting that Chinese investors do not shy away from countries with stricter employment regulations. In addition, higher scores on Sub-Index 5: Taxes, Tariffs and Property Ownership (Table A3.20) are predictive (with no controls) of more US FDI stocks and total FDI stocks.

Tables A3.14 and A3.21 show correlations of different measures of Chinese activity per country and deal quality measures. All correlations are low, with the by far "highest" correlation between "MOFCOM number of manufacturing projects" and the Ease of Doing Business (0.37, which is still relatively low).

3.5 Conclusion

Overall, the patterns highlighted around Chinese investments in Africa cast significant doubt on the Weak Bargaining Power Narrative that countries should impose very few requirements on investors if they do not want to deter capital from private Chinese investors. But the low correlation also means that we do not observe countries with stronger bargaining power always using that bargaining power. Why is that the case? To answer this question, I conducted two complementary conjoint experiments with the Nigerian government and private Chinese companies to directly test their preferences and exit thresholds around various policy changes. A summary is provided in the next chapter.

Appendix

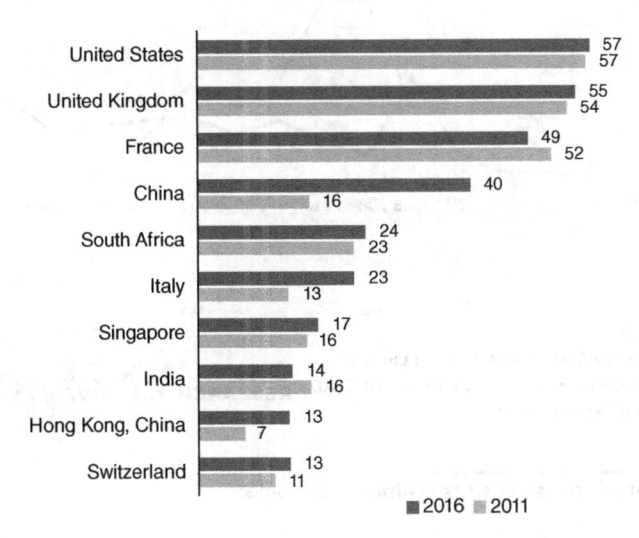

Country	2016	2011
United States	57	57
United Kingdom	55	54
France	49	52
China	40	16
South Africa	24	23
Italy	23	13
Singapore	17	16
India	14	16
Hong Kong, China	13	7
Switzerland	13	11

Figure A3.1 The Top Investor Economies in Africa 2011 and 2016 (Billions of Dollars).
Notes: Numbers presented in this figure are based on the FDI stock data of partner countries.

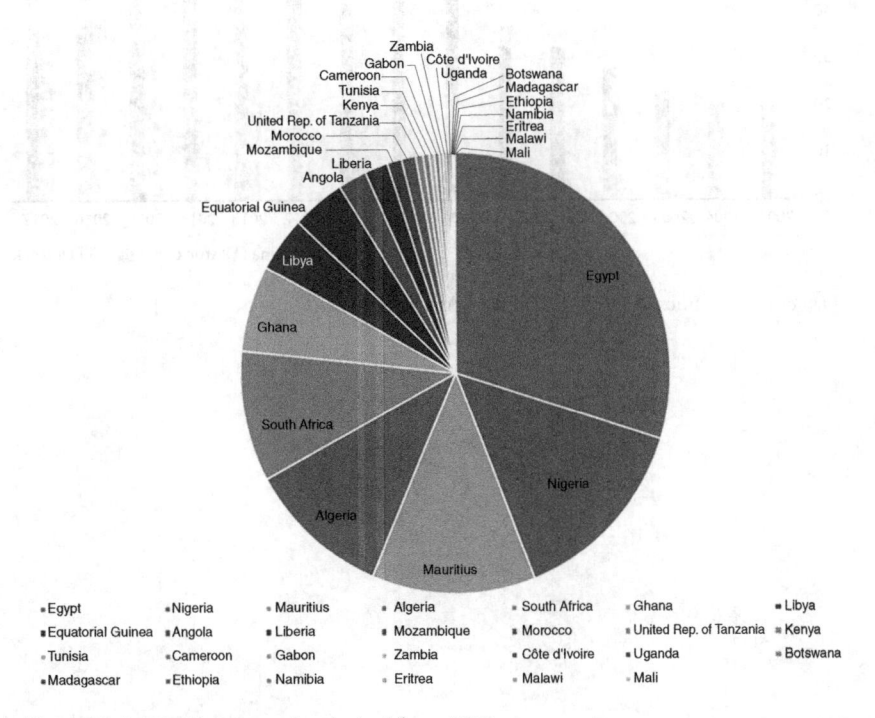

Figure A3.2 US: Investment Stocks in Africa, 2012.
Source: UNCTAD

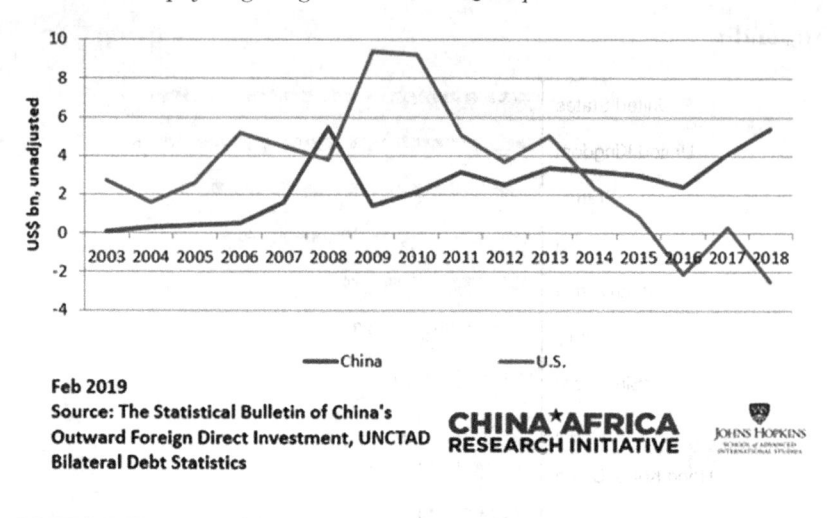

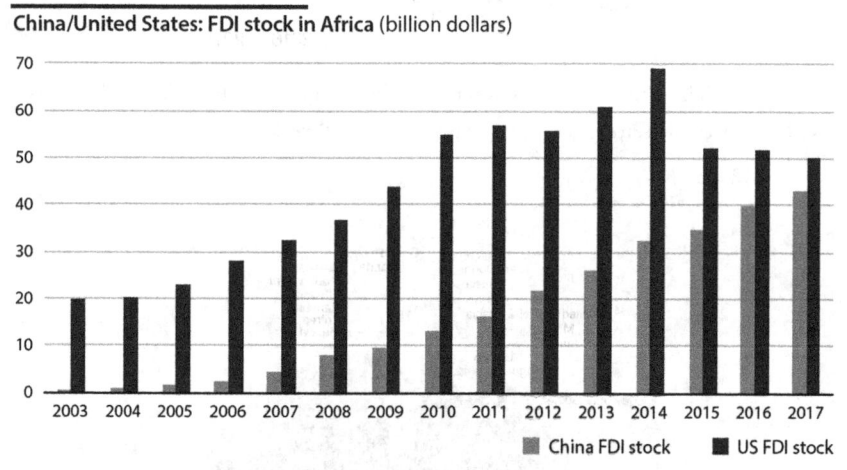

54 *Relationship of Bargaining Power & Deal Quality*

Feb 2019
Source: The Statistical Bulletin of China's
Outward Foreign Direct Investment, UNCTAD
Bilateral Debt Statistics

China/United States: FDI stock in Africa (billion dollars)

Figure A3.3 Chinese FDI vs. US FDI to Africa: Flow and Stocks.

Relationship of Bargaining Power & Deal Quality 55

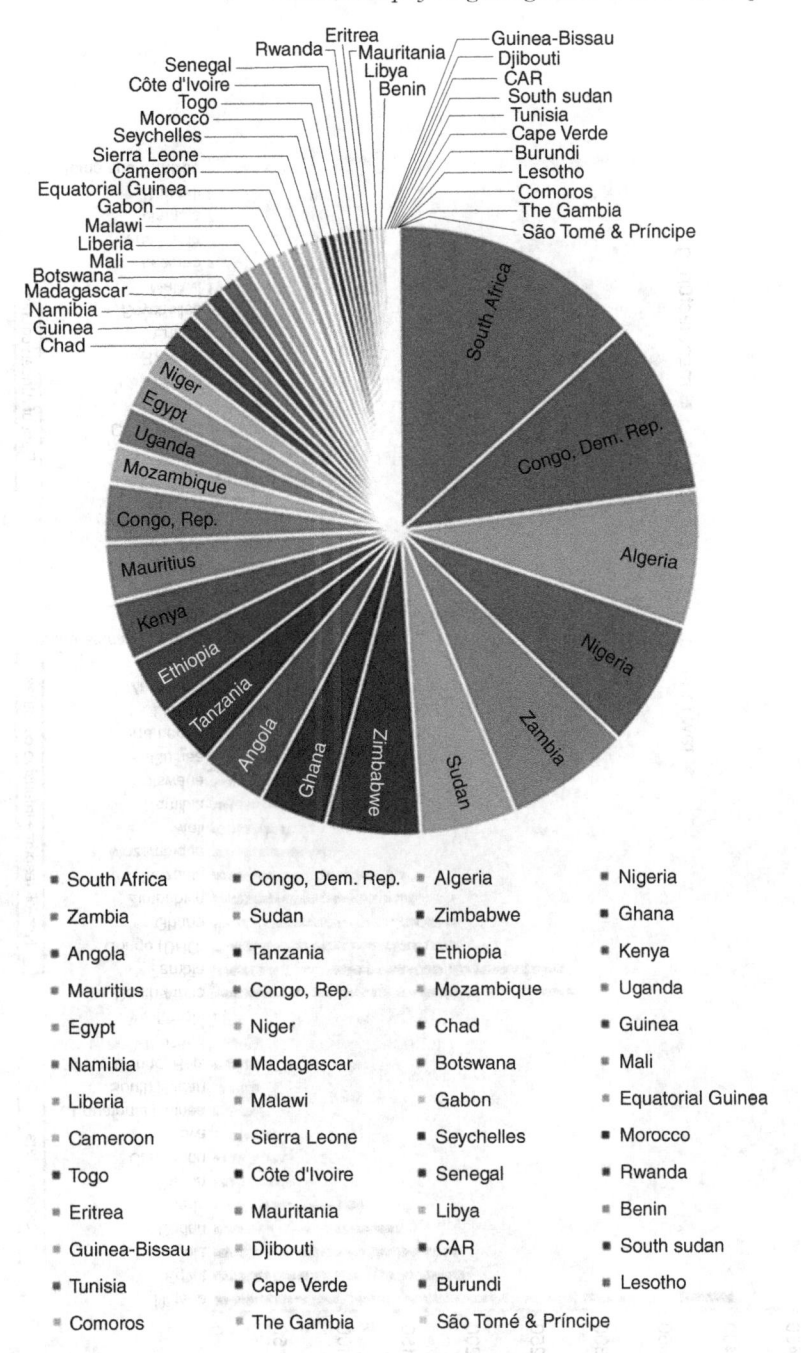

■ South Africa	■ Congo, Dem. Rep.	■ Algeria	■ Nigeria
■ Zambia	■ Sudan	■ Zimbabwe	■ Ghana
■ Angola	■ Tanzania	■ Ethiopia	■ Kenya
■ Mauritius	■ Congo, Rep.	■ Mozambique	■ Uganda
■ Egypt	■ Niger	■ Chad	■ Guinea
■ Namibia	■ Madagascar	■ Botswana	■ Mali
■ Liberia	■ Malawi	■ Gabon	■ Equatorial Guinea
■ Cameroon	■ Sierra Leone	■ Seychelles	■ Morocco
■ Togo	■ Côte d'Ivoire	■ Senegal	■ Rwanda
■ Eritrea	■ Mauritania	■ Libya	■ Benin
■ Guinea-Bissau	■ Djibouti	■ CAR	■ South sudan
■ Tunisia	■ Cape Verde	■ Burundi	■ Lesotho
■ Comoros	■ The Gambia	■ São Tomé & Príncipe	

Figure A3.4 Chinese Investment Stocks in Africa, 2015.
Source: CARI, Johns Hospkins University.

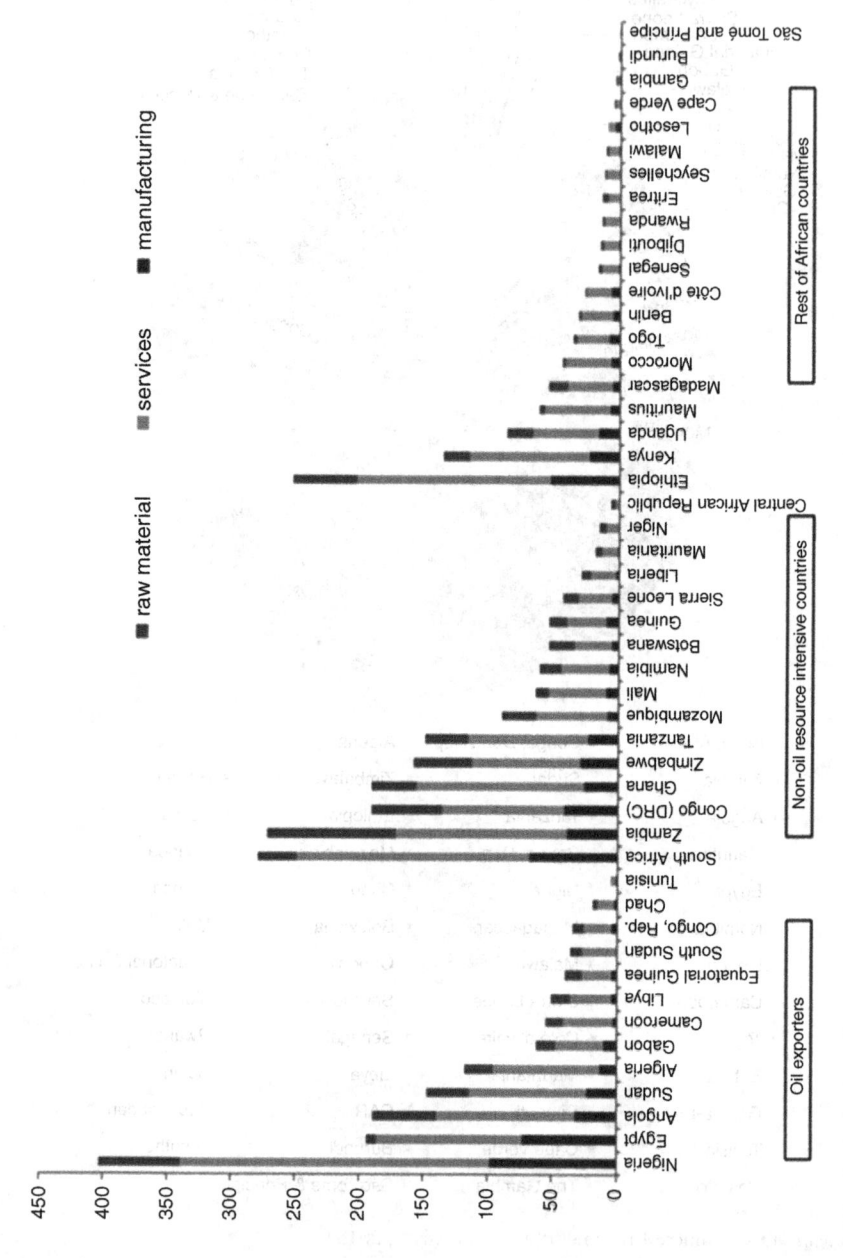

56 *Relationship of Bargaining Power & Deal Quality*

Figure A3.5 Distribution of Small and Medium Private Chinese Enterprises in Africa.

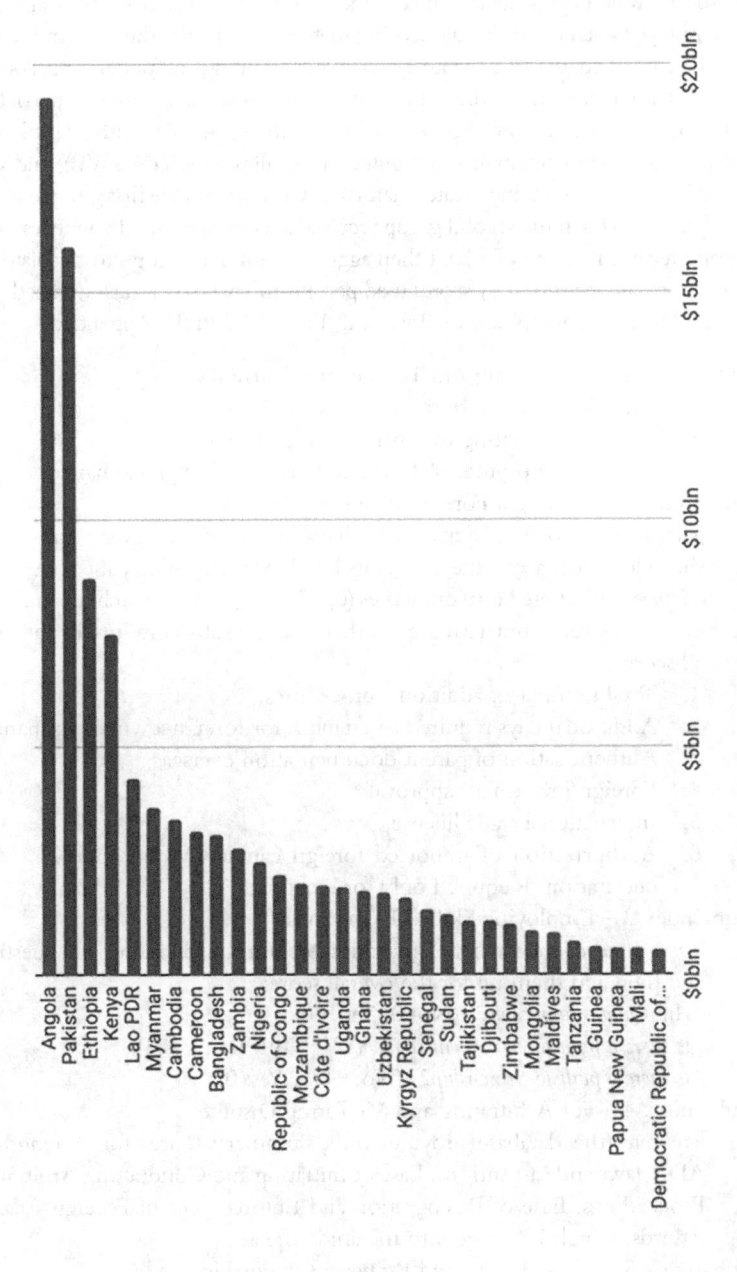

Figure A3.6 The 30 Low-Income Countries with the Most Debt to China.

Methodology

The IFC's "FDI Regulations" database provides summary scores (in italics below) for sub-questions. Wherever qualitative or outside data were used to describe a summary score, I employed a standard −5 scale scoring method to quantify the data. In order to do so, I first graphed the data or analyzed word groupings to understand country clusters and natural cut-offs before I then determined how many levels of restrictiveness (0, −5, −10 etc.) to use. For example, the three cut-offs with "tariffsscore" depended on the tariff rate (applied, weighted mean, all products (%) (WB)) and were 1.0–5%, 2.5–10%, and anything greater than 10%. Countries in the first group received a score of 0, countries in the second group received a score of −5, and countries in the third group received a score of −10. I then aggregate summary scores to calculate five Sub-Indices (please see summary scores used per sub-index below), that averaged, lead to the Deal Quality Score (please see Tables A3.1 and A3.2 in the Appendix).

I. Sub-Index 1 – Converting and Transferring Currency:
   a. *inflowscore* (receiving investment flows)
   b. *outflowscore* (repatriating investment and income)
   c. *payscore* (making payments abroad and holding foreign exchange)
II. Sub-Index 2 – Starting a Foreign Business:
   a. *foreignscore*: % foreign equity ownership allowed, where I average all ownership allowances across the 11 sectors listed for each country into one score
   b. *addprocscore*: where I give out scores (0, −5, −10, −15) for each sub-question based on level of restrictiveness. I then add the sub-scores up for the overall score:
      1. Total number of additional procedures
      2. Additional days required to establish for foreign-owned companies
      3. Authentication of parent documentation overseas
      4. Foreign investment approval
      5. International trade license
      6. Authorization of imported foreign capital (Actual approval, Mere declaration, Required only for incentives)
III. Sub-Index 3 – Employing Skilled Expatriates:
   a. *workpermwuotascore*: where I give out scores for the following sub-questions and then add them up for the overall score:
      "*Are Quotas applicable?*" (No: 0, Yes: −0.5)
      "*Is there a path to permanent residency?*" (No: −0.5, Yes: 0)
      "*Is there a path to citizenship?*" (No: −0.5, Yes: 0)
IV. Sub-Index 4 – For Arbitrating and Mediating Disputes:
   a. *amdscore* (the database provides three summary scores for: Strength of ADR laws and institutions, Ease of Initiating and Conducting Arbitration Proceedings, Ease of Recognition and Enforcement of Foreign Arbitral Awards, which I average into the amdscore
V. Sub-Index 5 – Taxes, Tariffs, and Property Ownership:
   Taxestariffsandpropertyownership: where I give out scores (0, −5, −10, −15) for the following sub-themes and then add them up for the overall score.
   a. taxscore
   b. tariffscore
   c. ffposcore

Table A3.1 Scoring

Country	Inflow Score	Outflow Score	Payment Score	Foreign Exchange Score	AMD Score	Additional Procedures Score	Work Permit/ Quota Score	Tax Score	Tariffs Score	Property Rights Score	Deal Quality (Raw Score)	Deal Quality (Final Score)
Algeria	25.00	41.25	50.00	37.50	62.00	50	95	100	95	90	64.58	90.28
Angola	20.00	20.00	43.75	56.25	63.67	45	85	90	95	90	60.87	99.73
Burkina Faso	100.00	56.25	68.75	12.50	80.67	75		95	95	90	74.80	64.23
Burundi	87.50	62.50	56.25	56.25	56.67	85		95	95	90	76.02	61.11
Cameroon	45.00	75.00	62.50	6.25	86.00	60	100	85	90	100	71.48	72.69
Chad	45.00	75.00	62.50	6.25	65.33	80	95	85	95	90	69.41	77.96
Congo, Dem. Rep.	100.00	100.00	87.50	75.00	74.67	55	95	85	95	90	85.72	36.40
Côte d'Ivoire	100.00	56.25	68.75	12.50	78.33	80	90	100	95	90	77.08	58.40
Egypt, Arab Rep.	100.00	100.00	100.00	100.00	69.00	80		100	95	100	93.78	15.86
Ethiopia	37.50	20.00	62.50	6.25	61.33	50	90	95	95	90	60.76	100.00
Ghana	100.00	75.00	75.00	56.25	84.33	55	95	100	90	100	83.56	41.90
Kenya	100.00	75.00	75.00	100.00	78.00	85	100	95	95	95	89.30	27.27
Liberia						65		100	90	90	86.25	35.04
Madagascar	57.50	100.00	93.75	53.75	75.00	100	90	95	95	95	85.50	36.95
Mali	100.00	56.25	68.75	12.50	73.67	70		100	95	100	75.13	63.38
Mauritius	100.00	100.00	100.00	100.00	75.00	70	90	95	100	95	92.50	19.11
Morocco	75.00	56.25	62.50	37.50	70.67	75	100	90	100	100	76.69	59.40
Mozambique	25.00	47.50	58.33	25.00	83.33	65	85	95	100	90	67.42	83.04
Nigeria	75.00	68.75	56.25	75.00	79.00	60	90	95	95	95	78.90	53.77
Rwanda	87.50	75.00	75.00	75.00	79.67	75	100	100	95	95	85.72	36.40
Senegal	100.00	56.25	68.75	12.50	81.33	70	90	90	95	100	76.38	60.19
Sierra Leone					50.67	75		95	95	90	81.13	48.08
South Africa	62.50	68.75	62.50	25.00	85.00	65	90	95	100	100	75.38	62.75
Tanzania	87.50	75.00	75.00	53.75	66.67	80	95	95	90	100	81.79	46.40
Tunisia	57.50	66.25	62.50	50.00	79.33		100	95	95	90	77.29	57.88
Uganda	100.00	100.00	100.00	100.00	83.00	70			95	90	92.25	19.75
Zambia	100.00	100.00	100.00	100.00	74.67	80	85		100	90	92.19	19.92

Table A3.2 Deal Quality Index and Sub-Indices

Country	Overall Deal Quality Index (Raw Score)	Country	Component 1 DQ Index: Converting and Transferring Currency	Country	Component 2 DQ Sub-Index: Starting a Foreign Business Across Sectors	Country	Component 3 DQ Sub-Index: Employing Skilled Expatriates	Country	Component 4 DQ Sub-Index: Arbitrating and Mediating Disputes	Country	Component 5 DQ Sub-Index: Taxes, Tariffs and Property Ownership
Egypt, Arab Rep.	93.78	Egypt, Arab Rep.	100.00	Madagascar	100.00	Cameroon	100	Cameroon	86.00	Egypt, Arab Rep.	98.33
Mauritius	92.50	Mauritius	100.00	Tunisia	95.58	Kenya	100	South Africa	85.00	Ghana	98.33
Uganda	92.25	Uganda	100.00	Burundi	92.50	Morocco	100	Ghana	84.33	Mali	98.33
Zambia	92.19	Zambia	100.00	Chad	90.00	Rwanda	100	Mozambique	83.33	South Africa	98.33
Kenya	89.30	Congo, Dem. Rep.	90.63	Zambia	90.00	Tunisia	100	Uganda	83.00	Mauritius	96.67
Liberia	86.25	Kenya	87.50	Kenya	89.58	Algeria	95	Senegal	81.33	Morocco	96.67
Congo, Dem. Rep.	85.72	Rwanda	78.13	Côte d'Ivoire	87.92	Chad	95	Burkina Faso	80.67	Rwanda	96.67
Rwanda	85.72	Ghana	76.56	Rwanda	87.50	Congo, Dem. Rep.	95	Rwanda	79.67	Algeria	95.00
Madagascar	85.50	Madagascar	76.25	Egypt, Arab Rep.	85.38	Ghana	95	Tunisia	79.33	Côte d'Ivoire	95.00
Ghana	83.56	Tanzania	72.81	Uganda	85.00	Tanzania	95	Nigeria	79.00	Madagascar	95.00
Tanzania	81.79	Nigeria	68.75	Senegal	84.79	Côte d'Ivoire	90	Côte d'Ivoire	78.33	Mozambique	95.00
Sierra Leone	81.13	Burundi	65.63	Morocco	84.63	Ethiopia	90	Kenya	78.00	Nigeria	95.00
Nigeria	78.90	Burkina Faso	59.38	Sierra Leone	84.58	Madagascar	90	Madagascar	75.00	Senegal	95.00
Tunisia	77.29	Côte d'Ivoire	59.38	Mauritius	83.33	Mauritius	90	Mauritius	75.00	Tanzania	95.00
Côte d'Ivoire	77.08	Mali	59.38	Burkina Faso	82.73	Nigeria	90	Congo, Dem. Rep.	74.67	Zambia	95.00

Relationship of Bargaining Power & Deal Quality   61

Morocco	76.69	Senegal	59.38	Mali	82.67	Senegal	90	Zambia	74.67	Burkina Faso	93.33
Senegal	76.38	Tunisia	59.06	Nigeria	80.00	South Africa	90	Mali	73.67	Burundi	93.33
Burundi	76.02	Morocco	57.81	Liberia	78.85	Angola	85	Morocco	70.67	Cameroon	93.33
South Africa	75.38	South Africa	54.69	Mozambique	78.13	Mozambique	85	Egypt, Arab Rep.	69.00	Ethiopia	93.33
Mali	75.13	Cameroon	47.19	Cameroon	78.04	Zambia	85	Tanzania	66.67	Kenya	93.33
Burkina Faso	74.80	Chad	47.19	South Africa	77.50	Burkina Faso	N/A	Chad	65.33	Liberia	93.33
Cameroon	71.48	Mozambique	38.96	Ghana	77.21	Burundi	N/A	Angola	63.67	Sierra Leone	93.33
Chad	69.41	Algeria	38.44	Tanzania	75.71	Egypt, Arab Rep.	N/A	Algeria	62.00	Tunisia	93.33
Mozambique	67.42	Angola	35.00	Congo, Dem. Rep.	74.71	Liberia	N/A	Ethiopia	61.33	Uganda	92.50
Algeria	64.58	Ethiopia	31.56	Angola	67.46	Mali	N/A	Burundi	56.67	Angola	91.67
Angola	60.87	Liberia	N/A	Ethiopia	58.75	Sierra Leone	N/A	Sierra Leone	50.67	Congo, Dem. Rep.	90.00
Ethiopia	60.76	Sierra Leone	N/A	Algeria	48.08	Uganda	N/A	Liberia	N/A	Chad	88.33

Table A3.3 Resource-Seeking Motivations of Chinese Investment

	Chinese FDI Stocks 2003–2007	Chinese FDI Stocks 2003–2007	Chinese FDI Stocks 2008–2017	Chinese FDI Stocks 2008–2017	Chinese FDI Stocks 2003–2017	Chinese FDI Stocks 2003–2017
	(1)	(2)	(3)	(4)	(5)	(6)
natresrents_lag	0.077***	0.040*	−0.354***	−0.349***	−0.166**	−0.186***
	(0.020)	(0.020)	(0.068)	(0.073)	(0.067)	(0.071)
manuvadded_lag	−0.012	−0.065**	−0.294**	−0.156	−0.569***	−0.412***
	(0.032)	(0.031)	(0.141)	(0.145)	(0.107)	(0.113)
electricity_lag		0.096		0.785***		0.972***
		(0.071)		(0.160)		(0.144)
agland_lag		0.310*		0.198		−0.001
		(0.174)		(0.517)		(0.421)
F Statistic	7.543***	3.744***	15.154***	14.355***	15.764***	19.893***
	(df = 2; 174)	(df = 4; 151)	(df = 2; 407)	(df = 4; 391)	(df = 2; 629)	(df = 4; 588)

*p < .1; **p < .05; ***p < .01.

Table A3.4 Resource- and Market-Seeking Motivations of Foreign Investment

	chinesefdistocks Chinese FDI Stocks 2003–2017	usfdistocks US FDI Stocks 2001–2012	totalfdistocks Total FDI Stocks 2003–2017
	(1)	(2)	(3)
natresrents_lag	−0.148**	−0.148*	−0.042
	(0.061)	(0.080)	(0.026)
manuvadded_lag	−0.228**	−0.128	−0.011
	(0.095)	(0.102)	(0.040)
electricity_lag	−0.196	−0.642**	−0.016
	(0.162)	(0.257)	(0.070)
imports_lag	0.865***	0.863***	0.817***
	(0.109)	(0.151)	(0.046)
gdp_lag	−0.137	0.774***	−0.126
	(0.209)	(0.281)	(0.089)
exports_lag	−0.021	−0.193	−0.124***
	(0.096)	(0.148)	(0.041)
pop	4.449***	−1.576	1.297***
	(0.817)	(1.331)	(0.345)
F Statistic	67.127***	28.136***	146.939***
	(df = 7; 577)	(df = 7; 342)	(df = 7; 583)

*p < .1; **p < .05; ***p < .01.

Table A3.5 Resource-, Market- and Efficiency-Seeking Motivations of Foreign Investment

	chinesefdistocks Chinese FDI Stocks 2003–2017	usfdistocks US FDI Stocks 2001–2012	totalfdistocks Total FDI Stocks 2003–2017
	(1)	(2)	(3)
natresrents_lag	−0.102	−0.154*	−0.065**
	(0.065)	(0.083)	(0.027)
manuvadded_lag	−0.214**	−0.117	0.031
	(0.102)	(0.110)	(0.042)
electricity_lag	−0.153	−0.653**	−0.029
	(0.167)	(0.270)	(0.070)
imports_lag	0.883***	0.856***	0.795***
	(0.111)	(0.161)	(0.046)
gdp_lag	−0.464**	0.851***	0.049
	(0.236)	(0.304)	(0.098)
exports_lag	−0.003	−0.191	−0.110***
	(0.098)	(0.155)	(0.041)
pop	5.342***	−1.808	0.815**
	(0.882)	(1.435)	(0.363)
inflation_lag	−0.0002	0.014	0.115***
	(0.075)	(0.032)	(0.033)
F Statistic	54.529***	22.861***	127.871***
	(df = 8; 538)	(df = 8; 315)	(df = 8; 544)

*p < .1; **p < .05; ***p < .01.

Table A3.6 Economic and Political Motivations of Foreign Investment

	Chinese FDI Stocks 2003–2017 (1)	Chinese FDI Stocks 2003–2017 (2)	chinesefdistocks Chinese FDI Stocks 2003–2017 (3)	Chinese FDI Stocks 2003–2017 (4)	Chinese FDI Stocks 2003–2017 (5)	usfdistocks US FDI Stocks 2001–2012 (6)	totalfdistocks Total FDI Stocks 2003–2017 (7)
regimetype_lag	0.267*** (0.082)				−0.119 (0.090)	0.326** (0.131)	0.015 (0.039)
rol_lag		0.298*** (0.104)			0.383*** (0.142)	−0.478*** (0.183)	−0.087 (0.061)
corr_lag			0.389*** (0.079)		−0.161* (0.085)	0.306*** (0.107)	−0.004 (0.036)
polstabviolterr_lag				−0.006 (0.065)	−0.004 (0.092)	−0.421*** (0.114)	−0.149*** (0.039)
natresrents_lag					−0.116 (0.071)	−0.209** (0.106)	−0.064** (0.031)
manuvadded_lag					−0.365*** (0.111)	−0.158 (0.130)	0.023 (0.048)
imports_lag					0.789*** (0.072)	0.550*** (0.076)	0.632*** (0.031)
gdp_lag					−0.118 (0.245)	1.427*** (0.361)	−0.003 (0.106)
pop					4.859*** (0.878)	−5.306*** (1.675)	1.283*** (0.378)
F Statistic	10.588*** (df = 1; 708)	8.192*** (df = 1; 730)	24.508*** (df = 1; 639)	0.009 (df = 1; 730)	54.911*** (df = 9; 524)	23.297*** (df = 9; 288)	104.248*** (df = 9; 530)

*p < .1; **p < .05; ***p < .01.

Table A3.7 Resource-Seeking Motivations of Chinese Investment (Hot-Deck)

	chinesefdistocks					
	Chinese FDI Stocks 2003–2007	Chinese FDI Stocks 2003–2007	Chinese FDI Stocks 2008–2017	Chinese FDI Stocks 2008–2017	Chinese FDI Stocks 2008–2017	Chinese FDI Stocks 2003–2017
	(1)	(2)	(3)	(4)	(5)	(6)
natresrents_lag	0.077***	0.048	−0.227***	−0.214***	−0.177***	−0.184***
	(0.020)	(0.116)	(0.044)	(0.043)	(0.054)	(0.053)
manuvadded_lag	−0.012	−0.018	−0.175**	−0.172**	−0.094	−0.105
	(0.032)	(0.172)	(0.085)	(0.084)	(0.082)	(0.080)
electricity_lag		0.022		0.291***		0.527***
		(0.191)		(0.080)		(0.067)
agland_lag		0.221		0.340		−0.052
		(1.049)		(0.374)		(0.331)
F Statistic	7.543***	0.061	14.867***	11.503***	5.511***	18.233***
	(df = 2; 174)	(df = 4; 212)	(df = 2; 484)	(df = 4; 482)	(df = 2; 916)	(df = 4; 914)

*p < .1; **p < .05; ***p < .01.

Table A3.8 Resource- and Market-Seeking Motivations of Foreign Investment (Hot-Deck)

	chinesefdistocks Chinese FDI Stocks 2003–2017	usfdistocks US FDI Stocks 2001–2012	totalfdistocks Total FDI Stocks 2003–2017
	(1)	(2)	(3)
natresrents_lag	−0.235***	−0.096*	−0.160***
	(0.046)	(0.049)	(0.022)
manuvadded_lag	−0.157**	−0.312***	−0.056*
	(0.070)	(0.067)	(0.032)
electricity_lag	0.068	−0.143**	−0.005
	(0.065)	(0.062)	(0.035)
imports_lag	0.626***	0.116	0.509***
	(0.085)	(0.103)	(0.037)
gdp_lag	0.219**	−0.142	0.197***
	(0.107)	(0.103)	(0.068)
exports_lag	0.056	0.340***	0.012
	(0.094)	(0.115)	(0.038)
pop	−0.090	2.131***	0.831***
	(0.381)	(0.502)	(0.248)
F Statistic	61.183***	23.451***	129.169***
	(df = 7; 911)	(df = 7; 530)	(df = 7; 788)

*p < .1; **p < .05; ***p < .01.

Table A3.9 Resource-, Market- and Efficiency-Seeking Motivations of Foreign Investment (Hot-Deck)

	chinesefdistocks Chinese FDI Stocks 2003–2017	usfdistocks US FDI Stocks 2001–2012	totalfdistocks Total FDI Stocks 2003–2017
	(1)	(2)	(3)
natresrents_lag	−0.234***	−0.096*	−0.161***
	(0.046)	(0.049)	(0.022)
manuvadded_lag	−0.158**	−0.308***	−0.056*
	(0.070)	(0.068)	(0.031)
electricity_lag	0.070	−0.146**	−0.002
	(0.065)	(0.063)	(0.035)
imports_lag	0.626***	0.113	0.502***
	(0.085)	(0.103)	(0.037)
gdp_lag	0.215**	−0.143	0.212***
	(0.108)	(0.103)	(0.068)
exports_lag	0.054	0.344***	0.026
	(0.094)	(0.116)	(0.038)
pop	−0.086	2.150***	0.820***
	(0.382)	(0.504)	(0.246)
inflation_lag	−0.006	0.010	0.125***
	(0.025)	(0.023)	(0.039)
F Statistic	53.489***	20.515***	115.614***
	(df = 8; 910)	(df = 8; 529)	(df = 8; 787)

*p < .1; **p < .05; ***p < .01.

Table A3.10 Economic and Political Motivations of Foreign Investment (Hot-Deck)

	Chinese FDI Stocks 2003–2017	Chinese FDI Stocks 2003–2017	chinesefdistocks Chinese FDI Stocks 2003–2017	Chinese FDI Stocks 2003–2017	Chinese FDI Stocks 2003–2017	usfdistocks US FDI Stocks 2001–2012	totalfdistocks Total FDI Stocks 2003–2017
	(1)	(2)	(3)	(4)	(5)	(6)	(7)
regimetype_lag	0.246*** (0.069)				−0.146** (0.064)	0.172** (0.071)	0.002 (0.028)
rol_lag		0.496*** (0.079)			0.225** (0.091)	−0.077 (0.092)	−0.056 (0.043)
corr_lag			0.160*** (0.044)		−0.020 (0.039)	0.047 (0.038)	−0.008 (0.018)
polstabviolterr_lag				0.095* (0.058)	−0.101* (0.050)	−0.068 (0.064)	−0.067** (0.026)
natresrents_lag					−0.210*** (0.046)	−0.124** (0.051)	−0.164*** (0.021)
manuvadded_lag					−0.144** (0.070)	−0.291*** (0.069)	−0.045 (0.031)
imports_lag					0.681*** (0.047)	0.368*** (0.042)	0.515*** (0.024)
gd p_lag					0.258** (0.105)	−0.102 (0.097)	0.259*** (0.067)
pop					0.004 (0.390)	2.059*** (0.521)	0.621** (0.242)
F Statistic	12.698*** (df = 1; 917)	39.492*** (df = 1; 917)	13.030*** (df = 1; 917)	2.713* (df = 1; 917)	48.816*** (df = 9; 909)	17.296*** (df = 9; 528)	104.316*** (df = 9; 786)

*p < .1; **p < .05; ***p < .01.

Table A3.11 Private Chinese FDI Stocks Rankings – Five Different Approaches

RANKING 1:

Mc Kinsey Case Studies	Number of Private Firms	McKinsey Private Ranking
Nigeria	874	1
Zambia	775	2
Tanzania	759	3
Ethiopia	620	4
South Africa	547	5
Kenya	317	6
Cote d'Ivoire	247	7
Angola	186	8

RANKING 2:

Countries	Number of Projects	Ranking, Number of Projects
Nigeria	404	1
South Africa	280	2
Zambia	273	3
Ethiopia	255	4
Egypt	197	5
DRC	193	6
Ghana	192	7
Angola	189	8
Zimbabwe	167	9
Tanzania	149	10
Sudan	148	11
Kenya	137	12

RANKING 3:

Countries	Projects in Services	Ranking, Projects in Services
Nigeria	241	1
South Africa	182	2
Ethiopia	152	3
Zambia	134	4
Ghana	131	5
Egypt	117	6
Angola	108	7
DRC	96	8
Tanzania	95	9
Kenya	94	10
Sudan	93	11
Zimbabwe	91	12

RANKING 4:

Countries	Projects in Manufacturing	Ranking, Projects in Manufacturing
Nigeria	98	1
Egypt	76	2
South Africa	69	3
Ethiopia	54	4
DRC	42	5
Zambia	39	6
Angola	32	7
Zimbabwe	32	8
Ghana	27	9
Sudan	24	10
Tanzania	24	11
Kenya	24	12

RANKING 5:

Countries	Projects in Raw Material	Ranking, Projects in Raw Material
Zambia	101	1
Nigeria	65	2
DRC	55	3
Ethiopia	50	4
Angola	49	5
Zimbabwe	44	6
Ghana	34	7
Sudan	31	8
Tanzania	30	9
South Africa	30	10
Mozambique	25	11
Algeria	22	12

Algeria	123	13	Algeria	89	13	Uganda	15	13	Botswana	21	13
Mozambique	94	14	Mozambique	60	14	Algeria	12	14	Uganda	20	14
Uganda	89	15	Mauritius	55	15	Gabon	10	15	Kenya	19	15
Gabon	71	16	Uganda	54	16	Mali	10	16	Gabon	18	16
Mali	68	17	Mali	49	17	Mozambique	9	17	Namibia	18	17
Namibia	66	18	Gabon	43	18	Guinea	9	18	Madagascar	15	18
Mauritius	65	19	Cameroon	42	19	Togo	7	19	Libya	15	19
Cameroon	60	20	Namibia	42	20	Namibia	6	20	Equatorial Guinea	15	20
Botswana	55	21	Madagascar	36	21	Mauritius	6	21	Cameroon	15	21
Madagascar	55	22	Morocco	36	22	Cote d'Ivoire	6	22	Guinea	13	22
Guinea	53	23	Libya	33	23	Sierra Leone	6	23	Sierra Leone	10	23
Libya	51	24	Guinea	31	24	Morocco	6	24	Mali	10	24
Morocco	45	25	Botswana	30	25	Botswana	4	25	Congo, Rep.	9	25
Sierra Leone	43	26	South Sudan	27	26	Madagascar	4	26	South Sudan	9	26
Equatorial Guinea	42	27	Sierra Leone	27	27	Benin	4	27	Liberia	7	27
South Sudan	36	28	Benin	25	28	Cameroon	3	28	Egypt	5	28
Togo	36	29	Togo	24	29	Congo, Rep.	3	29	Niger	4	29
Congo, Rep.	33	30	Equatorial Guinea	24	30	Lesotho	3	30	Eritrea	4	30
Benin	33	31	Congo, Rep.	21	31	Libya	3	31	Mauritania	4	31
Liberia	30	32	Liberia	19	32	Equatorial Guinea	3	32	Togo	4	32
Cote d'Ivoire	27	33	Cote d'Ivoire	19	33	Liberia	3	33	Mauritius	3	33
Chad	18	34	Chad	13	34	Chad	1	34	Benin	3	34
Mauritania	18	35	Senegal	13	35	Mauritania	1	35	Morocco	3	35
Senegal	18	36	Mauritania	12	36	Senegal	1	36	Seychelles	3	36
Niger	15	37	Djibouti	12	37	Tunisia	1	37	Chad	3	37
Djibouti	15	38	Rwanda	12	38	Djibouti	1	38	Senegal	3	38
Rwanda	13	39	Niger	10	39	Gambia	1	39	Cape Verde	1	39
Eritrea	13	40	Malawi	9	40	Burundi	1	40	Cote d'Ivoire	1	40
Seychelles	12	41	Eritrea	9	41	Malawi	1	41	Rwanda	1	41
Malawi	10	42	Seychelles	9	42	South Sudan	0	42	Djibouti	1	42

(Continued)

Table A3.11 (Continued)

RANKING 2:			RANKING 3:			RANKING 4:			RANKING 5:		
Countries	Number of Projects	Ranking, Number of Projects	Countries	Projects in Services	Ranking, Projects in Services	Countries	Projects in Manufacturing	Ranking, Projects in Manufacturing	Countries	Projects in Raw Material	Ranking, Projects in Raw Material
Lesotho	9	43	Lesotho	6	43	Niger	0	43	Malawi	1	43
Tunisia	6	44	Tunisia	4	44	Rwanda	0	44	Gambia	1	44
Cape Verde	4	45	Cape Verde	3	45	Eritrea	0	45	Tunisia	0	45
Gambia	3	46	Gambia	1	46	Seychelles	0	46	Burundi	0	46
Burundi	1	47	Sao Tome and Principe	1	47	Cape Verde	0	47	Sao Tome and Principe	0	47
Sao Tome and Principe	1	48	Burundi	1	48	Sao Tome and Principe	0	48	Lesotho	0	48

Table A3.12 Chinese FDI Stocks and Ease of Doing Business Index

	chinesefdistocks Chinese FDI Stocks 2003–2017	usfdistocks US FDI Stocks 2003–2017	totalfdistocks Total FDI Stocks 2003–2017
	(1)	(2)	(3)
edb_lag	9.26v9	62.600	10.150
	(6.325)	(106.801)	(69.183)
F Statistic	2.147 (df = 1; 301)	0.344 (df = 1; 39)	0.022 (df = 1; 299)

*p < .1; **p < .05; ***p < .01.

Table A3.13 Chinese FDI Stocks and Global Competitiveness Index: Pillar 6.2 – Foreign Competition

	chinesefdistocks Chinese FDI Stocks 2003–2017	usfdistocks US FDI Stocks 2001–2012	totalfdistocks Total FDI Stocks 2003–2018	chinesefdistocks Chinese FDI Stocks 2003–2017	usfdistocks US FDI Stocks 2001–2012	totalfdistocks Total FDI Stocks 2003–2018
	(1)	(2)	(3)	(4)	(5)	(6)
regimetype_lag				5.696	60.092	25.050
				(17.346)	(89.745)	(302.281)
rol_lag				602.109**	−692.394	−3,856.571
				(233.377)	(1,418.153)	(4,007.421)
corr_lag				−5.440	51.738	40.015
				(7.903)	(38.929)	(136.052)
polstabviolterr_lag				−226.750**	−1,191.129**	−5,322.571***
				(108.872)	(569.160)	(1,848.638)
natresrents_lag				−12.353**	−9.366	−160.723*
				(5.600)	(30.237)	(96.273)
manuvadded_lag				−26.612*	−18.986	287.227
				(15.059)	(65.901)	(260.605)
electricity_lag				5.321	8.997	145.456*
				(4.741)	(18.598)	(82.650)
gdp_lag				974.781***	1,997.128**	10,405.940***
				(127.360)	(845.186)	(2,204.933)
gci_lag	226.389**	691.517**	3,949.741***	−40.166	−254.983	1,702.391
	(94.604)	(317.756)	(1,483.910)	(97.372)	(454.294)	(1,694.154)
F Statistic	5.727**	4.736**	7.085***	16.630***	2.315**	8.921***
	(df = 1; 303)	(df = 1; 108)	(df = 1; 309)	(df = 9; 265)	(df = 9; 92)	(df = 9; 271)

*p < .1; **p < .05; ***p < .01.

Table A3.14 Correlation Between Chinese Activity and Global Competitiveness Index: Pillar 6.2 – Foreign Competition

	Global Competitiveness Index: Pillar 6.2 - Foreign Competition
McKinsey Number of Firms	−0.28
McKinsey Ranking	0.31
MOFCOM Number of Projects	−0.07
MOFCOM Ranking of Projects	0.00
MOFCOM Number of Manufacturing Projects	0.06
MOFCOM Ranking of Manufacturing Projects	0.00
MOFCOM Number or Service Projects	−0.06
MOFCOM Ranking or Service Projects	−0.03
MOFCOM Number of Natural Resources Projects	0.01
MOFCOM Ranking of Natural Resources Projects	0.04

Table A3.15 Chinese FDI Stocks and Deal Quality Index

	chinesefdistocks Chinese FDI Stocks 2012	usfdistocks US FDI Stocks 2012	totalfdistocks Total FDI Stocks 2012
	(1)	(2)	(3)
dq	−9.232	113.661	−132.593
	(22.480)	(84.347)	(787.538)
Constant	1,404.207	−6,759.973	33,364.430
	(1,787.515)	(6,684.966)	(62,476.250)
F Statistic	0.169 (df = 1; 22)	1.816 (df = 1; 22)	0.028 (df = 1; 23)

$^*p < .1; ^{**}p < .05; ^{***}p < .01.$

Table A3.16 Chinese FDI Stocks and Deal Quality Sub-Index 1: Converting and Transferring Currency

	chinesefdistocks Chinese FDI Stocks 2012	usfdistocks US FDI Stocks 2012	totalfdistocks Total FDI Stocks 2012
	(1)	(2)	(3)
dq1	−2.897	59.966	−87.519
	(10.908)	(39.916)	(382.364)
Constant	918.855	−1,714.911	30,158.510
	(758.276)	(2,758.404)	(26,423.420)
F Statistic	0.071 (df = 1; 20)	2.257 (df = 1; 21)	0.052 (df = 1; 21)

$^*p < .1; ^{**}p < .05; ^{***}p < .01.$

Table A3.17 Chinese FDI Stocks and Deal Quality Sub-Index 2: Starting a Foreign Business Across Sectors

	chinesefdistocks Chinese FDI Stocks 2012	*usfdistocks* US FDI Stocks 2012	*totalfdistocks* Total FDI Stocks 2012
	(1)	(2)	(3)
dq2	−24.613	−63.899	−428.277
	(19.092)	(76.082)	(687.996)
Constant	2,680.769	7,381.872	57,834.310
	(1,569.516)	(6,248.579)	(56,573.300)
F Statistic	1.662 (df = 1; 22)	0.705 (df = 1; 22)	0.388 (df = 1; 23)

*$p < .1$; **$p < .05$; ***$p < .01$.

Table A3.18 Chinese FDI Stocks and Deal Quality Sub-Index 3: Employing Skilled Expatriates

	chinesefdistocks Chinese FDI Stocks 2012	*usfdistocks* US FDI Stocks 2012	*totalfdistocks* Total FDI Stocks 2012
	(1)	(2)	(3)
dq3	−88.952*	−100.338	−1,130.760
	(48.220)	(126.658)	(1,788.174)
Constant	9,120.893*	11,230.850	131,388.300
	(4,494.470)	(11,805.370)	(166,669.900)
F Statistic (df = 1; 16)	3.403*	0.628	0.400

*$p < .1$; **$p < .05$; ***$p < .01$.

Table A3.19 Chinese FDI Stocks and Deal Quality Sub-Index 4: Arbitrating and Mediating Disputes

	chinesefdistocks Chinese FDI Stocks 2012	*usfdistocks* US FDI Stocks 2012	*totalfdistocks* Total FDI Stocks 2012
	(1)	(2)	(3)
dq4	21.350	−27.796	759.700
	(23.202)	(105.571)	(804.642)
Constant	−864.318	4,302.049	−32,396.740
	(1,712.524)	(7,913.804)	(59,631.200)
F Statistic	0.847 (df = 1; 21)	0.069 (df = 1; 21)	0.891 (df = 1; 22)

*$p < .1$; **$p < .05$; ***$p < .01$.

Table A3.20 Chinese FDI Stocks and Deal Quality Sub-Index 5: Taxes, Tariffs and Property Ownership

	chinesefdistocks Chinese FDI Stocks 2012	usfdistocks US FDI Stocks 2012	totalfdistocks Total FDI Stocks 2012
	(1)	(2)	(3)
dq5	129.860	797.858**	6,188.424**
	(88.380)	(318.436)	(2,952.784)
Constant	−11,629.540	−73,421.640**	−563,122.600*
	(8,377.193)	(30,183.310)	(279,712.500)
F Statistic	2.159 (df = 1; 22)	6.278** (df = 1; 22)	4.392** (df = 1; 23)

*$p < .1$; **$p < .05$; ***$p < .01$.

Table A3.21 Correlation Between Bargaining Power and Deal Quality Index

	FDI Regulations Index
MOFCOM Number of Projects	−0.03
MOFCOM Ranking of Projects	−0.00
MOFCOM Number of Manufacturing Projects	0.12
MOFCOM Ranking of Manufacturing Projects	0.00
MOFCOM Number of Service Projects	−0.05
MOFCOM Ranking of Service Projects	−0.00
MOFCOM Number of Natural Resources Projects	−0.06
MOFCOM Ranking of Natural Resources Projects	0.14

Notes

1 CARI has combined the ODI figures from both the China Statistical Yearbooks and Statistical Bulletins of China's Outward Foreign Direct Investment of various years.
2 Please see a list under JHU SAIS CARI Media.
3 For example, "In your country, how restrictive are regulations related to the hiring of foreign labor?" [1 = highly restrictive; 7 = not restrictive at all].
4 See, for example, the Ease of Doing Business Index Initiative by the World Bank Group, which rates countries' attractiveness to investors, or the Ernst and Young Africa Attractiveness Report (2019).
5 I had initially also included logistics, primary school enrolment, and secondary school enrolment but had to drop these variables due to severe cross-country missing data concerns (more than 25% of the data was missing for each variable). The data was still unbalanced, so I also employed hot-deck imputation to fill in for missing values (please see Table A3.21) in the Appendix for the results).
6 The last year for which UNCTAD US data is available.
7 Comparison between 2012 UNCTAD data on US FDI Stocks and 2012 CARI data on Chinese FDI Stocks.
8 Please note that I am using the raw score (before I reverted the order by subtracting each score from 100 and then rescaled) for the analysis in order not to skew correlations.

4 Bargaining Power and Deal Quality
Experimental Evidence from Nigeria

4.1 Introduction

Nigeria is often used as an example case for weak trade and investment deals between Africa and the rest of the world. There are two common explanations that academic literature, newspaper reports and policy advisors usually point to in order to elucidate why this is the case. The Weak Bargaining Power Narrative posits that if governments like Nigeria's strengthened FDI restrictions, foreign investors would either choose not to enter their markets or – if they are already operating in the markets – they would exit. The bargaining space for these governments to influence deal conditions is therefore effectively very limited, and they are best advised to cater with their policies exclusively toward the needs and preferences of foreign investors if they want to kick-start growth and development.

A second perspective points toward corruption and the lack of accountability as the sources of weak economic outcomes in Africa, and particularly in Nigeria. With the small bargaining power they have, governments could simply choose to use it for personal gain rather than to put in place conditions that would benefit their populations. Solving the issue of corruption would therefore be the first and most important step toward achieving a higher quality of investment deals.

Both explanations described above assume that governments have perfect knowledge on how much bargaining power they possess with foreign investors. But is that truly always the case? While bargaining literature is rich and has expanded to address particularities within the contexts of developing countries, it has paid comparatively scant attention to the role of information and the difference between perceived versus actual bargaining power as predictive of negotiation outcomes. A few studies shine light on the importance of information, notably Wolfe and McGinn (2005), who analyze the effect of (perceptions of) relative power on both the distribution of resources and the integrity of bargaining outcomes. They use experimental games and find that negotiating pairs who perceived a smaller difference in relative power reached agreements of greater integrativeness than pairs who perceived a greater power difference, which we would also expect in the context studied here.

Regarding the African region, the role of information has been studied for high-level negotiations between state actors. For example, Weinhardt and Moerland (2017) offer a reconceptualization of Putnam's (1988) two-level game

DOI: 10.4324/9781003308768-4

by conducting a case study on the Economic Partnership Agreement negotiations between the EU and the West African and the Caribbean regions. They argue that

> [l]imited institutional capacities for collecting and transmitting information about the domestic win-set may prevent domestic constituents from exerting influence on the negotiator. This perspective sheds new light on the outcomes of negotiations in two-level games, as they do not necessarily reflect actual win-sets, but more likely the negotiator's (mis)perceptions or (mis)representations thereof.
>
> (p. 1)

Finally, and perhaps most related to the study conducted here, Berge and Stiansen (2016) analyze the influence of states' experiences around bilateral investment treaty (BITs) negotiations. They use novel text-as-data analysis and leverage states' public regulatory preferences, as expressed through model BITs, to argue that bargaining power stems from expertise in states' bargaining institutes that can be found in effective and meritocratic bureaucracies, rather than be predicted by economic resources alone.

Since expertise can also be treated as a form of "information", these findings shine some light on the influence of cues as a key variable for bargaining outcomes. Yet, evidence from the semi-structured interviews that I conducted with African government officials and managers of private Chinese and Western companies across five countries show that high level state-to-state agreements and BITs have played no significant role in private Chinese companies' decisions to enter African markets. Instead, they listed governments' national FDI policies and conditions offered in case-by-case negotiations with government officials as essential pull-factors for foreign investment inflows.[1] How governments think about FDI policies and how companies decide to enter markets based on these policies often takes place in an isolated context, where parties do not directly face each other. This process can still be understood as a form of negotiation since two parties are weighting and basing their demands and decisions on each other's' perceived alternatives to the negotiated agreement.

To my knowledge, no study to date has analyzed the importance of the perceptions of bargaining power versus competing existing explanations for the outcome of investment negotiations with private companies in developing countries with weak formal institutions. Scholars consequently do not know what role information on bargaining power plays for investment outcomes in this particular setting. In order to fill this gap, I therefore designed and implemented two complementary conjoint experiments in Nigeria in the spring and summer of 2020.

The first experiment (Experiment 1) was conducted in cooperation with a Nigerian NGO. We hired and trained a Nigerian survey team that then interviewed technical advisors and key investment negotiators of the Nigerian federal government and of the Lagos State government. The second experiment (Experiment 2) was conducted in cooperation with a Nigerian company based in Lagos that provides services for Chinese businesses. Similar to Experiment 1, we also hired and trained a Chinese survey team to interview senior managers of private Chinese companies in the service and manufacturing sectors, located in Lagos and Ogun State. Both parties (government and company respondents) were asked to rate hypothetical investment deals with randomly assigned policy attributes that capture "deal quality" including ownership, employment, taxes and licenses, facilitation payments,[2] property rights, environmental regulations, government assistance, and longevity of the policy horizon. In addition, several attributes capturing investment location, sector, the presence of a competitor, type of company (US or Chinese), and entry/exit negotiations were included as part of the deals to vary the background scenarios of the deals.

The experiments allow us to measure for the first time how technical advisors and key negotiators of the Nigerian federal government and Lagos State government assess their bargaining power with Chinese and Western investors, how Chinese companies in Nigeria assess their bargaining power with the Nigerian government, and finally how the government and the companies consequently act or do not act on their bargaining power. By asking Nigerian and Chinese respondents separately about their deal preferences, the study purposefully excludes the influence of negotiation and persuasion techniques that would be salient in face-to-face negotiations. I am, therefore, able to isolate the effects of actual and perceived bargaining power without psychological disturbances through the presence of the other party.

The findings show that while the Nigerian government accurately assesses how sensitive Chinese companies are around revenue generating attributes (e.g. taxes and licenses), there is a statistically significant gap between how much the Nigerian government is asking for, and how much Chinese companies would be willing to give, regarding local participation requirements (local ownership and employment). While government respondents rated the likelihood of both parties signing a deal with an average score of 1.06 (scale: 0–3), company respondents rated the attractiveness of deals with an average score of 1.34 (scale: 0–3). The 0.28-point gap between the two ratings largely exists because government respondents overestimated the importance that Chinese companies ascribe to local participation requirements. Through the complementarity of the two experiments, I am able to show that this gap can be primarily attributed to the Nigerian government's distorted perceptions about their own bargaining leverage. Overall, these findings suggest that the theory proposed in Chapter 1 holds for Nigeria – Chinese companies would be willing to comply with stricter local participation requirements if the Nigerian government asked for them.

In order to explain why some governments may underestimate their bargaining power with China around local participation, I complemented the experiment with a survey. The aim was to better understand the number of actors involved in the negotiations; how they cooperate or compete with each other on each side, and what creates well-coordinated versus poorly-coordinated teams that induce (or fail to induce) free flow of information about sources of bargaining power (e.g. the role of national and state governments; or the formation of national ministries); the role of regime type and electoral politics (e.g. how electoral cycles change politicians' incentives and demands to gain access to information about bargaining power); and the importance of third-party advisors and information shocks (e.g. Western advisors, international organizations, and NGOs). Chapters 6 and 7 describe in detail how the findings travel from Nigeria to the other four case studies, and tease out the causal mechanisms that distinguish governments that hold perceptions of high bargaining power (e.g. Ethiopia, Tanzania) from governments that hold perceptions of medium bargaining power (e.g. South Africa) to those that hold beliefs of low bargaining power (e.g. Nigeria, Kenya).

4.2 Case Selection

I selected Nigeria for the experiment because the Nigerian federal government imposes relatively few requirements on foreign investors while it is ranked among the top receivers of Chinese investments across Africa. "You can't negotiate with the Chinese!"[3] was among the most common phrases I gathered in my interviews with government officials in Abuja, Nigeria in the summer of 2019. At the same time, my interviews with Chinese companies in Nigeria reveal that, in fact, a high readiness exists to comply with stricter regulations since "the Nigerian market is so good" that they "would stay under any kind of policy restrictions."[4] Consequently, there may exist an important gap between what the Nigerian side believes it is able to ask for, and what the Chinese side is, in fact, willing to give. Nigerian politics is also corruption-ridden and its economic ideology may have been significantly influenced by the international capitalist regime, notably since the 1990s. Nigeria is therefore an appropriate case to test my theory and alternative hypotheses on why Nigeria maintains an open FDI regime despite its high attractiveness, relative to other countries on the continent, to Chinese investors.

It is also an appropriate case to test whether my interview results overlap with the experimental results. Since a growing body of literature points to the influence of identity, gender, and foreigner effects in international research (Baldwin et al. forthcoming, Adida et al. 2016, Blaydes and Gillum 2013, Campbell 1981), respondents may be more open to discuss issues related to the government with their co-ethnics rather than with a white foreign woman. For this purpose, I hired a fully Nigerian staff (four members; two male and two female) to conduct the interviews with the technical advisors to the Nigerian government, and a fully Chinese staff (two members; both male[5]) to conduct the interviews with Chinese companies in Lagos and Ogun State.

4.3 Variables That May Influence the Quality of Deals

Below, I describe different theories on why governments may negotiate weak deals with foreign investors, and predictions on how each mechanism should play out in the conjoint experiments.

4.3.1 Weak Bargaining Power Narrative

Following classic work on the poverty trap (Sachs et al. 2004), the first mechanism describes governments' behavior under the assumption that they have perfect knowledge over their bargaining power with Chinese investors and that this bargaining power is simply weak. If Chinese companies exited, or did not enter an African market when stricter policy requirements were set in place, the government has simply no option but to agree to whatever conditions the Chinese side is asking for. We would consequently expect government respondents, who believe that Nigeria is negotiating from a position of weakness, to sign weaker deals in Experiment 1. In addition, we would also expect Chinese companies in Experiment 2 to sign deals that grant them significant freedom and benefits, and to leave little bargaining space to the African side across all policy attributes.

4.3.2 Lack of Accountability and Corruption

The second mechanism concerns how governments think about their direct relationship to voters, and whether they believe constituents can punish them for signing deals whose outcomes are unfavorable for the population. If governments believe that their constituents will not change their vote based on official FDI regulations, or specific conditions present and absent in deals signed with foreign investors, governments may be more likely to sign deals that are in their own self-interest rather than those that take into account their voters' preferences. Deals in Nigeria could consequently grant foreign investors relatively more freedom because the government is aware of their bargaining power but chooses this bargaining power to ask for personal payments. Such self-interested decision-making could be especially likely in an environment like Nigeria, where ethno-regional identity (Olayode 2015) and vote-buying (Francis et al. 2015) largely determine the outcome of elections; and where the government generally does not provide public information on investment deals. While governments may not try to cater to all voters, they could still take into account the preferences of special-interest groups that contribute to election campaigns (Grossman and Helpman 1996). As a result, I test for governments' accountability sentiments toward both voters and special-interest groups.

In particular, I included four questions on corruption/lack of accountability in the government survey:

1. *Have voters in the past asked your office about the conditions specified in the deals? If yes, what were they interested in? (please circle one and take notes if answered with yes)*
2. *Judging from your past experience, what are important drivers of voters' decision-making during elections?*
3. *(If not mentioned in the list above) Are investment deals an important driver of voters' decision-making during elections? (If respondent says no) – Why not? (please circle one and take notes if answered with no)*
4. *Judging from your past experience, have Nigerian businessmen asked your office about investment deals set up by your government office with foreign investors? If yes, what were they interested in? (please circle one and take notes if answered with yes)*

If either question 2 did not include foreign investment deals in the response, and/or question 3 was answered with no, and questions 1 and 4 were both answered with no, I coded the "corruption/lack of accountability" variable as 1, otherwise as 0.

4.3.3 Perceptions on Bargaining Power

Finally, the third possible mechanism describes government behavior under the assumption that their bargaining power with Chinese investors is strong, but that the government underestimates this power. If the government believes that it has little bargaining leverage to influence deal conditions, it would be willing to sign deals that are highly favorable to the investors to lure them into their markets, even if, effectively, the Chinese companies would also be entering and/or staying under stricter regulations.

There is an important difference between the first and third causal mechanism: In the first case, government responses of what they think they are able to demand, and what Chinese companies are in fact willing to give, should overlap. In contrast, under the third causal mechanism, we should observe a gap between the two. The complementarity of the two conjoint experiments, therefore, helps us to understand respective levels of bargaining power between the companies and the government, how the Chinese side thinks about the Nigerian investment climate, and whether Chinese companies would be willing to agree to stricter FDI regulations.

I asked the following background questions on low (coded as 0) versus high (coded as 1) perceptions of bargaining power with China on the government survey:

1. In your opinion, does Nigeria receive little, same or a lot of Chinese money compared to the rest of the African continent?
2. Does Nigeria have no, few or a lot of competitors for foreign investment on the continent? Who are they?
3. Which of the following statements do you think are true? (please show them the list, printed on a separate document, and let them circle what is appropriate to them. Please attach the form to this survey at the end of the interview.)
   a. It is easier to negotiate with Western investors than with Chinese ones.
   b. It is easier to negotiate with Chinese investors than with Western investors.
   c. Nigeria and the West are equal partners.
   d. Nigeria and China are equal partners.
   e. Nigeria offers land, labor, or raw material but foreign investors bring the money. So foreign investors should have most of the say in investment negotiations.
   f. Nigeria is a dwarf and China is a giant.
   g. Nigeria has little say in investment deals with the West.
   h. Nigeria has little say in investment deals with China.
   i. The Chinese are everywhere in Africa, and very aggressive, they will not come to your country if they don't get their way, so you can't negotiate with them.

If Question 1 is answered with "receive little" or "receive the same", it is coded as 0. If Question 2 is answered with "a lot of competitors", it is coded as 0.

Table 4.1 Summary of Predictions of Each Mechanism

Attributes predicted to condition effects of including local participation in mock deal with Chinese investors	Corruption and Lack of Accountability	Weak Bargaining Power Narrative: Correct Perceptions of Bargaining Power under the Assumption that Bargaining Power is Small	Distorted Perceptions of Bargaining Power
Believe population and/or special-interest groups cannot punish them based on choice to sign the deal	√		?
Believe they negotiate from a position of weakness		√	√
Expect Chinese partner to be willing to pay bribes	√		
Expect Chinese partner to be willing to agree to stricter deal conditions	√		
Chinese respondents agree to the same level of deal strictness that government respondents predict	√	√	
Chinese respondents agree to stricter deals than government respondents believe			√

If statements 3e, 3f, 3h or 3i are answered with "yes", they are each coded as 0. If out of Question 1, 2, 5, and 3e, 3f, 3h and 3i, at least four are coded as 0, I code the person as 0, "low perceptions of bargaining power with China." Table 4.1 summarizes predictions of each mechanism.

4.4 Survey Experiment Design: Conjoint Analysis

The empirical innovation of this research threefold. First, I use for the first time an experimental design to complement the few existing observational studies on negotiation behavior around trade and investment in China–Africa relations (Soulé 2019). Blair and Roessler (2018) use survey experiments and experimental games to examine the effects of Chinese aid on the legitimacy of African states but, to the best of my knowledge, no experiment has been conducted to better understand motivations, policy sensitivity and exit thresholds of different types of Chinese companies in Africa.

Second, the study's design, for the first time, shines light on how the Nigerian government and Chinese private companies perceive each other. This feature allows us to understand the validity of the Weak Bargaining Power Narrative versus the new Power of Weak Economies Theory advanced in this book. The central power of the experiment therefore arises from comparing the results of the two experiments and from drawing inferences for players' levels of (perceived) bargaining power.

The third innovation of this research in the context of China–Africa relations is that it is an original choice-based conjoint survey experiment. Conjoint designs allow for studying individuals' preferences on multidimensional policies. They have been applied to a range of topics that are of interest to political science, including voting behavior (Franchino and Zucchini 2014), mass attitudes toward immigration (Hainmueller and Hopkins 2014) or tax policy preferences (Ballard-Rosa et al. 2017), among others. Yet, this is to my knowledge the first time that a conjoint analysis is used to study investment deal preferences. A conjoint analysis is useful in this case for two reasons: First, investment deals typically include a multitude of attributes that are a reflection of countries' FDI policies and case-by-case deal requests. A conjoint design allows us to estimate the causal effects of multiple treatment components and to assess several causal hypotheses simultaneously. It helps us to answer questions such as: How much value do companies place on the amount of tax versus local ownership requirements when deciding where to invest? In addition, a conjoint design is useful in this context since one of the competing alternative hypotheses concerns corruption, a variable that is difficult to measure. The conjoint design will therefore reveal corrupt practices (if they do play a role) without direct questions on the matter.

4.4.1 Background Variables

In Experiment 1, government respondents were first asked to answer a series of background questions on regional origin (North Central, North East, North West, South East, South South or South West), education (domestic or abroad), age (< or = 50, > 50) and gender (F/M). In Experiment 2, Chinese respondents were asked to answer questions on industry (manufacturing or services), business environment (competitive/not competitive), number of employees (0–5, 6–10, 10+), years of operations (less than a year, 1–5 years, 5+ years), and located in industrial park (Yes/No) to better understand the influence of these background variables on measured outcomes.

4.4.2 Investment Deal Rating

Each respondent in Experiments 1 and 2 was then given two hypothetical investment deal pairs with several features that were independently randomized. Respondents were asked to rate each deal on a scale of 0–3, and also asked which deal they would prefer to sign. Figure 4.1 provides a template for the deals that were presented to all respondents.

Imagine that a [U.S. company[vi] / Chinese company] [is interested in running / has been for a year running] [a microloan business / a foam factory / a keke ride hailing service] in [Lagos State / Oyo State / Kano State].

[blank / Another company is also interested in entering the market with the same idea.]

Imagine now that the conditions for the [U.S. company[vii] / Chinese company] to [operate / keep operating suddenly] were the following:

- [The company can be 100% foreign owned. (status quo) / The company must set up a contractual joint venture with a local partner. / The company must be 51% locally owned.]

- [No local employment requirements apply. (status quo) / The company can hire non-Nigerians only if all efforts have been explored to obtain a local expert and must propose a succession plan to train and hire a citizen for the same position. / The company must hire at least 30% locals for executive and senior management positions.]

- [A five year tax holiday applies. / A corporate income tax of 30% applies. (status quo)/ A corporate income tax of 35% applies.]

- [No license fees apply. / A license fee of N2 million annually applies.]

- [No facilitation payments apply / One-time facilitation payments of 180,000 Naira apply.]

- [The company may acquire and own immovable property. Property rights will be enforced by the Nigerian government. (status quo) / The company may lease all immovable property from the government.]

- [There are no water or air pollution restrictions imposed on the company. (status quo)/ The company will need to stick to strict water and air pollution regulations, including emission restrictions set forth by the Nigerian government.]

- The company will need to obtain standard business licenses, work permits, land acquisitions and visas if applicable. (status quo) / The government, through the Nigerian Investment Promotion Commission (NIPC), will expedite delivery times of business licenses, work permits, land acquisitions and visas for the company. In addition, the government will assist the company in labor strike settlements, facilitation of resettlements and compensation negotiations.

- [The company is guaranteed the same conditions to hold over the next two years after which the conditions may change or stay the same. / The company is guaranteed the same conditions to hold over the next five years after which the conditions may change or stay the same.]

Government Signature   **Company Signature**

Figure 4.1 Investment Deal [Template].

Each combination of components corresponds to a realistic policy attribute in line with the conditions that I found in my qualitative interviews to be important to foreign investors and governments. In addition, several background variables were also randomized to test the influence on deal outcomes. A short description of each attribute is offered in the Appendix.

After the experiment, respondents in both Experiment 1 and 2 were asked a list of follow-up questions. Given the overlap of the experiment with the Covid-19 outbreak in the spring of 2020, I included questions on the impact of Covid-19 on perceived bargaining powers in the follow-up questions for surveys conducted after March 30, 2020 (the beginning of the lockdown in Nigeria). The full surveys can be found in the Appendix.

There are certainly benefits and drawbacks in including a variety of attributes in the hypothetical investment deals. Most importantly, on the drawbacks, respondents may not understand the wording of the deals, mix up attributes, or lose interest before they have finished reading the scenarios. In order to mitigate these concerns, survey teams received detailed instructions on how to present the deals, to ensure that respondents, in fact, read the deals, and were directed to ask after the deals were read whether anything was unclear. We also sent out both teams to conduct pilots with government respondents and Chinese companies prior to conducting the experiments, where we alternated the number of attributes from three to fifteen. We did not observe any differences in willingness to participate, respond or complete the rating of two investment deal pairs, which is why we chose to include all attributes that were commonly mentioned as important in my interviews with government officials and companies prior to conducting the experiment. Including more attributes does not pose a threat to power in conjoint experiments, only including more levels does. I, therefore, kept the number of levels to a maximum of three, and usually only had two per attribute.

To respond to the concern that participants might not carefully read the deals, I included a Keke ride hailing service as one of the sectoral scenarios. As mentioned above, the Lagos State government banned all Kekes and Okadas on February 1, 2020. The ban was widely publicized via the news, social media, and posters on the street and led to protests on Lagos mainland. We would therefore expect respondents to be generally aware of the ban, and – if presented with a Keke ride hailing service scenario in Lagos – to bring up the new regulations. Finally, a few studies show that the order in which attributes are presented influences decision making processes when respondents' familiarity with the attributes is low (Kumar and Gaeth 1991). Since all attributes listed in the deals are informed by interviews that I had conducted with stakeholders, I assume that respondents were generally familiar with these attributes. In addition, randomizing order of attributes per deal would also come at some costs. Most importantly, since we are asking respondents to compare deals, keeping an order within the list of attributes may help them to compare differences per condition more easily. I consequently decided to keep the order of attributes fixed.

4.4.3 Outcome Variables

Deal Rating (0–3): I code a variable Deal Rating that takes a value of 0, 1, 2 or 3, depending on how likely the respondent believes the government/the company/both together would sign the deal.

Sign deal (Yes/No): I code a binary outcome variable Sign Deal that takes a value of 0 or 1, depending on whether the respondent would sign the deal.

4.4.4 Hypotheses

I conduct three types of analyses. First, the central hypothesis tested through the experiments with the Nigerian government and Chinese companies is as follows:

Hypothesis 1:

Technical advisors and key investment negotiators to the Nigerian government will underestimate the government's bargaining power with Chinese companies. This means that they will estimate Chinese companies' sensitivity around all policy attributes to be higher and thus companies' willingness to sign deals as lower compared to their own willingness and to what Chinese companies report themselves. (Testing the Weak Bargaining Power Narrative and the Perceptions of Bargaining Power Theory).

Second, I analyze potential Average Marginal Component Effect for both government and company responses. As summarized in Table 4.1, I expect the following:

Hypothesis 2:

For government respondents that indicate having low perceptions of bargaining power, the gap between what deals they believe to maximize the likelihood of both the government and the company signing, and what the Chinese company would in fact be willing to sign will be larger than for respondents that have high perceptions of bargaining power (Testing the Perceptions of Bargaining Power Theory).

Hypothesis 3:

Government respondents who are of type "corruption/lack of accountability" will prefer deals that include facilitation payments, and will also believe that Chinese companies are willing to sign these deals (but not US companies due to the Anti-Corruption Act), compared to respondents who are not of that type. (Testing the Lack of Accountability and Corruption Theory).

Third, since the experiment was conducted during the global Covid-19 outbreak, I also included questions on the implications of the virus for bargaining power at the end of the survey for respondents who took the survey after March 30, 2020 (when the Federal Government announced a total lockdown of Lagos and Abuja due to Covid-19) to test the following hypothesis:

Hypothesis 4:

Government respondents who took the survey after March 30, 2020 will report lower/higher levels of bargaining power across attributes, compared to pre-March 30 government respondents. Company respondents who took the survey after March 30 will report lower/higher levels of bargaining power across attributes, compared to pre-March 30 respondents.

4.5 Sampling and Implementation

For both Experiment 1 and Experiment 2, the research teams employed snowball sampling to identify suitable research subjects. For the government survey, the Nigerian research team reached out to all technical advisors within the federal

Table 4.2 Set of Respondents and Total Number of Ratings

	Pre-Covid-19 Number of Respondents	Post-Covid-19 Number of Respondents	Total Number of Respondents	Total Number or Ratings
Government Respondents	85	49	134	512
Company Respondents	71	71	142	526

government of Nigeria as well as for the Lagos State governments, who then gave us contact with more research subjects involved in investment and trade negotiations. We contacted each person at most twice. In total, we recruited 134 government respondents. 122 respondents rated both deal pairs, 12 respondents chose to only rate one deal pair. In total, we therefore have 512 ratings (Table 4.2).

For the Chinese company survey, the Chinese research team used contacts from the Nigerian company that was leading the project with me, who then gave us contact with more research subjects who were managing Chinese companies in Lagos and Ogun State. In addition, our research team also drove around the city of Lagos and small villages in Ogun State to look for Chinese company signs and then approached them directly. We specifically targeted clusters of Chinese companies (but not Ogun Guangdong and Lekki FTZ Zone) outside of Lagos, and focused on single Chinese companies in the Lagos area. We recruited 142 company respondents, with 121 respondents rating both deals and 21 choosing to only rate one deal pair. In total, we collected 526 ratings (Table 4.2).

Both survey experiments were supposed to be implemented between February and May 2020. Yet, the first official Covid-19 cases emerged in Nigeria at the beginning of March and the Nigerian government implemented a lockdown in Lagos and Abuja on March 30, 2020. We had conducted 85 surveys with the government and 71 surveys with companies by that time. We then had to pause the experiments while waiting for further instructions from the Nigerian government and the Yale Faculty of Arts and Sciences Dean's Office on in-person research. To protect the safety of the research teams, we eventually decided to switch completely to phone interviews. The Chinese research team resumed work on April 15, while the Nigerian research team resumed work on June 10. Both survey experiments were completed by July 10, 2020.

The exogenous Covid-19 shock could have significantly influenced causal processes that this book aims to study. We therefore included Covid-19 related questions in the interviews conducted after March 30 to be able to deal with the shock as a potential "treatment". The Covid-19 related questions can be found in the questionnaires in the final Appendix.

4.6 Results

Since the deal attributes are conditionally independent randomizations, the Average Marginal Component Effect (AMCE) and the Average Component Interaction Effect (ACIE) are non-parametrically identified and are estimated using a regression of the outcome variables on indicator variables corresponding to the values taken by each attribute (Hainmueller et al. 2013, Hainmueller and Hopkins 2014). Standard errors are clustered at the respondent level to account for the non-independence of multiple choices made by each respondent. I employ Ordinary Least Squares (OLS) throughout the analysis. Research subjects in Experiment 1 and Experiment 2 are hereafter called "government respondents" and "company respondents", respectively.

4.6.1 Analysis 1: Comparison Between Government Perceptions and Actual Behavior of Chinese Companies

The first and core analysis concerns responses to the following questions:

Government Respondents (Experiment 1):

1. In scenario X, how likely do you think the government and the company would be to both sign the deal? (0 = definitely not sign, 3 = definitely sign)?
2. Do you think the government in scenario X would sign the deal?
3. Do you think the company in scenario X would sign the deal?

Company Respondents (Experiment 2):

4. How likely on a scale from 0–3 would you be to sign deal X (0 = definitely not sign, 3 = definitely sign)?

A comparison of these four questions shines light on government respondents' perceptions of their own and Chinese companies' behavior (Question 1, 2 and 3), and whether Chinese companies would, in fact, agree to deals with the government (Question 4).

Figure A4.1 in the Appendix summarizes the main results for how government respondents rated the likelihood of both the government and the company signing the deal (Question 1) and 95 percent confidence intervals for each attribute. The first finding is that government respondents rated the likelihood as significantly lower if everything else equal, the deal included ownership ["Joint Venture" (−0.22) and "51 percent locally owned" (−0.26)], and employment restrictions ["Succession Plan" (−0.11) and "At least 30 percent local for executive and senior management" (−0.15)], if the deal included facilitation payments (−0.10), license fees (−0.058), if the deal was made in Kano State (−0.15) or if the corporate income tax was raised to 35 percent (−0.12). In contrast, government respondents rated the likelihood of both parties signing the deal as higher if the government provided extra assistance (0.10) or if there was a competitor present (0.13).

Importantly, respondents also made no distinction in their likelihood ratings between whether the company was a Chinese or US one, indicating that they assessed both types of companies to be equally likely to sign or not sign deals with the government. None of the Average Component Interaction Effects (ACIEs) were statistically significant, which could be an issue of small sample size.

The average rating of the likelihood of signing a deal was a mere 1.06. If the cut-off between signing a deal or not were 1.5 (since the scale was 0–3), this implies that government respondents believed most deals would be rejected by at least one of the parties. The assumption is that respondents have evaluated both the government and the company's likelihood to sign the deal, and then based their assessment of overall likelihood of signing the deal on whatever likelihood of the two parties they believed to be lower. So, whose perceived preferences are driving this low rating? In other words, are government responses based on what they believe to be Chinese or Nigerian government preferences?

In order to answer this question, the survey had government respondents answer separately whether they thought that first, the state government and second, the company would sign the deal. Figure A4.2 in the Appendix provides a summary of government respondents' opinions about the state government decisions and 95 percent confidence intervals for each attribute. Since most attributes are beneficial to the government, the percentage of deals that state governments are perceived to be willing to sign is unsurprisingly high (79 percent).

Figure A4.3 in the Appendix summarizes government respondents' perceptions of whether a company (either Chinese or US) would sign a deal or not. Of the deal presented, respondents estimated that companies would sign a mere 18.55 percent.[6] Similar to their response on Question 1 (the overall likelihood of both parties signing the deal), government subjects indicated that they believed companies are less likely to sign deals if they included ownership (−0.175 and −0.206, respectively for each level) and employment restrictions (−0.161 and 0.215 respectively for each level), if there were facilitation payments (−0.069), if the deal was made in Kano State (−0.216) or if corporate taxes were raised to 35 percent (−0.129).

Importantly, the coefficient on type of company is small (0.03) and not significant, indicating that the government believes US and Chinese companies are about equally likely to sign deals. The results largely overlap with the responses to Question 1, except the coefficient on license fees remains statistically insignificant here and the coefficient on tax holidays is now large and significant (since Question 3 is explicitly about company preferences only).

These findings provide important information on how government respondents assess company's preferences, and how these perceived preferences translate into the overall likelihood of the government being able to strike a deal with investors. According to government respondents, the government would be likely to sign most deals while companies strongly favor deals with fewer restrictions and, importantly, are also unlikely to give in to government demands. Overall, the low average rating suggests that there was a general pessimism about companies signing, which translates into a very low average rating for the likelihood of a deal signed by both parties.

The central question of this analysis is: How do these government perceptions of Chinese company behavior compare to companies' actual behavior gathered from the company survey that was conducted with managers of Chinese businesses in Lagos and Ogun State? The results in Figure A4.4 in the Appendix show that there is a quite striking gap between the deals government respondents believe

Chinese companies would sign and the deals Chinese companies would in fact sign. Most centrally, companies rated deals with an average of 1.34 (on a 0–3 scale), which is 0.28 points higher than what government respondents had indicated on Question 1 (1.06).

A key comparison in Figure 4.2 between Question 1 and Question 4 shows that government respondents severely overestimated the importance of ownership (by 0.12 points for "51 percent locally owned" and the coefficient for "Joint Venture" is only large and statistically significant in the government survey results) and employment restrictions (by 0.03 points for "At least 30 percent local for executive and senior management" while the coefficient for "Succession Plan" is only large and significant for the government survey results). The government slightly underestimated the importance of a deal being signed in Kano (by 0.04 points) and of license fees (by 0.02 points).

On the positive attributes to investors, government respondents underestimated the importance of providing government assistance (by 0.04 points), and believed that the presence of a competitor and facilitation payments would influence the likelihood of a deal being signed ratings, which is not reflected in the company results. Government and company responses largely overlapped, however, for (estimated) sensitivity to 35 percent tax. Finally, the government believed that facilitation payments, the presence of a competitor and whether the deal was signed in Lagos State mattered to Chinese companies (which they did not). In addition, the government did not indicate that environmental restrictions, tax holiday, or sector (Keke ride hailing service) would matter for Chinese companies (which they did). A comparison between Question 3 (government perceptions of whether the company would sign a deal) and Question 4 (company responses on whether they would sign the deal) shows very similar results (please see Appendix).[7]

As a second check, on the company survey I included the question: "What would have to happen so that you take the decision to leave Nigeria; and where else would you go?" at the very end of the survey. Interestingly, my research team reported back to me that many respondents were confused about this question in particular, and said that they did not intend to leave, even if the overall business environment got difficult. "I don't understand, I don't want to leave", "I'm not leaving, my business is here, we always face difficulty with the government or the currency or electricity but [it is the] same in China, I prefer to be here, I can make better money here", and "There is no place like here I can go to."

25 percent of company respondents said that they would leave if taxes increased significantly, if they started to make losses, or if the security situation got significantly worse, and that in that case, they would go back to China. Interestingly, none of the respondents mentioned that they would leave if they suddenly had to employ locals, and only five said that they would leave if they had to set up a Joint Venture with a local company.

Is the difference in how the government and companies perceive local participation requirements statistically significant? In order to answer this question, I combined government and company responses and interacted each of the variables "ownership" and "employment" with type of respondent. Figures 4.3 and 4.4 present the results. The Average Component Interaction Effects (ACIEs) for both

90 *Bargaining Power and Deal Quality*

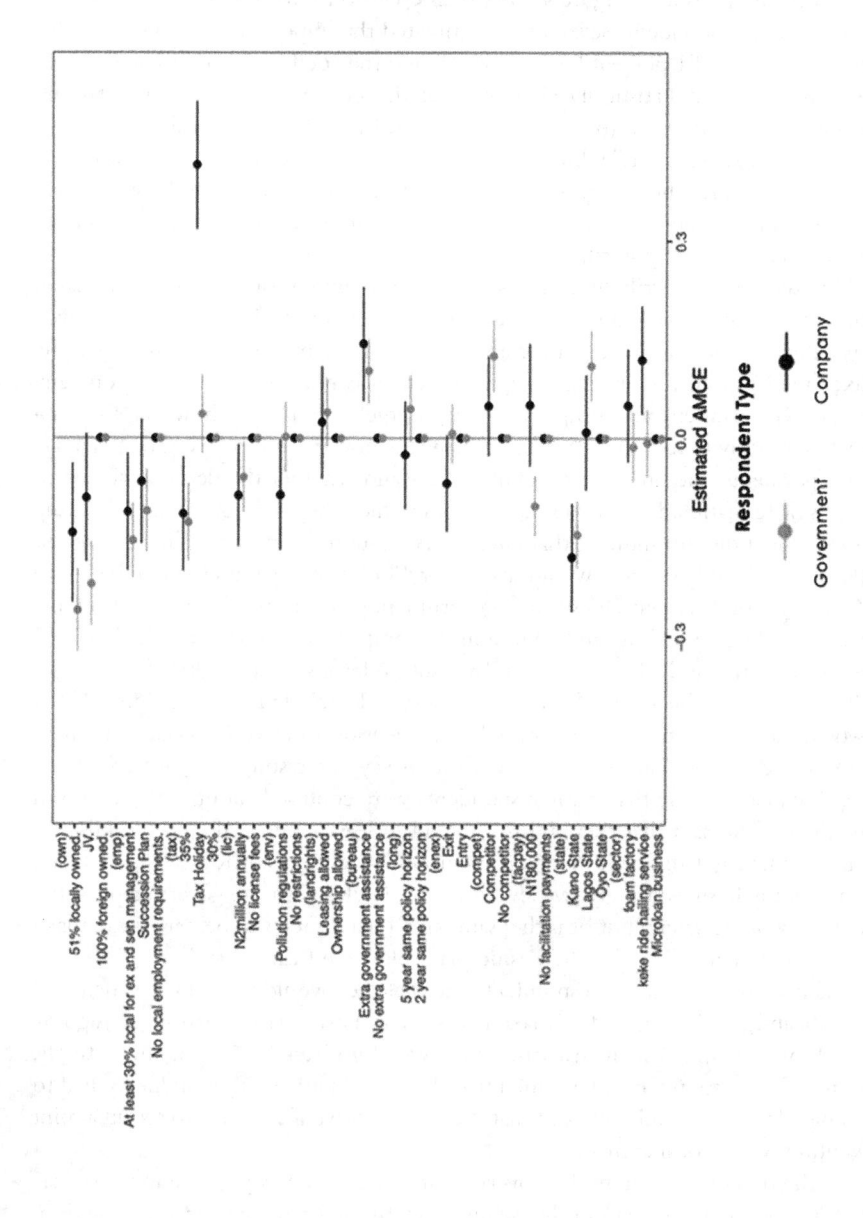

Figure 4.2 Comparison Between Question 1 (Government Responses) and Question 4 (Company Responses): Likelihood to Sign the Deal.

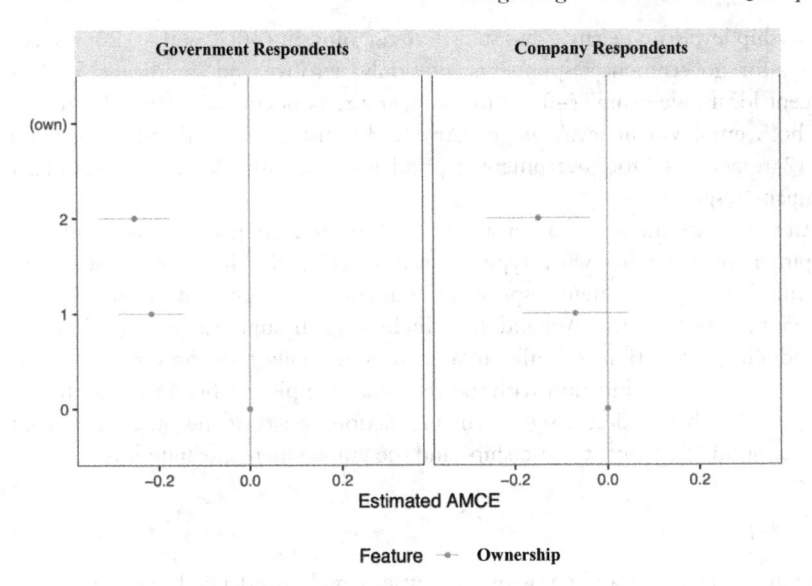

Figure 4.3 Interaction Effects (ACIEs) Between Ownership and Type of Respondent.

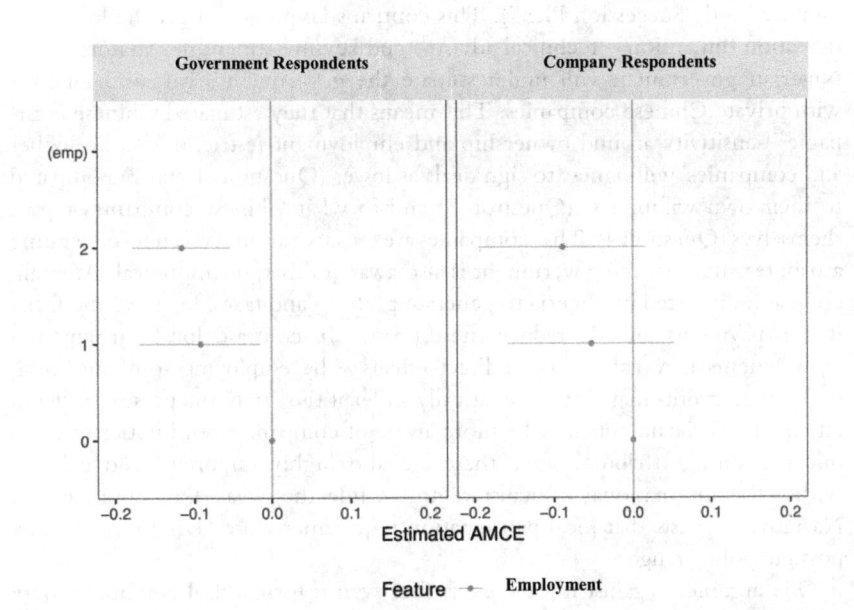

Figure 4.4 Interaction Effects (ACIEs) Between Employment and Type of Respondent.

ownership levels are negative and statistically significant (−0.22 and −0.25, respectively) for government respondents, but only negative and significant for "51 percent local ownership" (−0.15) for company respondents. Similarly, the ACIEs for both employment levels are negative and statistically significant (−0.09 and −0.12, respectively) for government respondents, but neither level is significant for company respondents.

After re-introducing all other attributes and interacting each ownership and employment variables with type of respondents, the interaction of "Joint Venture" and "government respondent" remains significant and positive (please see Figure A4.5 in the Appendix), which is again supporting Hypothesis 1. Introducing interactions of different attributes generally hurts power in conjoint experiments. In combination with the very small sample size here, we may, therefore, not be able to detect significant interaction effects of the other interacted levels around "51 percent ownership" and the employment attribute levels.

4.6.1.1 Discussion

Overall, government and company responses largely overlapped regarding revenue generating attributes (e.g. taxes, licenses, facilitation payments) but there appears to be an important gap between what the government thinks they can ask in terms of local participation (ownership and employment) and what Chinese companies are in fact willing to give, especially on the first levels ("Joint Venture" and "Succession Plan"). This confirms Hypothesis 1 for the local participation dimension – technical advisors and key investment negotiators to the Nigerian government will underestimate the government's bargaining power with private Chinese companies. This means that they estimated Chinese companies' sensitivity around ownership and employment restrictions to be higher and companies' willingness to sign deals as lower (Questions 1 and 2) compared to their own willingness (Question 3) and to what Chinese companies report themselves (Question 4). That companies are sensitive around revenue-generating attributes, and that the government is also aware of that, seems logical. After all, companies invested in Nigeria to generate profits – and taxes, licenses, and facilitation payments directly reduce these profits. In contrast, local participation requirements may have more indirect effects – by employing someone local, companies' profits may not automatically suffer if they train the person well and efficiently. Governments may be more aware of companies' sensitivities to revenue generating attributes since these are also highly important and debated within the international capitalist regime while the Weak Bargaining Power Narrative suggests that local participation requirements are "lying outside" any possible policy range.

One argument against my theory is that even if formal deal conditions were aggressive, companies know that the government has limited capacity to effectively enforce these conditions. The results that companies are sensitive around taxes is therefore particularly interesting – the Nigerian government may be enforcing tax collection at least well enough so that Chinese companies are in fact sensitive to an increase.

Another interesting observation is that government respondents believed Chinese and Western companies were sensitive to facilitation payment (corruption) when at least the Chinese ones are, in fact, not. My interviews with Chinese managers in Nigeria also confirm that Chinese companies tend to view personal payments as a way to facilitate transactions and that they were used to these payments from the Chinese market. The fact that the Nigerian government is less aware about this again suggests that they may equate Chinese company behavior with Western company behavior, where there are clear and prominent Anti-Corruption Acts in the West that prevent Western companies from engaging in corrupt behavior with government officials.

4.6.2 Analysis 2: Subgroups

As indicated earlier, the first part of the conjoint experiment included a survey on background covariates to test whether different "subgroups" of government respondents reacted differently to the presented investment deals. Since the subgroups are not randomly assigned, the differences in effects across the subgroups are only descriptive rather than causal, and may be sensitive to sampling variability. Below I present responses to Question 1: "In scenario X, how likely do you think the government and the company would be to both sign the deal?", categorized by "perceived bargaining power", "corrupt", and "liberal ideology" for government respondents. Please find all other subgroup results in the Appendix.

4.6.2.1 Perceptions of Bargaining Power

Figure A4.6 in the Appendix shows that among government respondents, low perceivers of bargaining power are more pessimistic than high perceivers around the likelihood of a deal signed by both parties if it included "51 percent local ownership", an "employment succession plan", "at least 30 percent local for executive and senior management", "35 percent income tax", "license fees", and if the deal was made in Kano State. In contrast, high perceivers were more pessimistic around "Joint Venture" requirements. High perceivers were optimistic that "government assistance" would increase the likelihood of both parties signing a deal and pessimistic around "facilitation payments", while the coefficients on both variables for low perceivers were not statistically significant. Low perceivers were optimistic that a deal situation around an "exit" versus an "entry" decision would increase the likelihood of both parties signing a deal, while the coefficient was not statistically significant for high perceivers. In addition, low perceivers were also more optimistic of a deal being signed than high perceivers if there was a "competitor" present.

Overall, these results support the argument advanced here that low perceivers of bargaining power believe that companies will be more sensitive to a variety of policy restrictions, compared to high perceivers. At the same time, even the high perceivers underestimated how much Chinese companies were willing to comply around local participation. Interestingly, and in stark contrast with my government interviews, the majority indicated in their responses that Nigeria has bargaining power (104 out of 134). Government respondents therefore seemed to be more open with me than with the Nigerian interviewers, and there may have been more interviewees of the type "low perceivers" than they self-identified to the interview team. This could be because admitting to their co-ethnic peers or citizens that they believe Nigeria has weak bargaining power might be politically more difficult than having an open conversation with a foreigner. This was also confirmed by a head of a federal government agency, who I interviewed, and who said that "officially to the press", they would say that Nigeria has bargaining power but to me they can "openly say" that they "don't have any power" and that "everyone in the government is aware of that."[8]

4.6.2.2 Corruption/Lack of Accountability

Regarding "corruption, lack of accountability", 80 out of 134 respondents were coded as "corrupt." Most respondents said that deal outcomes did not matter for elections, and that neither voters nor companies had inquired with them about the conditions specified in any past investment deal. Interestingly, Figure A4.7 in the Appendix shows that respondents coded as "corrupt" were more pessimistic across a variety of attributes compared to the "non-corrupt" ones, also regarding companies' sensitivity to facilitation payments. I would have expected the opposite – if respondents believed that deal conditions were not accessible to the public, and that deal outcomes would matter very little for elections, then governments could have preferred to sign deals that included personal benefits, such as facilitation payments, and cared little about the rest of the conditions. Yet, in fact, respondents of type "corrupt" perceived the overall likelihood of a deal being signed by both parties as lower if facilitation payments were part of the deal, compared to the type "not corrupt". These results point against the corruption hypothesis, that the government would be willing to sign "weak deals" in exchange for personal benefits.

4.6.3 Analysis 3: Covid-19 as an External Shock

As mentioned earlier, both experiments were conducted in the spring and summer of 2020. The global Covid-19 outbreak and the beginning of the lockdown in Abuja and Lagos on March 30 forced the team to put the experiments on a hold when we had collected 85 and 71 of completed government and company survey forms, respectively. We switched to phone interviews thereafter.

Figures A4.9 and A4.10 in the Appendix show that the conjoint experiment results reveal no striking differences between pre-and post-Covid-19 induced lockdown for the likelihood of signing deals. In order to better understand the potential impact of the shock, I also included survey questions on Covid for respondents who took it after the lockdown decision was announced (please see final appendix for details).

The majority of government respondents indicated that the falling oil prices and the devaluation of the naira would affect Nigeria's relation with China and the rest of the world "negatively" and that their image of China has not changed due to the outbreak. Overall, this indicates that perceived bargaining power did not shift, or because the Nigerian economy took a severe hit in the second quarter of 2020, shifted in favor of China.

The majority of company respondents, and especially those in the manufacturing industry, said that the Covid-19 outbreak did affect their business in Nigeria, mainly because of supply shortages in raw materials imported from China, because of a decline in consumer demand in Nigeria, or because of distribution difficulties due to the inter-state travel and transportation ban imposed by the government during parts of the lockdown. Responses to the second question varied and were perhaps surprising: Factory managers said that they would like to diversify away from importing only from China, and try to source raw material locally. In addition, several managers in service-based industries said that they would need to have an even stronger focus on the Nigerian market to better understand what drives demand in a depressed economy. Only five respondents said that they were considering exit from the market due to the Covid-19 outbreak. Overall, it therefore seems like the outbreak has (so far) not significantly negatively affected the attractiveness and bargaining power of the Nigerian government; in fact, company responses indicated that they are considering an even more Nigeria-focused strategy that may also cover procurement of raw materials in the future.

4.7 Long-Term Learning

One central limitation to the experiments conducted here is that while they provide us with a "snapshot" of how governments and companies perceive bargaining power at one point in time, they tell us very little about how these perceptions change over time with information updates that could lead to longer-term learning and shifts in perceptions around respective bargaining power. To respond to this concern to a very limited extent, I included the following "information treatment" after the survey team had presented both deal pairs to the government respondents:

> Studies show that Nigeria is the #1 investment destination on the continent for small and medium private Chinese firms. Chinese firms like the cheap land, labor, and the large market size in Nigeria that is unparalleled on the continent. Naturally, the most common response in a survey conducted by us among Chinese manufacturers in Nigeria was along the lines of "Labor is so cheap here, I would stay under any policy regulations. (+show graph below from Chen et al. (2015). This shows that Chinese companies really want to invest and operate in the Nigerian market."
>
> Knowing this, would you want to impose stricter local participation requirements on them, or not? Why/Why not?

Of the 134 government respondents, 98 (73 percent) indicated that they would indeed impose stricter local participation requirements. The most common reasons listed were: "I didn't know that we had that many small private firms here", "I didn't know Nigeria was ranked #1". 21 respondents even asked whether they could read the full report on the survey that was conducted. 36 respondents indicated that they would still not impose stricter regulations. Asked why, the most common responses were that "Maybe we are #1 because we don't have these restrictions" and "It isn't good to have too many regulations, investors don't like it".

While the results point toward my hypothesis, certainly, this "information treatment" has severe limitations. For example, respondents could have felt pressured to say yes, but kept supporting their original stance on local participation policies. In addition, we also do not know for how long this "information treatment" lasted, and how many treatments would be needed to update respondents' perceptions more permanently. This is therefore only a first attempt at measuring learning about bargaining power that future research should undertake more systematically and rigorously.

4.8 External Validity

External validity questions concern the similarity between the experiment setting and real-world experiences of deal negotiations between investors and governments. The first concern is that negotiation partners were not sitting in the same room, and that if respondents had faced their negotiation partner, they would have rated deals differently. This concern is mitigated by the fact that in situations where both parties are present, intimidation practices may influence individuals more than without the negotiation partner actively present. As a result, both parties could be acting more boldly separately than if they were in a room together and one party was intimidating the other one. Governments granted Chinese investors much leeway even without them present in the room. These findings indicate that the government would be likely to grant them the same or even more if the investor was actually present. On the Chinese side, the reasoning is similar – even without a government official present, Chinese companies indicated that they would be willing to sign more deals than the government respondents believed.

A second concern is that government respondents may have been highly aware of Nigeria's current official national FDI policies, and felt reluctant to sign any deal that deviated from the official law, even if they felt that companies would agree to stricter regulations. This concern is mediated through two forces. First, the year prior to conducting the experiments, I conducted semi-structured interviews with 45 Nigerian government officials at the federal and state level. The majority of interviewees (87 percent) agreed with the statement that "it was possible to adjust national policies in case-by-case situations where local realities required such changes." I also heard of multiple examples of state governments effectively setting their own conditions in deal negotiations around land rights, facilitation payments, or license fees. Second, I included the survey question: "How many of the following changes would you make to maximize the chances of the company in scenario 4 signing the deal?", with a list of individual attributes below. Responses vastly overlapped with the regression results found for Question 1.

A final concern is about how the results travel cross-nationally. I had interviewed Chinese companies in the manufacturing and service sectors across all countries that I visited in the year prior to conducting the experiment; responses largely overlapped across countries, with companies confirming a high likelihood of agreeing to stricter deals. These interview findings were in fact the motivating force behind also identifying the gap in government perceptions versus reality within an experimental setting.

4.9 Conclusion

This chapter makes an important contribution to China–Africa literature by, for the first time, highlighting a gap between perceived and actual negotiation power of the Nigerian government with Chinese companies regarding local participation. The existence of this gap stands in stark contrast to the Weak Bargaining Power Narrative, which claims that perceptions and reality of respective levels of bargaining power perfectly overlap, and that there is simply very little room for governments to impose stricter regulations if they want to attract any types of investors.

The experiment serves as a fitting test to show *that* the gap exists. However, it leaves important questions unanswered on *why* exactly the gap exists. At the core, the Nigerian government does not receive accurate or complete information on its bargaining power. Yet, what are the causal mechanisms through which governments continue to receive this information that then translates into wrong perceptions of bargaining power? In order to answer this question, I conducted 218 semi-structured interviews across five African countries to shine light on the political economy around information flows that influence governments' perceptions of their own bargaining power. Chapters 5, 6, and 7 summarize these findings and respond to external validity concerns that are posed by any experimental setting.

Appendix

Policy Attributes

- *Foreign Ownership*: One of three conditions appears on each deal – "The company can be 100 percent foreign owned (status quo). / The company must set up a contractual joint venture with a local partner. / The company must be 51 percent locally owned." The first option describes the status quo in Nigeria, the second option was informed by policies across several sectors in China, and the third option reflects policies (still) practiced in e.g. Algeria and Zimbabwe. In general, we would expect companies to be more sensitive to an increase in local ownership restrictions, but the cases of Algeria and Zimbabwe show that Chinese companies continued to increase investments over time even after the 51 percent local ownership policies were set in place. As a result, this attribute is included here to test how the Nigerian government thinks about how sensitive Chinese companies in Nigeria would be to such restrictions, and what these companies indicate themselves.
- *Foreign Employment*: Similar to the first attribute, respondents are presented with one of three conditions: "No local employment requirements apply

(status quo). / The company can hire non-Nigerians only if all efforts have been explored to obtain a local expert and must propose a succession plan to train and hire a citizen for the same position. / The company must hire at least 30 percent locals for executive and senior management positions." The first option again describes the status quo in Nigeria, the second option is practiced in other countries such as Tanzania, and the third option describes a more extreme case to test a possible threshold at which Chinese companies decide not to enter or exit a market. We would again expect companies to be more sensitive to stricter employment regulations but they may be less sensitive than government respondents believe.

- *Corporate Income Tax*: The options were the following: "A five-year tax holiday applies. / A corporate income tax of 30 percent applies (status quo). / A corporate income tax of 35 percent applies." I included the first option to study how much companies value tax holidays compared to how much they want to avoid the costs of other requirements. Tax holidays are already formally practiced in several special economic zones across Africa, as well as informally in villages with clusters of Chinese companies across Nigeria. The second option describes status quo tax levels in Nigeria, and the third option is a stricter variation as practiced, for example, in Zambia.
- *License Fees*: The options were as follows: "No license fees apply. / A license fee of N2 million annually applies." License fees can be placed on companies on a case-by-case base. For example, in the summer of 2019, two Keke ride hailing service providers entered the Lagos market. One company was Nigerian (Gokada) while the other one was Chinese-owned (OPay). The Lagos government asked both to pay a license fee of N25 million (about US $70,000) annually per 1,000 Kekes. I kept the license fee amount far more conservative at N2 million (around US $5,500) to account for the fact that background characteristics include three different industries. I also only included an annual fee that is not dependent on output levels.
- *Facilitation Payments*: One of the two following conditions appeared on the deals: "No facilitation payments apply. / One-time facilitation payments of 180,000 Naira apply." While Western companies need to adhere to strict anti-corruption acts in their home countries, Chinese companies are not bound by the Chinese government to restrict corrupt behavior. We would expect government respondents to have experience with this and ask for facilitation payments only from Chinese companies; and Chinese companies to be willing to pay facilitation payments, although sensitivity around the amount may exist.
- *Property Rights*: The two possible conditions were: "The company may acquire and own immovable property. Property rights will be enforced by the Nigerian government (status quo). / The company may lease all immovable property from the government." We would expect that companies would be more willing to sign deals where property rights are ensured, and that the government is also aware of that. Yet, although Nigeria officially enforces property rights, some cases of government expropriation exist. So it may be the case that

companies have experience with expropriation cases in Nigeria and may be indifferent to what the formal law states.
- *Environmental regulations*: The options were the following: "There are no water or air pollution restrictions imposed on the company (status quo). / The company will need to stick to strict water and air pollution regulations, including emission restrictions set forth by the Nigerian government." My interviews with Nigerian brokers and Chinese companies reveal that some Nigerian regions such as Kogi State have seen a massive influx of Chinese firms in environmentally sensitive sectors such as ceramics due to China's increasingly strict environmental regulations and Nigeria's loose policies. Since these policies were apparently a pull-factor to attract companies, we would expect that Chinese companies are sensitive around environmental regulations and that technical advisors may be aware of that as well.
- *Government assistance with investment procedure and settlements*: One of the following conditions appeared on each deal: "The company will need to obtain standard business licenses, work permits, land acquisitions and visas if applicable (status quo). / The government, through the Nigerian Investment Promotion Commission (NIPC), will expedite delivery times of business licenses, work permits, land acquisitions and visas for the company. In addition, the government will assist the company in labor strike settlements, facilitation of resettlements and compensation negotiations." Although the NIPC has recently tried to play a more active role in attracting investment and facilitating investment procedures (e.g. by setting up a one-stop shop service), Nigeria overall still keeps a hands-off approach to foreign investors relative to other countries such as Ethiopia or Tanzania where their one-stop services play a much more active role in politics. Including government assistance as an attribute will, therefore, help discern whether Chinese companies prefer assistance, and how the Nigerian government thinks about the usefulness of assisting foreign investors in setting up and running a business in their country.
- *Policy Uncertainty*: The options were the following: "The company is guaranteed the same conditions to hold over the next two years after which the conditions may change or stay the same. / The company is guaranteed the same conditions to hold over the next five years after which the conditions may change or stay the same." I included policy uncertainty as an attribute following my interviews with Chinese companies across the continent. "Policy uncertainty" was one of the top 3 complaints reported, so we would expect longer promised policy horizons to also influence Chinese company behavior in the experiment.

Background Characteristics

- *Type of Investor*: Governments were presented with deals with either a US company or a Chinese company. Chinese companies were only presented with deals about Chinese companies. The Weak Bargaining Power Narrative suggests that Western companies are sensitive around a variety of investment deal conditions. As a result, I include two types of investors to better understand whether, and to what extent, government respondents are aware of how policy preferences differ between Western and Chinese companies.

- *Sector*: Deals described scenarios in one of three sectors: a foam factory, a Keke ride hailing service, or a microloan business. These sectors were chosen to describe scenarios that were the closest possible to companies' real life situations. Most Chinese businesses in Lagos and Ogun State are small and private, and either produce goods in a factory or provide services.
- *Entry/Exit Negotiations*: The hypothetical investment deals either described an entry or an exit scenario: In the entry scenario, a company is interested in opening a business in Nigeria, and then the deal describes the conditions under which that would be possible. In contrast, in the exit scenario, a company has been operating in Nigeria for a year, and suddenly the policy conditions change to what the deal describes. This attribute is meant to test companies' sensitivities to sudden policy changes as experienced in Zimbabwe in 2008 and in Algeria in 2007. Since companies that are already operating in Nigeria have already set up factories or offices in Nigeria, they may incur more costs from exiting the market compared to those who are simply thinking of entering Nigeria. As a result, we would expect companies already in operation to be less sensitive to stricter policies than those who have not yet entered Nigeria.
- *Competitor*: In each investment deal, there was either a competitor present or absent. We would expect companies to be more willing to agree to deals with stricter conditions if a competitor is present because it indicates that the sector is lucrative. At the same time, my interviews reveal that Chinese companies' sensitivities were similar regardless of whether their sector was competitive or not. Therefore, this also helps us to test whether African governments have weak bargaining power with Chinese investors because there are no exit options for governments, or if Chinese investors always behave the same way regardless of how competitive the environment is.

Finally, I test for potential interaction effects between the following variables:

Type of Investor & Facilitation Payments: Since US companies need to adhere to strict anti-corruption laws in their home economy, I expect Nigerian government respondents to know that US companies will be less willing to sign deals that include facilitation payments. In contrast, since Chinese companies are not constraint by such laws, they may be more willing to provide these payments, and from experience, government respondents may also be aware of that.

Sector & State: On February 1, 2020, Lagos State implemented a ban on Kekes and okadas. As a result, I expect government respondents and Chinese respondents to rate the likelihood of both sides signing deals describing a hypothetical scenario of a Chinese Keke company in Lagos to be low.

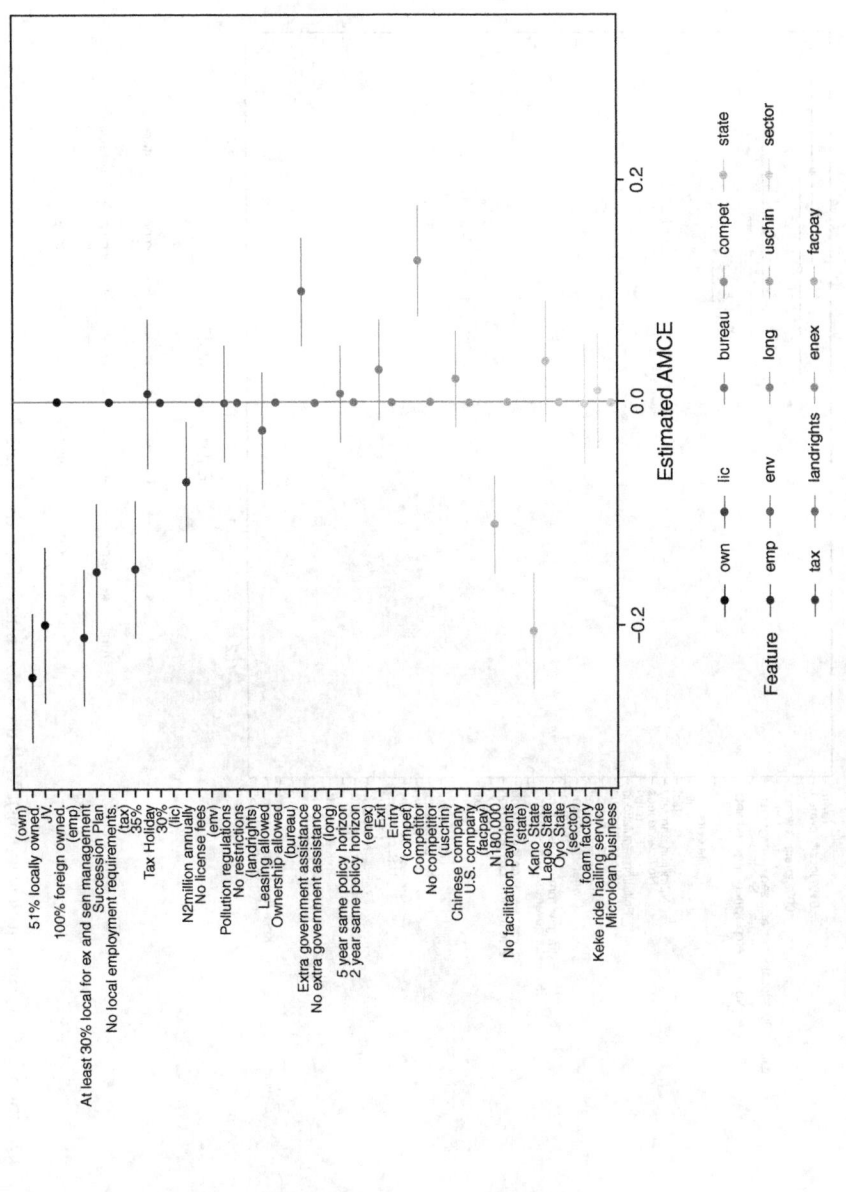

Figure A4.1 Question 1 (Government Perceptions): Perceived Likelihood of Both Parties Signing the Deal (0–3).

102 *Bargaining Power and Deal Quality*

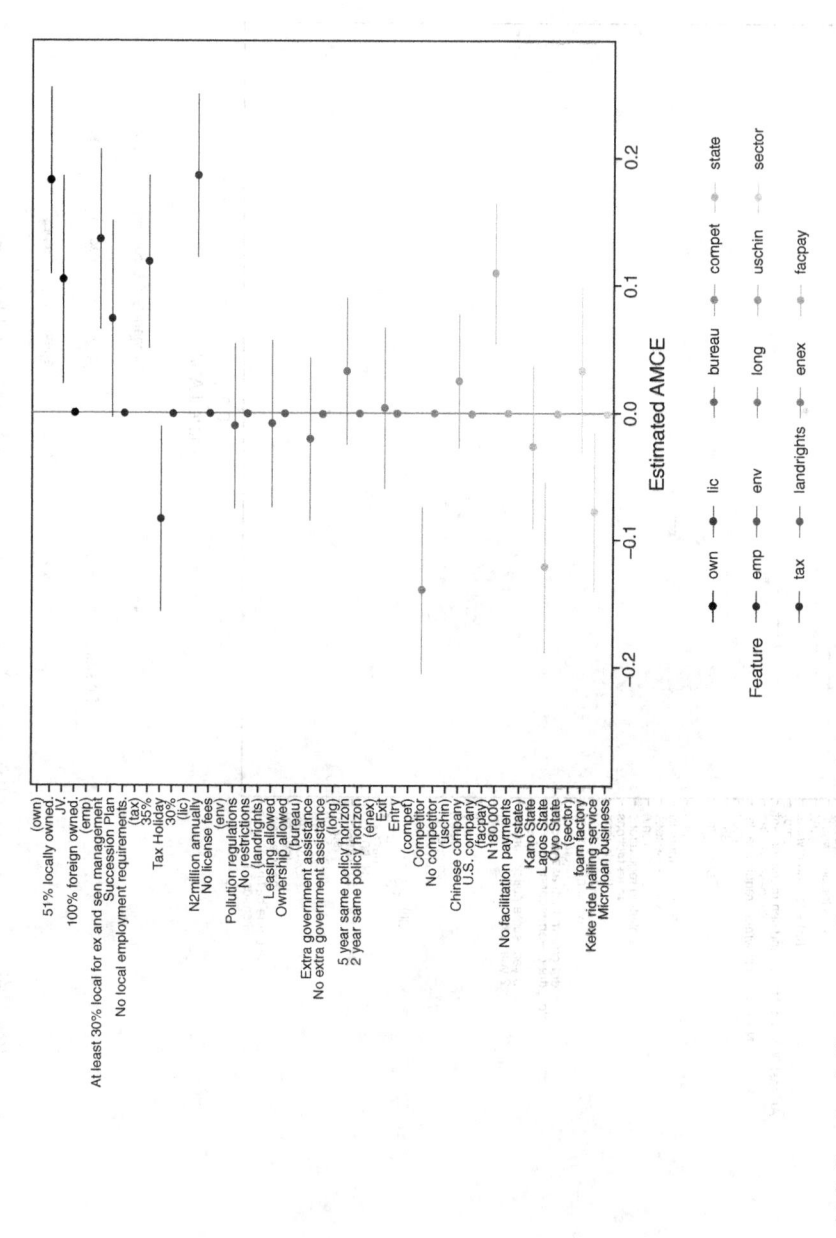

Figure A4.2 Question 2 (Government Perceptions): Will the Government Sign the Deal? (Y/N).

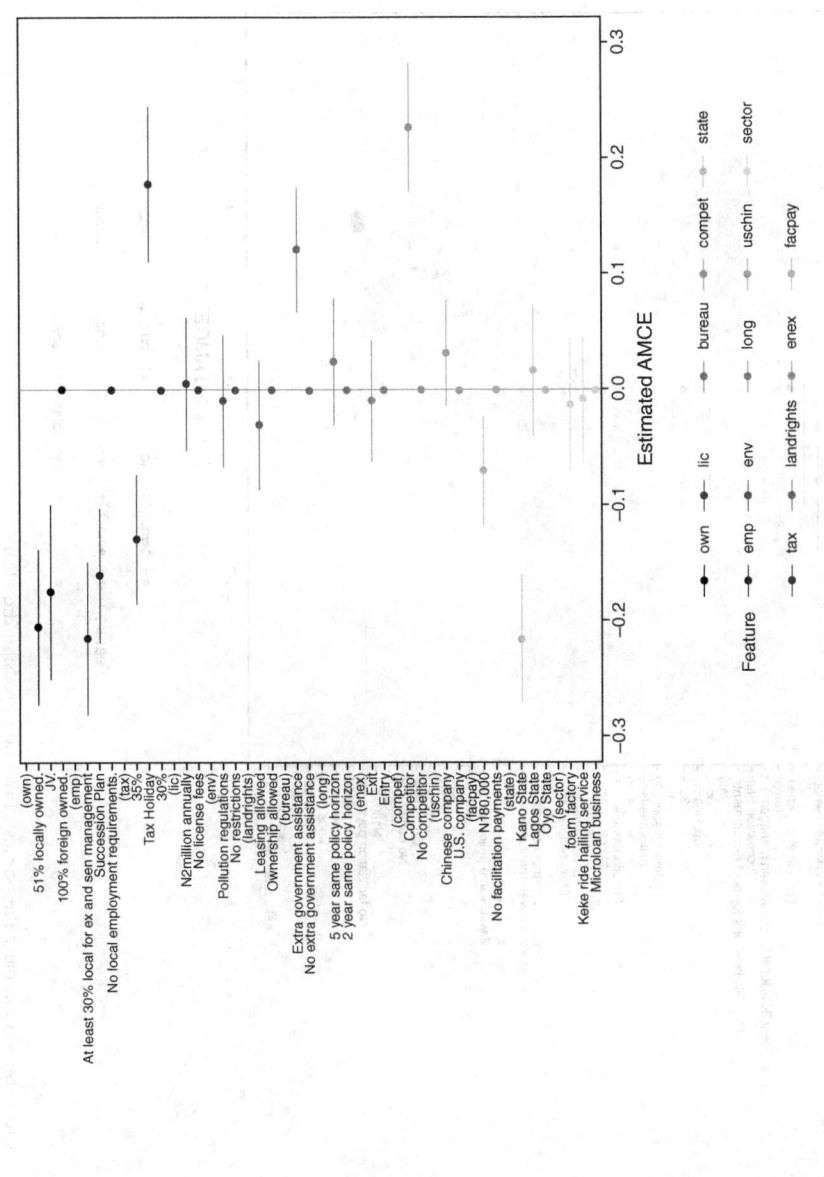

Figure A4.3 Question 3 (Government Perceptions): Will The Company Sign the Deal? (Y/N).

104 *Bargaining Power and Deal Quality*

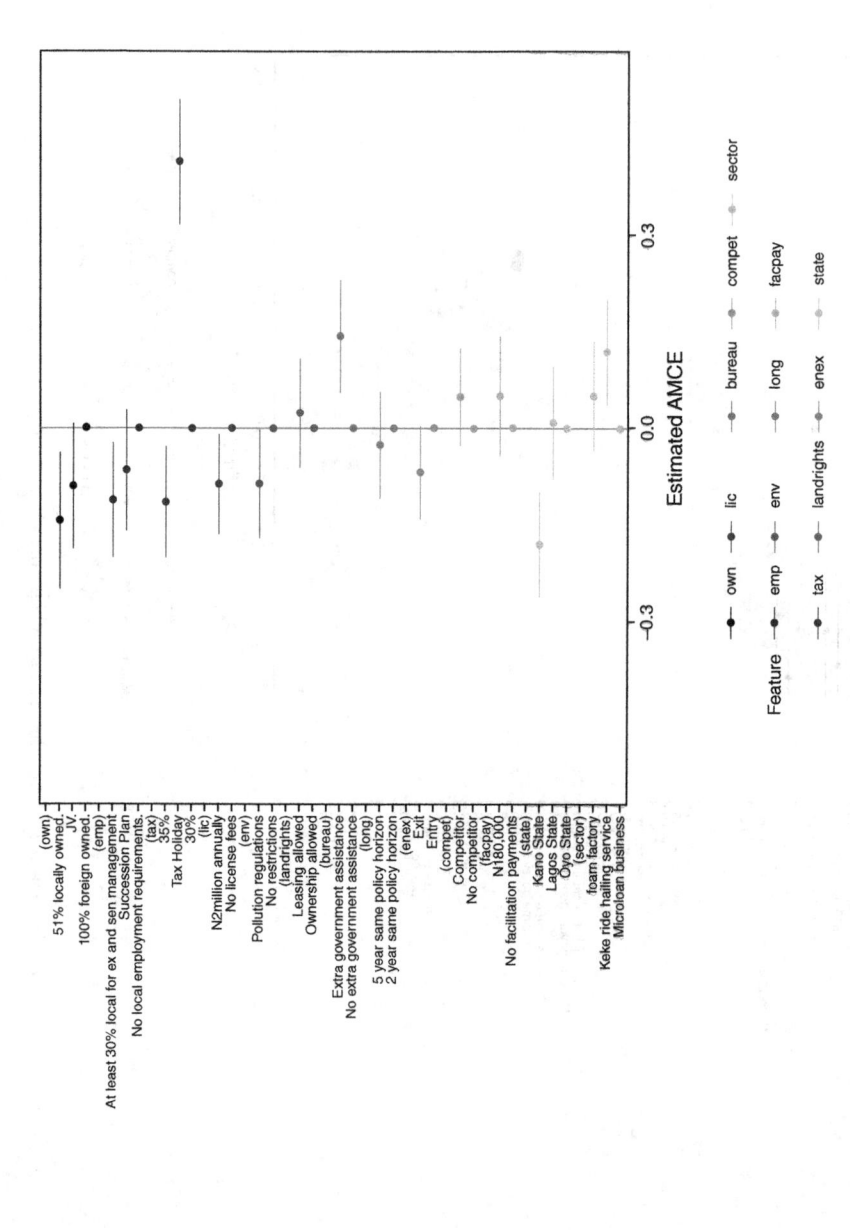

Figure A4.4 Question 4 (Company Responses): Likelihood to Sign the Deal (0–3).

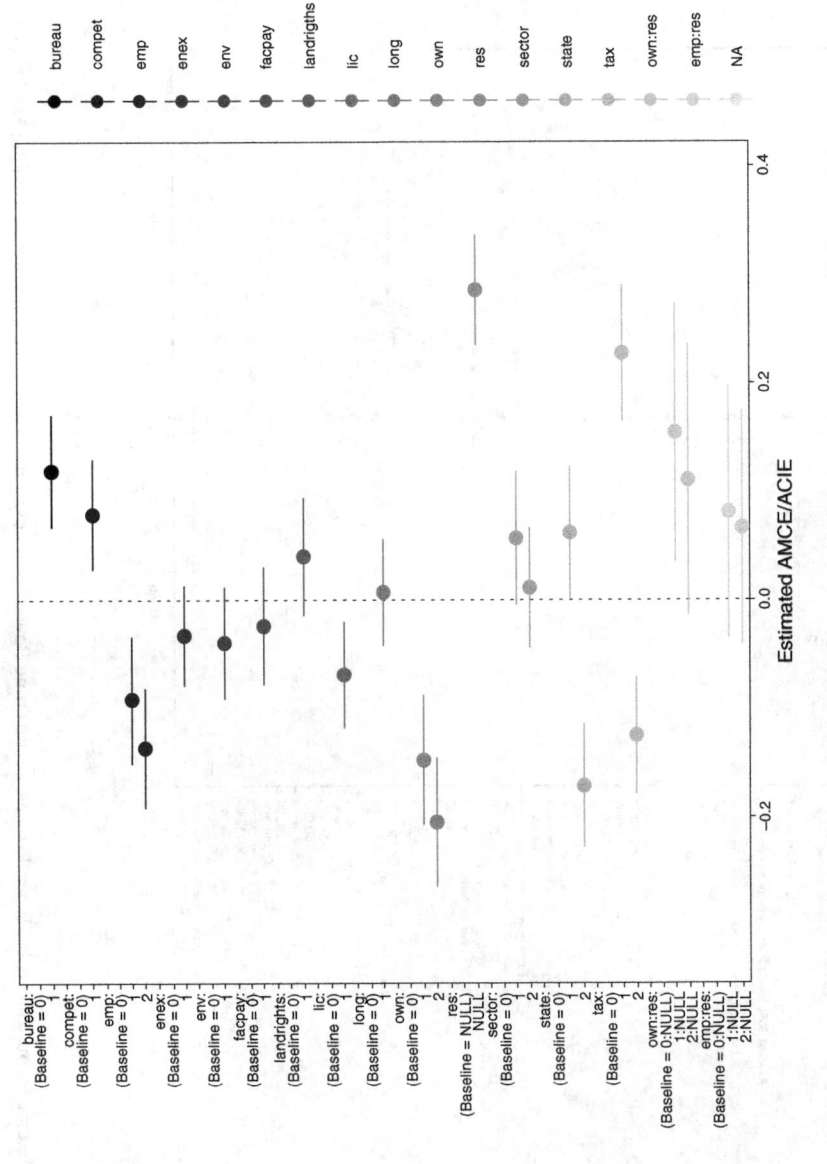

Figure A4.5 Differential Effect of Attribute on Chinese Respondents' Reports of Whether Company Would Sign.

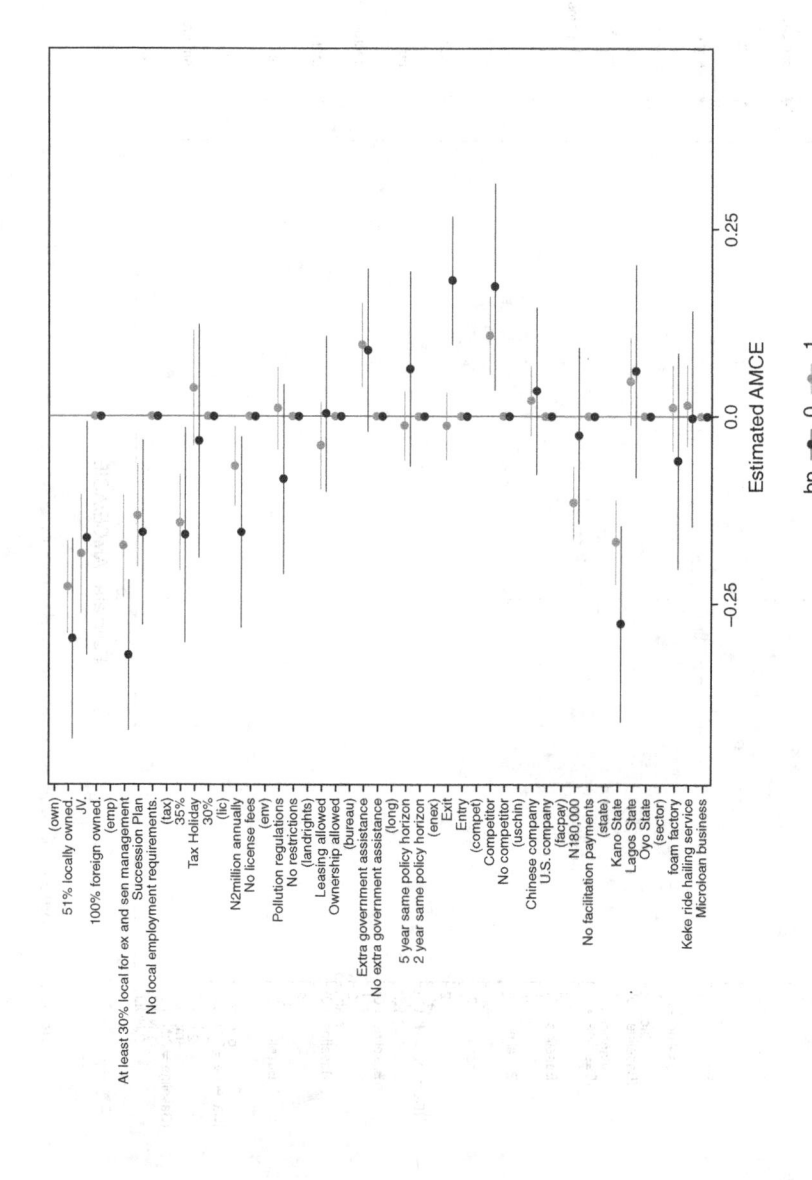

Figure A4.6 Heterogeneous Effects by Type "Perceived Bargaining Power" (0 = low perceived bargaining power, 1 = high perceived bargaining power).

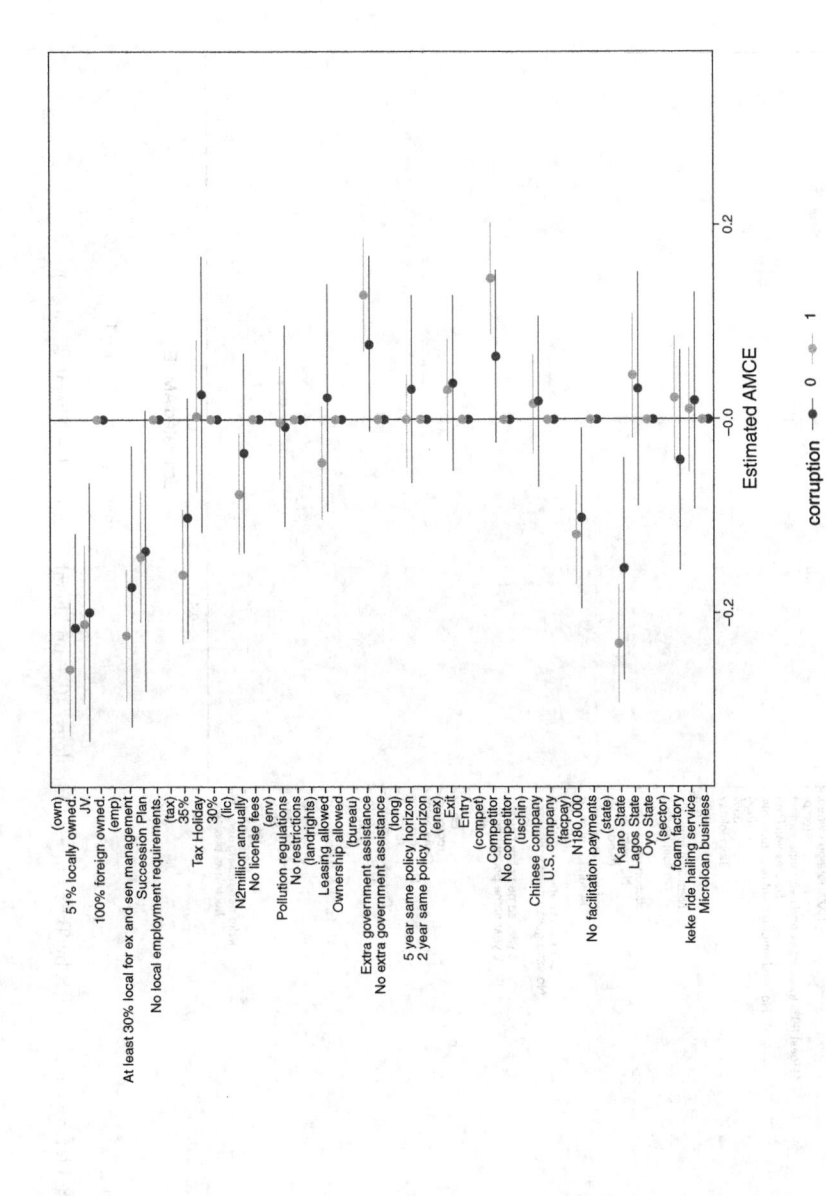

Figure A4.7 Heterogenous Effects by Type "Corrupt" (0 = not corrupt, 1 = corrupt).

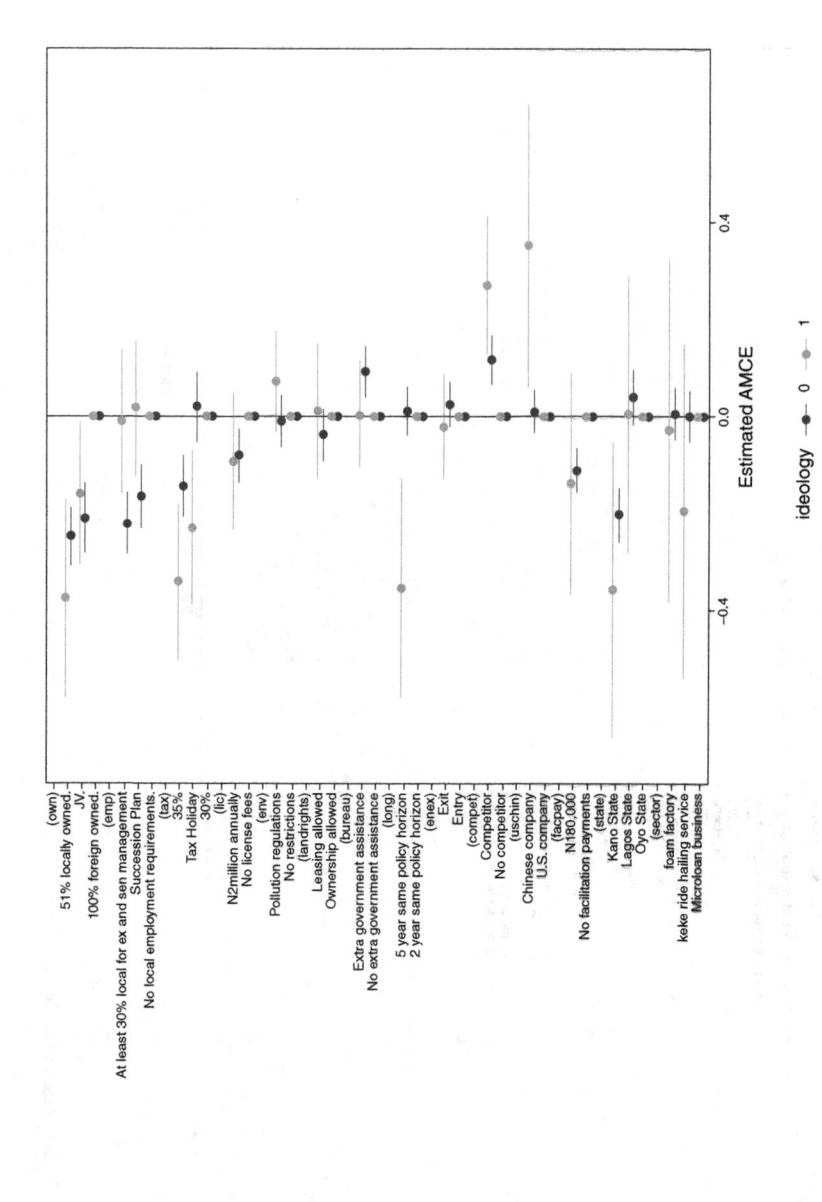

Figure A4.8 Heterogenous Effects by Type "Liberal Ideology" (0 = no liberal ideology, 1 = liberal ideology).

Bargaining Power and Deal Quality 109

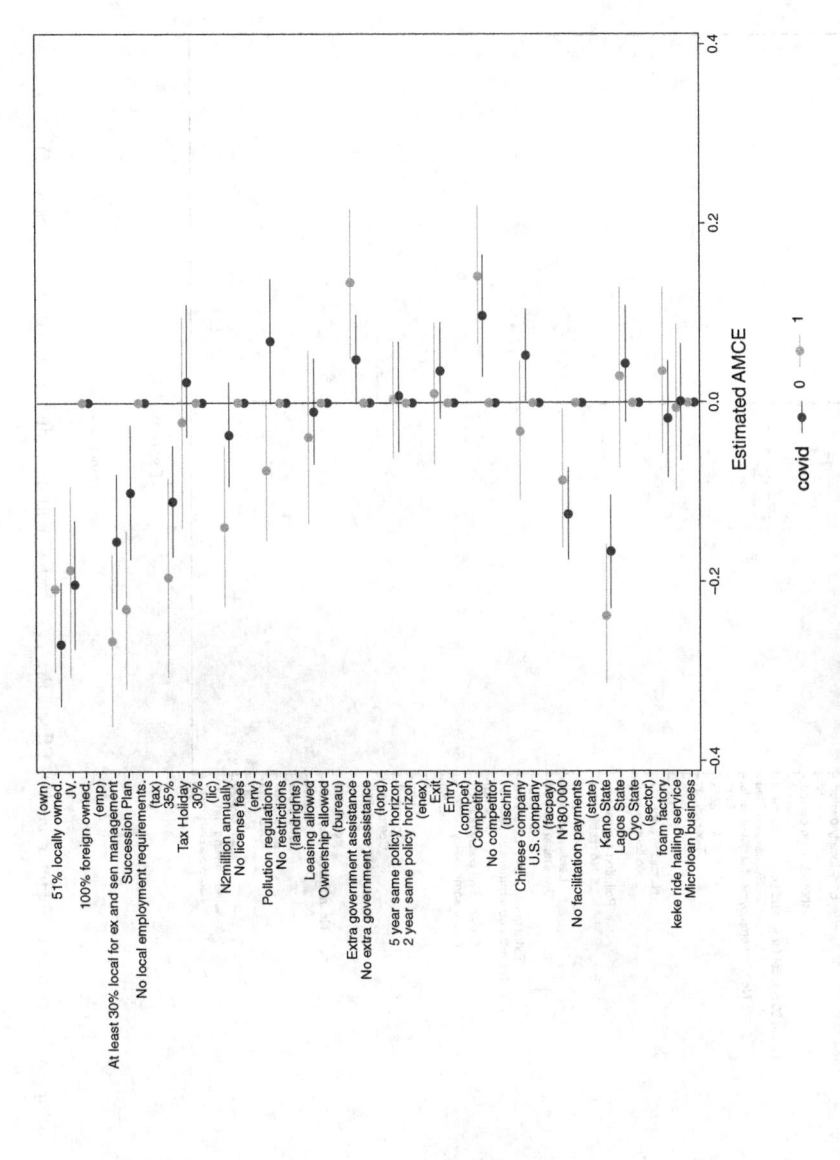

Figure A4.9 Government Respondents – Heterogenous Effects Pre- Vs. Post-Covid-19 Induced Lockdown (Question 1).

110 *Bargaining Power and Deal Quality*

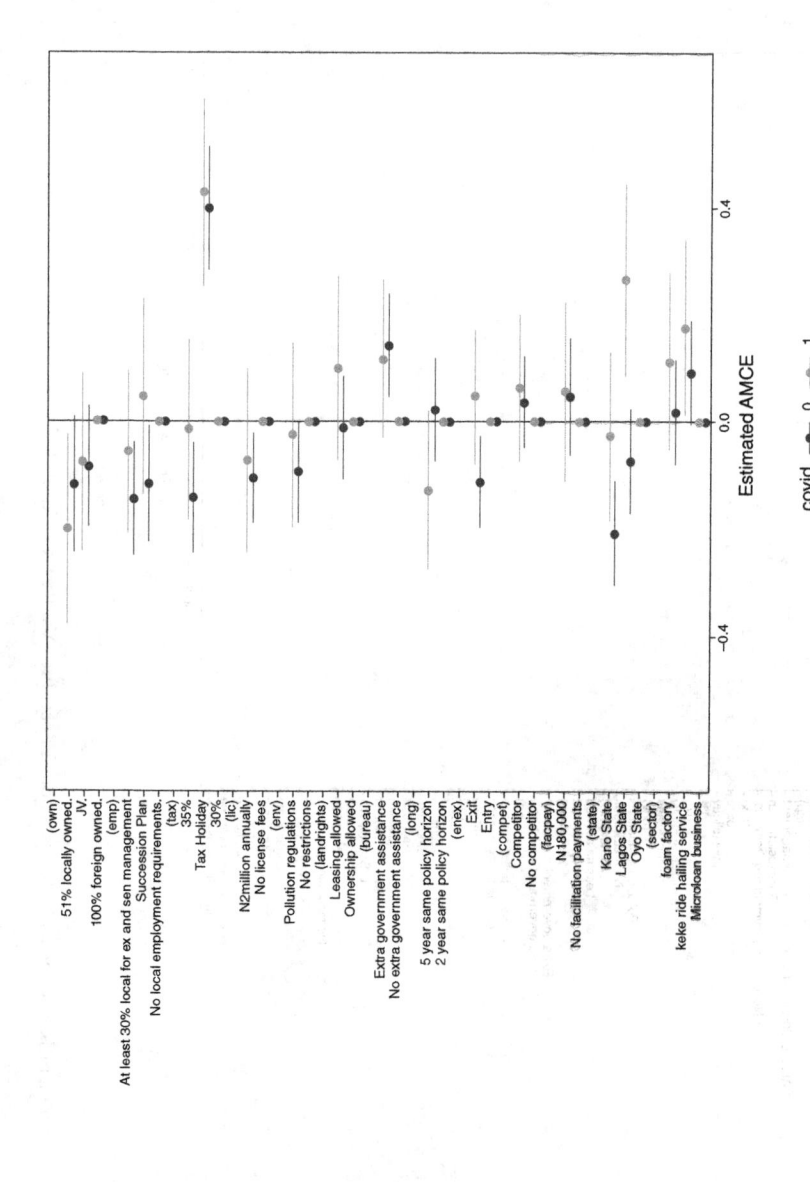

Figure A4.10 Company Respondents – Heterogenous Effects Pre– Vs. Post-Covid-19 Induced Lockdown (Question 4).

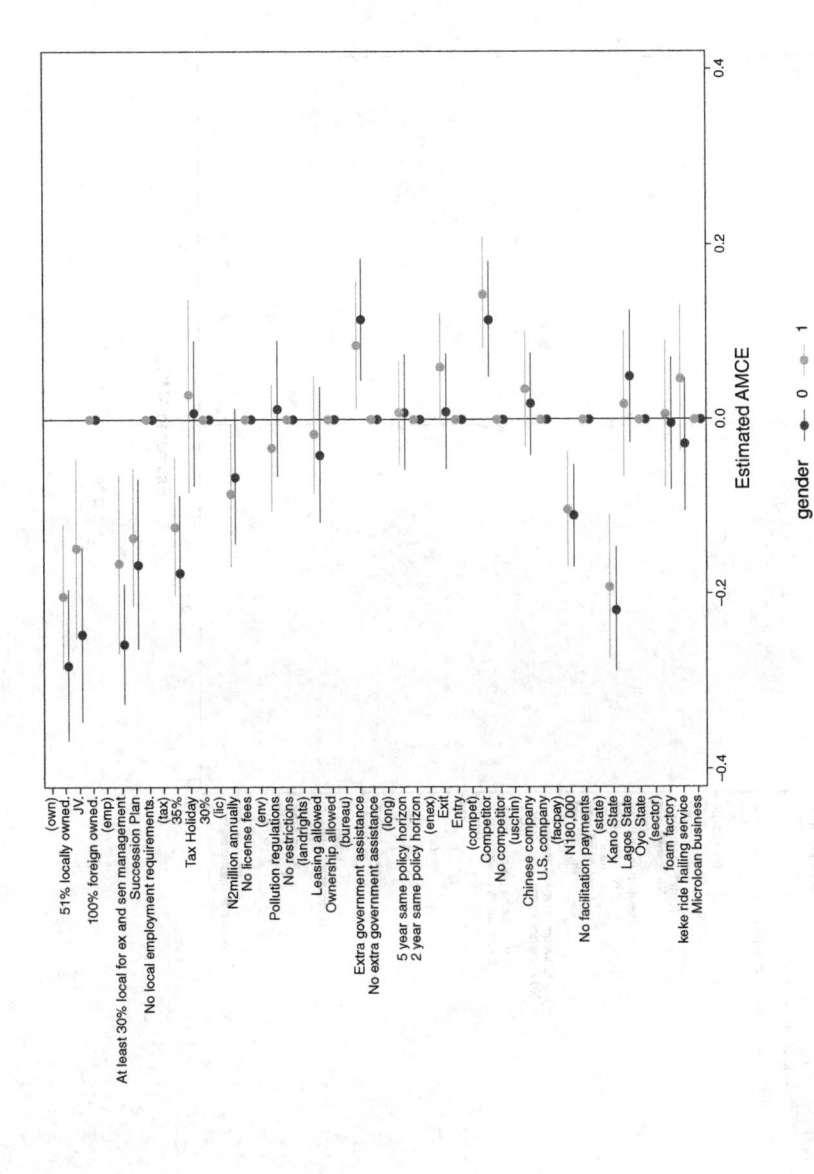

Figure A4.11 Subgroup Results by Remaining Government Background Variables.

112 Bargaining Power and Deal Quality

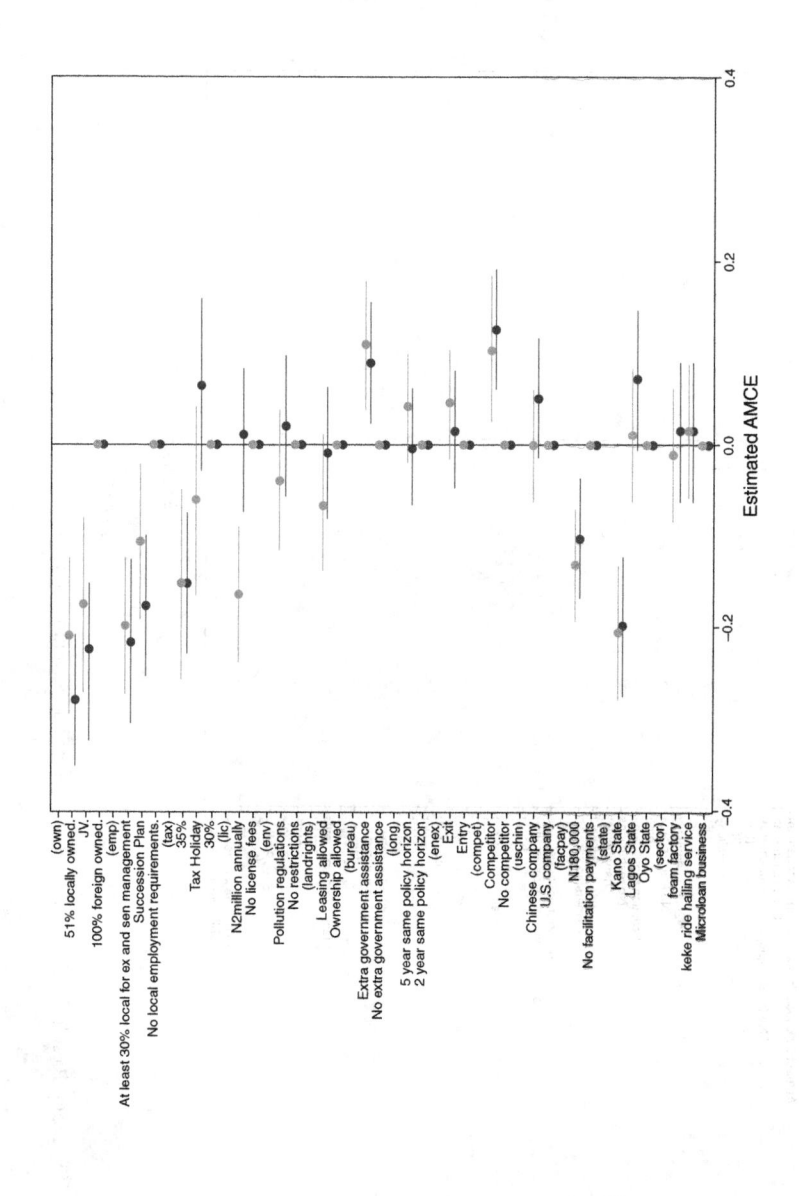

Figure A4.11 (Continued).

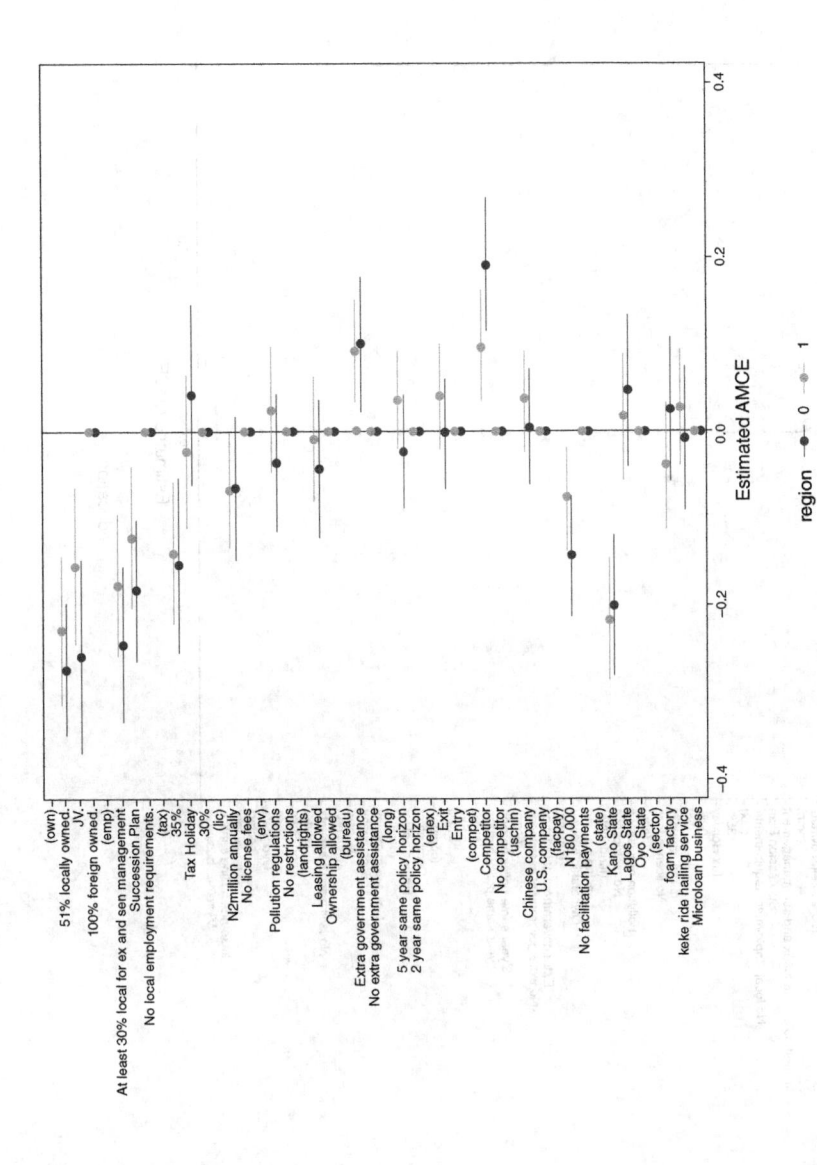

Figure A4.11 (Continued).

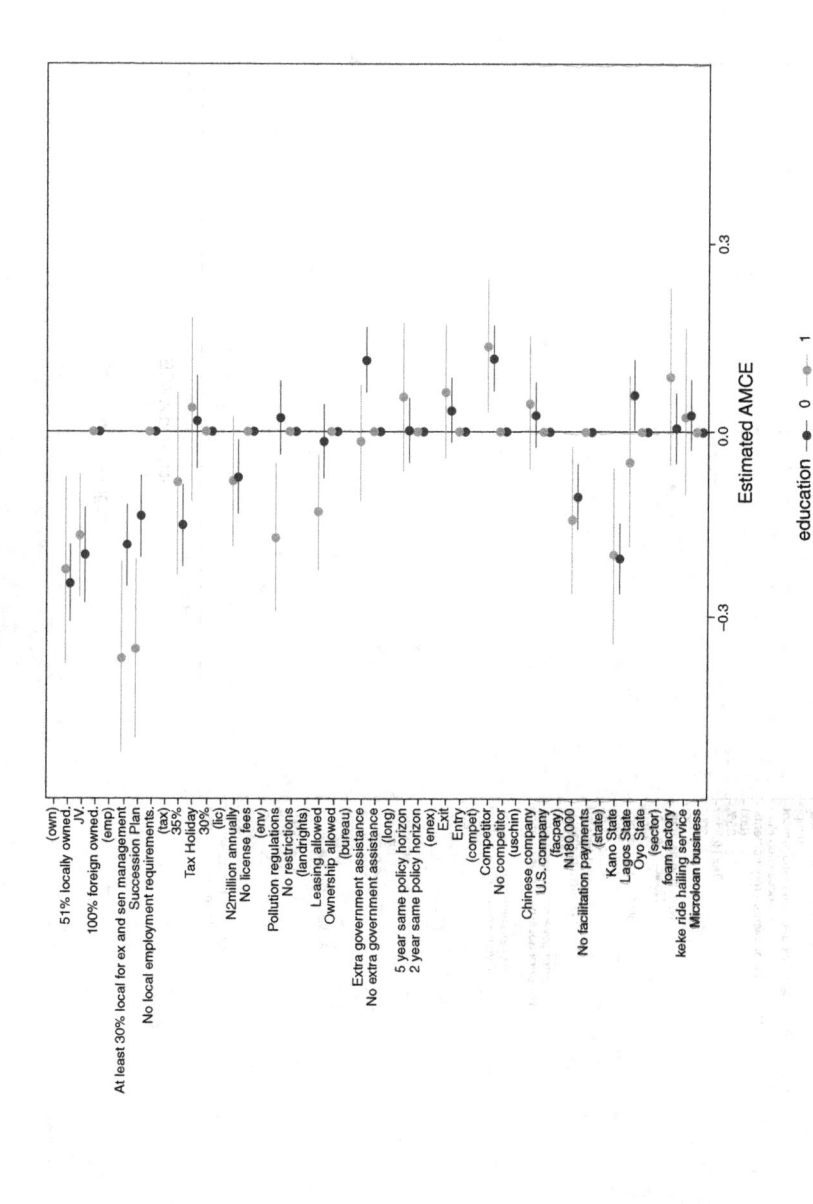

Figure A4.11 (Continued).

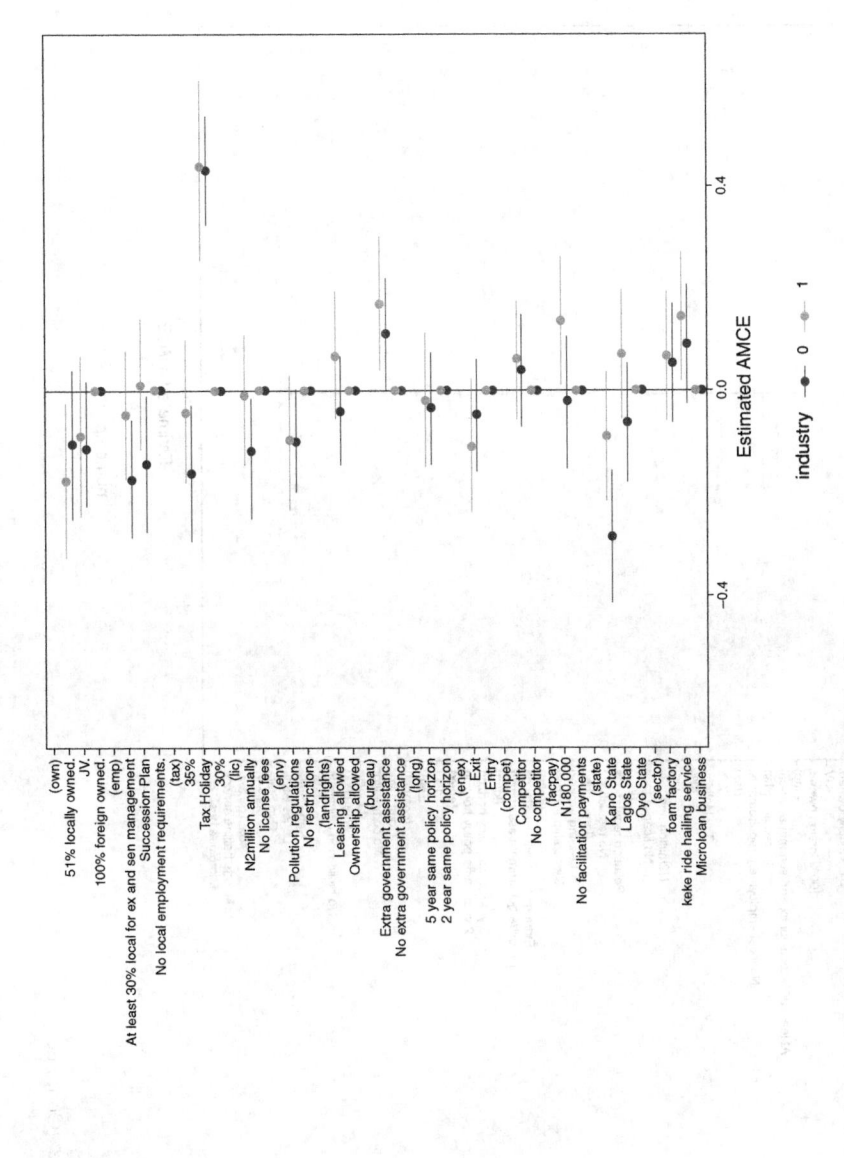

Figure A4.12 Subgroup Results by Company Background Variables.

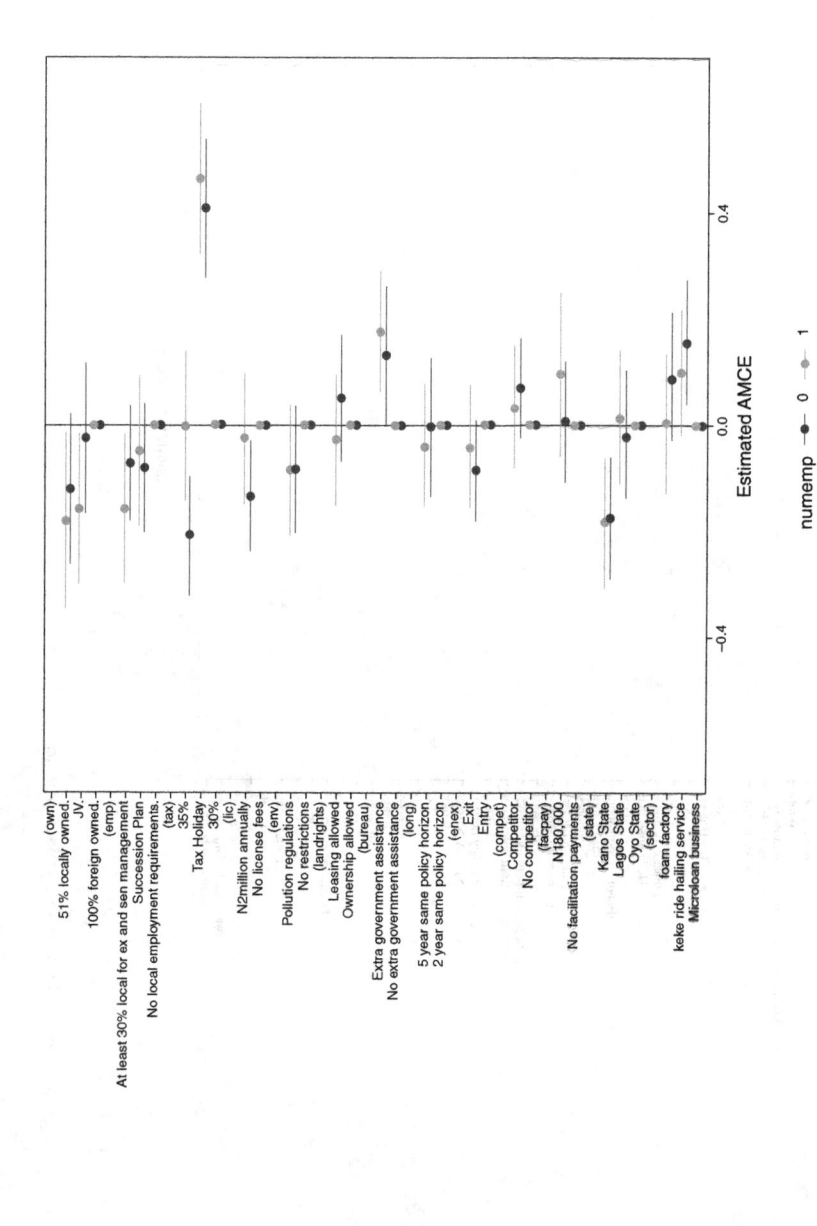

Figure A4.12 (Continued).

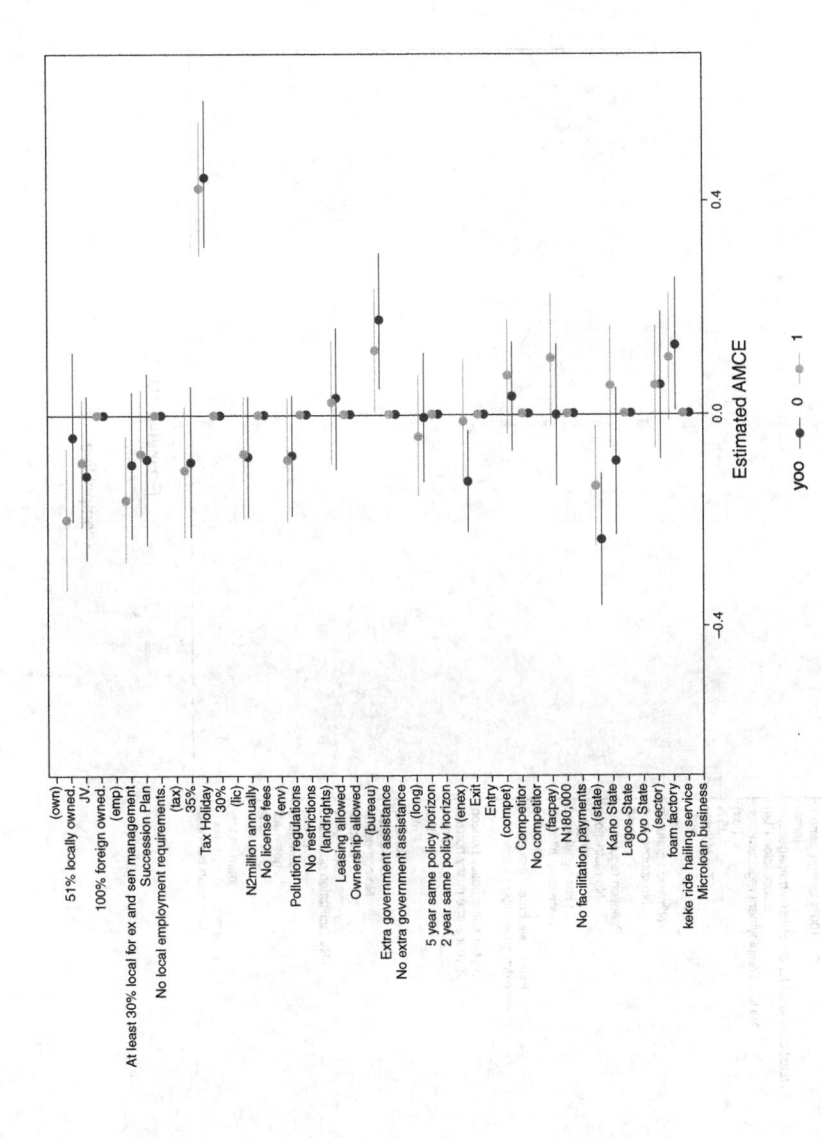

Figure A4.12 (Continued).

118 *Bargaining Power and Deal Quality*

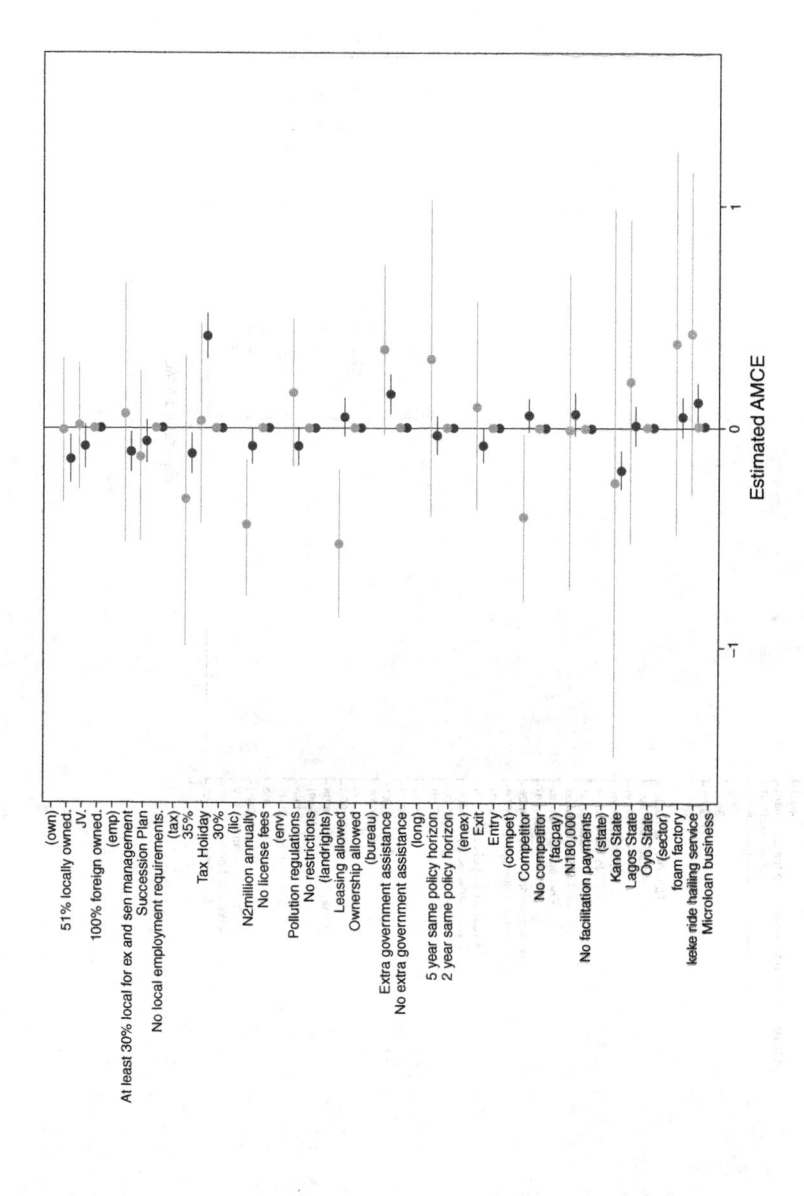

Figure A4.12 (Continued).

Notes

1 e.g. L44, DS2, DS9, N5, N19, P15, AA1, AA7.
2 I used the term "facilitation payments" to refer to corrupt payments.
3 e.g. A2, A3, A15.
4 O15.
5 I would have preferred to hire one male and one female but finding Chinese interlocuters was extremely difficult, also due to the Covid-19 pandemic.
6 Assumed cut-off rating between signing/not signing: 1.5.
7 Question 3 asks for a Y/N answer while Question 4 asks for a rating. For a comparison, we need to view the 0–3 scale as a Y/N, with 1.5 as the decision point.
8 L17.

5 Perceptions of Bargaining Power

5.1 Introduction

This study aims to assess the degree of African bargaining power and why it does, or does not, translate into how aggressive African governments negotiate with private Chinese investors around local participation. One of the major challenges when making claims about the scope of "African bargaining power" is as follows: Ideally, one should define a large enough universe of comparable countries for analysis (see Chen et al. 2018). At the same time, it is also important to pay enough attention and time to studying each country well enough to understand idiosyncrasies in countries' negotiation behavior that may otherwise be overlooked (e.g. see Chen 2020, Lauria 2020).

Faced with an inherent tradeoff between depth and breadth, this book takes three approaches to studying African bargaining power: First, the cross-country panel regression analysis conducted in Chapter 3 provided a first bird's eye-view on the overall bargaining landscape in Africa. Yet, while a cross-country analysis is useful as a first step, it does not allow us to understand causal mechanisms behind the detected correlations in the panel data.

Chapter 4 then presented, as a second approach to studying African bargaining power, a conjoint experiment conducted in Nigeria to highlight the rationale behind investment negotiations in one single case to understand how causal drivers of weak deals with Chinese companies play out on the national level. Nigeria is arguably one of the more difficult cases to test the theories presented here due to high levels of corruption as well as its close economic ties to the West. It is, therefore, a fitting case to assess the new 5ting alternative explanations.

Chapters 6 and 7 will offer a third approach to studying African bargaining power by drawing on qualitative interviews and homing in on why some of them negotiate more aggressively than others around local participation. This chapter, therefore, provides the justification for the case selection of five countries (Nigeria, Ethiopia, South Africa, Kenya, and Tanzania) that I deem appropriate to study for making larger claims about "African bargaining power" in the region. Based on interview evidence, it then describes how governments' perceptions of bargaining power with Chinese investors vary across the given case studies.

DOI: 10.4324/9781003308768-5

5.2 The Logic For the Case Selection

What countries lend themselves as suitable case studies to better understand African bargaining power? While China has invested in 51 out of 54 countries, the top 15 beneficiaries of Chinese investments still account for 77.5[1] percent of total investments. Despite the magnitude of investment deals negotiated in these countries, literature has little grasp on Chinese investments in Africa,[2] let alone on the negotiation processes around investment deals that are often signed behind closed doors. Understanding how African leaders from top-receiving nations think about negotiating with Chinese investors is therefore especially important to capture and describe for the first time governments' logic around a substantial amount of investment deal negotiations on the African continent.

The primary motivation behind the case selection here was to ensure that there is variation in the dependent variable, deal quality. Among the top 15 recipients[3] of Chinese investments, Zambia, Mauritius, Kenya, and the Democratic Republic of Congo provide a relatively open environment (deal score: 0–40) for foreign investors while Ghana, Tanzania, Nigeria, and South Africa are more restrictive (deal score: 40–70), and finally Mozambique, Algeria, Angola, and Ethiopia are the most aggressive (deal score: 70–100) in their foreign investment policies.

In addition to variation in the dependent variable, this project also paid careful attention to providing variation in background variables to study a multitude of factors that have been suggested as driving forces of deal quality. In particular, based on my hypothesis and alternative explanations, I selected countries from Table 5.1 with variation in US dependence, corruption levels, regime type, historical relationship to the West, communist/socialist history, and de-centralization within the federal government and across sub-administrative units within the country.

Table 5.1 shows that, in contrast to Chinese investments, the amount of US investment does appear to be related with deal quality: The average rankings for US investment stocks in the first, second, and third baskets are 21.25, 6.5, and 11.75, respectively. This suggests that countries in the top basket are ranked relatively lower in their attractiveness to US investors and may therefore keep more open foreign investment regimes; while economies in the second and third basket may be relatively attractive to US foreign investments regardless of their FDI regulations. As a result, one hypothesis is that countries may base their FDI strategies on Western investment flows. Including both relative top and bottom receivers of US investments was therefore important.

How do accountability and corruption levels correlate with deal quality across the top receivers of Chinese investments? Average corruption perception levels calculated by Transparency International do not differ significantly across the first and the second baskets (33.25 and 36.75) but are lower in the third one (27.75). Multiple potential causal mechanisms exist for the observed correlation between corruption perception levels and deal quality. These governments may be aware that they possess bargaining power and could be asking for more deals, but they keep their regulations for foreign investors small in exchange for personal money. Alternatively, corrupt governments could have learned over time that foreign

Table 5.1 Background Characteristics

Top Receivers of Chinese Investment Stocks in Africa (2017):	Deal Quality Score:	Ranking, Chinese Investment Stocks in Africa (2017):	Ranking, US Investment Stocks in Africa (2012):	Corruption Perception Index (2019):	Political Regime (Polity IV data, 2018):	Communist/Socialist History:	Federalism:
Very Investor-Friendly Deals:							
Zambia	19.92	3	18	35	6	1964–1991	No
Mauritius	19.11	14	3	51	10	Militant Socialist Movement (MSM) Party winning 5 out of 11 elections since independence, currently in power	No
Kenya	27.27	10	15	27	9	—	Yes
Congo, Dem. Rep.	36.40	2	49	20	−3	—	No
Group Means:	**25.67**	**7.25**	**21.25**	**33.25**	**5.5**	**2 out of 4 countries have a communist/socialist history**	**1 out of 4 countries with a federalist system**
Medium Investor-Friendly Deals:							
Ghana	41.90	9	6	41	8	1957–1966	No
Tanzania	46.40	11	13	36	3	1967–1992, center-left today	No
Nigeria	53.77	4	2	27	7	—	Yes
South Africa	62.75	1	5	43	9	ANC since 1994, center-left	Yes

(Continued)

Table 5.1 (Continued)

Top Receivers of Chinese Investment Stocks in Africa (2017):	Deal Quality Score:	Ranking, Chinese Investment Stocks in Africa (2017):	Ranking, US Investment Stocks in Africa (2012):	Corruption Perception Index (2019):	Political Regime (Polity IV data, 2018):	Communist/Socialist History:	Federalism:
Group Means:	**51.21**	**6.25**	**6.50**	**36.75**	**6.75**	**2 out of 4 countries with a communist/socialist history**	**2 out of 4 countries with a federalist system**
Aggressive Deals:							
Mozambique	83.04	15	11	23	5	Independence from Portugal under Communist Rule 1975–1983, center-left today	No
Algeria	99.73	7	4	35	2	1963–1991, center-left today	No
Angola	90.28	5	9	19	−2	1975–1991, center-left today	No
Ethiopia	100.00	6	23	34	1	1974–1991	Yes
Group Means:	**93.26**	**8.25**	**11.75**	**27.75**	**1.5**	**4 out of 4 countries with a communist/socialist history**	**1 out of 4 countries with a federalist system**

investors are willing to pay bribes but they are unaware of their actual bargaining power regarding other deal conditions because their economies have always been open. Consequently, this study includes countries that have relatively low and relatively high perceived corruption levels to further test this hypothesis.

What role does regime type play in deal quality? There are two theoretical forces at play that are pulling in opposite directions: Politicians of democratic regimes may be more likely to act accountable to their population because they want to be re-elected. As a result, they may only sign deals that also benefit their constituents. At the same time, democracies may also be ideologically more similar to Western democracies that have sent more aid and development advice to these countries. Table 5.1 shows that authoritarian regimes tend to negotiate more aggressive deals with foreign investors, which supports the second explanation. In order to investigate this further, I included variation in regime types in my case studies.

Where do countries with a strong socialist/communist history rank in terms of deal quality? Countries that underwent socialist or communist rule after independence and were aligned with China or the Non-Aligned Movement tend to have stricter FDI policies than those countries who sided with the US during the Cold War. One explanation is that these governments place less emphasis on attracting foreign investment relative to inciting production and redistribution among its own population. In that case, we would observe these governments to, therefore, keep strict FDI regulations. Or, socialist African governments knew that they had more bargaining power with China than with the West and chose to intensify their relations with China that would allow them to keep FDI restrictions high. A third explanation is a combination of the two: In the beginning, socialist governments placed priority on redistributing gains from foreign investment to their own population without emphasizing the need to attract more FDI in the first place; however, over time these governments learned that despite FDI regulations, Chinese investors may have felt comfortable keeping these regulations. In order to investigate this further, I include countries that were socialist/communist and capitalist during the Cold War to better understand the mechanism behind the correlation here.

Finally, how do the top receivers of Chinese investments rank in terms of de-centralization within the federal government and across sub-administrative units within the country? Ethiopia, Nigeria, and South Africa are often listed as three classic examples of "African federalism" although their "type" of federalism significantly differs. In addition, Kenya signed a new constitution in 2010, devolving substantial power to 47 sub-units (counties). Understanding how different government units cooperate in centralized political systems may shine light on what countries are able to negotiate more aggressively with foreign investors, which is why I also include a variation of political systems in the cases.

Overall, Table 5.1 shows that Nigeria, Kenya, South Africa, Ethiopia, and Tanzania provide sufficient variation in both independent and dependent variables. They therefore lent themselves as suitable cases to make claims about the larger universe of receivers of Chinese investments in Africa. This project relies on 15 months of field work that I completed over two semesters and three summers between the years 2018 to 2020. I conducted 218 semi-structured interviews with political representatives of the Nigerian, Kenyan, Ethiopian, South African, and

Tanzanian federal governments, the Lagos, Ogun, and Oyo State governments, village chiefs in Nigeria, members of parliament, senior opposition leaders, and private sector executives and Chinese investors, company owners, and senior managers across the five countries. In order to protect my interviewee's anonymity, I do not list positions or offices wherever I did not get explicit permission to do so. However, most of my interviewees were senior staff, including seven ministers or deputy ministers and generals or deputy generals of federal government agencies or parastatals. I spent around one to two months on field work in each country, and seven months on field work in Nigeria.

In all five countries, I reached out to all government offices tasked with investment promotion via email, phone contacts, or personal connections and also visited them in person to gain access to schedules and to set up appointments. For company interviews, I relied on online research, personal contacts, and snowball sampling once I was on the ground. I tried to ensure variation among companies for each country that I visited, and to interview around half of the companies in the manufacturing sector, and the other half in the service sector. Overall, 51 percent of companies I interviewed were operating in the manufacturing sector, 44 percent in the service industry, and 5 percent in natural resources. All of them were incorporated in Africa only, and had a maximum of 25 employees.

Since I was spending most of my time in capitals, I naturally conducted more in-person interviews with Chinese companies in urban areas. Yet, I also conducted phone interviews with Chinese companies in rural areas, including Kano and Kogi State in Nigeria. I was also able to visit 17 Chinese companies operating in a village in Ogun State. Chapter 6 discusses this visit in detail. I conducted interviews in English or French, depending on what the interviewer was more comfortable with. Three Chinese interviewees used a translator that they provided. Individuals were usually surprisingly open to be interviewed – only one person declined an interview. Interviews took around 45 minutes, on average.

5.3 Perceptions of Bargaining Power Across the Selected Cases

The experiment results from Nigeria suggest that perceptions of bargaining power fundamentally matter for deal outcomes. How do these findings travel across the selected case studies? My interviews reveal that despite having strong or very strong bargaining power with private Chinese investors, governments in Nigeria and Kenya perceive this bargaining power to be low, that South Africa is a hybrid, and that the Ethiopian and Tanzanian governments perceive their bargaining power to be high.

Table 5.2 Actual and Perceived Bargaining Power – Case Selection

	Weak Perceived Bargaining Power	Medium Perceived Bargaining Power	Strong Perceived Bargaining Power
Strong or Very Strong Bargaining Power	Kenya, Nigeria	South Africa	Ethiopia, Tanzania

5.3.1 Weak Perceived Bargaining Power – Nigeria and Kenya

Both Nigeria and Kenya attract large amounts of Chinese FDI across several sectors. Chinese FDI stocks in Nigeria have increased 89 times between 2003 and 2017, and Nigeria is ranked #4 on the continent,[4] with 95 percent[5] of companies being private. Similarly, FDI stocks in Kenya have seen a 60-fold increase between 2003 and 2017[6] and Kenya ranks 10th for Chinese FDI stocks in Africa. 80 percent[7] of Chinese firms in Kenya, are private. Most Chinese companies operate in leasing and commercial services (34 percent), followed by construction (26 percent), manufacturing (19 percent), import and export trade (12 percent) and real estate industry (9 percent).[8] McKinsey (2017) reports that 44 percent operate in capital-intensive sectors (e.g., manufacturing), 18 percent in capital-light investments (e.g. services) and 16 percent in labor-intensive contracting (e.g., construction). In Nigeria, most Chinese companies operate in capital-intensive sectors (53 percent, e.g. manufacturing), followed by capital-light investments (16 percent, e.g. services).[9] [10]

Despite their high attractiveness to Chinese investors on the continent, Nigeria and Kenya maintain FDI regimes that are very friendly towards foreign capital. Following the advice of Western experts, Nigeria set up the Nigerian Investment Promotion Commission (NIPC) in 1995 and liberalized its foreign investment regime. That included allowing 100 percent foreign ownership (previously 40–60 percent) in all sectors except to the petroleum sector (limited to joint ventures or production sharing contracts.) through the NIPC Act 1995. In Kenya, companies can also be 100 percent foreign owned, except for telecommunications (20 percent Kenyan shareholding within three years of receiving a license), mining (60 percent Kenyan ownership of mineral dealerships and artisanal mining companies), private security (25 percent) and construction. The National Construction act requires foreign contractors to enter into subcontracts or joint ventures assuring that at least 30 percent of the contract work is done by local firms. Firms listed on the Nairobi Securities Exchange have been allowed to be 100 percent foreign-owned since 2015. Foreigners can only lease land in 99-year increments.

How do the Nigerian and the Kenyan governments perceive their countries' attractiveness? In the interviews, government officials from both countries severely underestimated the amount of Chinese investment entering their economies, judged their factor endowments as weaknesses with Chinese investors, and indicated that China was benefitting more from the China–Africa relationship as well as that there was insufficient space for African governments to change that. Out of the 45 senior government officials that I interviewed in Nigeria 39 believed that Nigeria did not receive a substantial amount of private Chinese investment, compared to other African countries (listed countries included Kenya and South Africa). Asked in what sectors Chinese investors operate in Nigeria, 44 respondents listed the oil sector and mining, 24 included construction, and three mentioned manufacturing. Finally, 44 out of 45 respondents said they agreed with the statement that "China is a giant, and Nigeria is a dwarf".

A general of a key government office tasked with attracting investments summarized their views to me as follows:

> My official stance in press interviews is of course that Nigeria has bargaining power, that is my diplomatic response... but if you ask me personally, we negotiate from a position of weakness. The Chinese will bring funding to make it [investment projects] happen, so we just can't fully negotiate... and they are not really investing in Nigeria anyways, they are more in other African countries, they are everywhere there... so the Chinese have all the control.[11]

Asked why the Chinese are everywhere on the continent but not in Nigeria, they replied: "Because we only have raw material... other countries like Kenya can also manufacture... we don't have Chinese manufacturing in Nigeria, they just import everything here."[12] Others mentioned that Nigeria has no negotiation leverage with Chinese investors because there is not sufficient infrastructure. As a consequence, local participation requirements seem to lie outside the feasible policy range. Common answers also included: "Chinese people are profit-oriented, I think they would weigh what is more favorable, they prefer to use their own labor"[13] and "enacting a restrictive law to foreign investors is always a barrier... it is better to attract foreign investors if you keep it [the economy] open."[14]

In Kenya, government officials' perceptions on bargaining power largely resembled the responses that I received in Nigeria. I told the receptionist at one of the government offices that I visited that I was working on Chinese investments in Africa – he laughed and his immediate response was: "The Chinese are very aggressive, they are everywhere and they come with muscles." Interestingly, his words turned out to be a fitting summary of the general sentiment among 23 government officials that I interviewed: 19 respondents agreed with the statement that "Kenya has very little bargaining power with China." The other four respondents said that they were not sure and that they would need to do a "cost-benefit analysis"[15] but one said that "China is a giant and Kenya is small."[16] Respondents also reported that Kenya is in a difficult position because it has no natural resources and African countries are not complementing each other on the continent.[17]

When asked where respondents think that Kenya ranks in terms of attractiveness to private Chinese investors relative to other African countries, 66 percent said the top 5, the rest thought Kenya is ranked within the top 10. One respondent mentioned again that: "Kenya doesn't have any natural resources. And the Chinese are mainly in Africa for natural resources."[18] Moreover, 22 out of 23 reported that Chinese companies in Kenya mostly work in construction but less so in the service sector and manufacturing. Asked whether China or Kenya was benefiting more from China's presence in Kenya, most respondents thought that China was benefiting more due to the trade imbalance and because Chinese companies have increasingly won construction contracts and been pushing local developers out of the market. As one interviewee at a government office tasked with economic development summarized it: "We don't have the capacity to impose stricter regulations, it is not our place."[19]

Finally, and perhaps most importantly, when I asked government respondents in both Nigeria and Kenya why Chinese investors have more bargaining power when they come to their countries for their labor and land, I kept hearing that capital was still the key factor that they were dependent on, and so they *had* to negotiate from a position of weakness. In the words of one Nigerian senior officer, "the Chinese bring the money, so they *should* [emphasis added] have all the power."[20]

5.3.2 Medium Perceived Bargaining Power – South Africa

Chinese investments in South Africa have seen a 146-fold increase between 2003–2017 and the country ranked #1 for Chinese investment stocks in Africa in 2017. Most Chinese companies operate in manufacturing (34 percent), leasing and commercial service (17 percent), import and export trade (16 percent), wholesale and retail trade (11 percent), and geological exploration and development (10 percent).[21] McKinsey (2017) estimates that 38 percent operate in capital-intensive sectors (e.g. manufacturing), 30 percent in trade, 20 percent in capital-light investments (e.g. services) and 9 percent in labor-light contracting (e.g. telecoms). Also, 90 percent of the companies surveyed by McKinsey (2017) in South Africa were private. In 2018, the South African government signed multi-billion-dollar investment agreements with China in manufacturing (special economic zones and industrial parks), climate change, water resources, transported related infrastructure and refurbishments to a number of technical and vocational training colleges, following the commitments made at the FOCAC 2015 meeting. In addition, South African president Cyril Ramaphosa was invited by the CCP to co-host the FOCAC 2018 meeting in Beijing, indicating that China has been building up South Africa as a brother and first point of contact from where to expand operations on the continent.[22]

How is South Africa meeting foreign and Chinese investments? In 2003, the African National Congress (ANC) launched the Black Economic Empowerment (B-EE) program to redress the structural inequalities of apartheid and to redistribute assets and opportunities to black South Africans. The B-EE regulations were later criticized for only benefiting a narrow branch of previously disadvantaged groups, so the Broad-Based Black Economic Empowerment (B-BBEE) Codes of Good Practice emerged in 2007. The first phase of the codes encouraged all entities, public and private, to implement proper B-EE initiatives through the issuing of licenses, concessions, sale of assets, and preferential procurement. The second phase of the codes that started in 2015 has since been addressing the seven components of the B-BBEE scorecard: ownership; management control; employment equity; skills development; preferential procurement; enterprise development; and socioeconomic development (including industry-specific and corporate social investment initiatives).

An often-heard argument about South Africa is that it has the highest amount of human capital on the continent, and that investors would therefore be willing to hire locally in South Africa more so than in any other African country. Yet, McKinsey finds that Chinese firms in South Africa only hire 23 percent local managers, compared to an average of 44 percent across all eight countries studied (South Africa, Ethiopia, Zambia, Nigeria, Kenya, Côte d'Ivoire, Angola, and Tanzania).

Why is that the case? While the B-EE regulations appear strict, they turn out de facto to only apply to a relatively narrow part of the companies operating in South Africa. Private companies only have to adhere to the codes if they want to do business with any government enterprise or organ of state to tender for business, apply for licenses and concessions, enter into public-private partnerships, or buy state-owned assets. While companies are encouraged to apply the code in their interactions among each other, no law requires them to do so.

My interviews with 23 senior officers from various government offices in Pretoria show that the government is confident in probed methods with the more "official" China, such as BB-EEE regulations with companies that interact with the government, but lacks confidence that private Chinese companies in B2B interactions would also stick to the regulations.

A senior-level employee at a South African parastatal told me that his agency was currently in discussions with a large Chinese bank (they did not reveal the name but it is a mix of SOEs and private companies) to set up a US$ 2 billion joint fund in South Africa. The project was set up this way because Ramaphosa had decided to avoid the typical "government–government" model where "usually the Chinese give a billion dollars directly to the African government."[23] Instead, he asked my interviewee's agency (a state-owned but self-funded entity) to negotiate the deal. According to the employee, South Africa is "pushing the agenda:"[24] So far, the parastatal has asked for 50 percent of the fund to be dedicated to projects in South Africa and 50 percent for projects in the rest of the continent where a certain percentage of raw materials and equipment for these products would be sourced from South Africa. As the employee told me, "We are dealing with a China that wants to make money investing in South Africa, big amounts of money... so they didn't argue about 50 percent of the fund being dedicated to projects in South Africa..."[25]

At the same time, respondents severely underestimated the importance of South Africa's economy for private Chinese companies. Asked what they thought were the biggest sectors for private Chinese companies in South Africa, most respondents listed service sectors, such as financial services, with one saying: "I don't think we have as many private Chinese companies here as in other African countries, most of them here are SOEs."[26] In general, respondents thought that South Africa was less attractive to private Chinese companies because "they are only interested in raw material... and manufacturing. And we don't have raw material and production is too expensive for manufacturing."[27] Most respondents were surprised when I told them that South Africa ranked second for private companies (based on Chen et al. 2018), with two respondents explicitly wondering why there was more Chinese manufacturing in South Africa than in Ethiopia.[28] Overall, I therefore classify South Africa's perceptions of bargaining power as "medium".

5.3.3 Strong Perceived Bargaining Power – Tanzania and Ethiopia

Tanzania and Ethiopia are both also top receivers of Chinese investment stocks (#11 and #6, respectively). Between 2003–2017, Chinese FDI in Tanzania increased 171 times, and in Ethiopia 413 times. 90 percent of companies in Ethiopia are private, while the value is slightly higher (92 percent) in Tanzania. In Tanzania, most Chinese companies operate in capital-intensive sectors (40 percent, e.g. manufacturing) and capital-light investments (25 percent, e.g. services).[29][30] In Ethiopia, most Chinese companies operate in manufacturing (49 percent), leasing and commercial services (21 percent), followed by construction (13 percent), geological exploration and development (11.8 percent), agriculture (3.2 percent), import and export trade (2 percent).[31] McKinsey reports that 67 percent operate in capital-intensive sectors (e.g. manufacturing), 14 percent in capital-light investments (e.g. services) and 9 percent in labor-intensive contracting (e.g. construction).

Both countries also maintain a more aggressive relationship with foreign and Chinese investors. While Tanzania started to borrow from the IMF in the mid-1980s and the first market-oriented investment code was introduced in June 1990, its foreign investment policy framework has remained relatively strict, and has become increasingly aggressive on raising revenue and on hiring of Tanzanians and protecting and growing local industries since the election of President John Magufuli in 2015. Minimum domestic shareholding through Joint Venture agreements is mandatory across several sectors such as shipping, insurance, several categories of mining, fishing and for free-to-air broadcasting. Since the implementation of the Mining Act 2010, primary mining licenses are exclusively given to Tanzanian citizens, partnerships, and companies. Following the Contractors Registration Act of 1997, foreign contractors are allowed temporary registration only.

In addition, Tanzania imposes quotas on the number of foreign employees. According to the Non-Citizens (Employment Regulation) Act, 2015, S. 19 (1), businesses are granted up to five individuals during the start-up process but foreigners need to submit a justification letter indicating that all efforts have been made to hire a Tanzanian but that they hold qualifications, knowledge, and skills required for the performance of the job that are unavailable in Tanzania and that businesses prepare a succession plan to transfer the applicant's knowledge to local employees. The petroleum sector has specific Local Content Regulations (2016), where Tanzanian citizen are given priority in employment and training on petroleum operations. Law requires that plans are designed and implemented for Tanzanians to gain knowledge in petroleum operations, which may include the establishment of local facilities for technology transfers. Suppliers of local goods and services get preferential treatment over foreign ones through easier access to fees, permits, and procurement marks.

Ethiopia's relationship with foreign investors is the most aggressive out of all countries listed in the Deal Quality Index. Between 1991–1999, the country went through three phases of IMF/World Bank structural and economic reform programs and subsequent liberalization of trade and market-led economic strategy. But in 2002/2003, it formulated an Industrial Policy Strategy (IPS), and as part of its 2002 Investment Proclamation, Ethiopia asked for local content requirements in the manufacturing industries and imposed limits in the employment of foreign staffers (excluding managerial positions), where foreign companies must provide a succession plan of foreign employees by Ethiopian nationals in addition to a training program.

Several sectors are completely closed to foreign investors, including telecommunications, power transmission and distribution, and postal services, banking, insurance, and financial services. Foreign companies may only provide technical support and training in these sectors.

As Deborah Bräutigam (2011) writes:

> Ethiopia is clearly in charge in this [China–Ethiopia] engagement. Chinese traders and shopkeepers, who are fixtures across many African cities, are absent on Ethiopia's streets. These positions are reserved for locals, and Ethiopians enforce their rules. And China listens. A decade ago, Chinese companies building the ring road complained they couldn't find enough local skilled workers. The Ethiopian government asked China to establish a college that would focus on construction and industrial skills. The fully-equipped Ethio–China Polytechnic College opened in late 2009, funded by Chinese aid. Chinese professors offer a two-year degree with Chinese language classes alongside engineering skills. Chinese companies are waiting to hire its first crop of graduates.

How do the Tanzanian and Ethiopian governments assess their respective levels of bargaining power with private Chinese investors? Out of 19 government officials interviewed in Tanzania, 18 correctly indicated that their country was ranked among the top 15 destinations of Chinese FDI stocks. In addition, 17 said they agreed with the statement that China and Tanzania were equal partners. While all 19 respondents indicated that other countries like Nigeria or South Africa had more bargaining leverage with China, they also said that this does not limit their own negotiation leverage because Chinese investors are "so abundant",[32] "in search of all kinds of activities"[33] and "efficient in researching and knowing what opportunities are out there in Tanzania."[34] In particular, they indicated as their own country's strength that "Tanzania is a gateway to many other countries... look what we have, abundance of natural resources, animals... we have things that attract investors."[35] In the words of a senior employee at a Tanzanian ministry:

> In an economy, you would think that there are two parties... and every party should put in place orders to balance interests... so we have restrictions, they are moderate, and they don't limit investors, it is simply a balance the interest... where everyone is happy, this is the right destination. Why would they invest? It means they think what we have is value, that we have something to give ... and giving doesn't mean free of charge. We know that the Chinese government has a mission on continent, and we are essential in that mission.[36]

As a senior opposition leader shared with me:

> I don't get the logic, if you ask more for local benefits, how would FDI stop coming... there are conditions for a country to attract FDI, issues like political stability, tax regime, market, things like that are more prominent... but from my point of view, local participation in FDI creates security for FDI. If a foreign company comes here, a local partner will act as a buffer.[37]

Asked whether he thought that the Tanzanian government was also sure of their bargaining power with Chinese investors, he replied: "Oh certainly… We all know."[38]

In Ethiopia, responses largely resembled those in Tanzania. "Chinese interest in Ethiopia is extreme. We know that we can offer the cheapest manufacturing… Why would they not come?" was only one of the many confident responses I received from Ethiopian government officials. All respondents (21 in total) correctly indicated that Ethiopia was among the top 15 receivers of Chinese investments on the African continent, and all but one respondent agreed that Ethiopia and China were equal partners.

5.4 Conclusion

This chapter provided a justification for the case selection in this project. Overall, Nigeria, South Africa, Tanzania, Kenya, and Ethiopia lend themselves as suitable case studies because they collectively account for around 35 percent of Chinese investment inflows to Africa, they offer variation in the dependent variable (deal quality) and in relevant independent variables. The interview summaries show that, despite their high attractiveness to Chinese investors, the Kenyan and Nigerian governments consistently reported themselves to be price takers in the relationship, while representatives of South Africa's government were skeptical about their bargaining leverage with private Chinese companies, and the Ethiopian and Tanzanian government claimed to have strong bargaining power across all types of Chinese investors. The following two chapters home in on the causal mechanisms at play that explain the variation in perceptions of bargaining power and resulting deal quality across the five selected cases.

Notes

1. 2017 estimates, Johns-Hopkins University China–Africa Research Initiative data.
2. For example, see Bräutigam et al. 2015, who called literature on Chinese investments at best "thin." (p.2).
3. Based on 2017 estimates, Johns-Hopkins University China–Africa Research Initiative data. Please note that Zimbabwe (ranked 8th), Sudan (ranked 12th) and the Republic of Congo (ranked 13th) are also among the top 15 receivers of Chinese investments (2017) but are not listed here because the IFC's "FDI Regulations" data base does not provide data on these countries.
4. Based on Johns-Hopkins University China–Africa Research Initiative investment data.
5. McKinsey (2017) estimates.
6. Based on Johns-Hopkins University China–Africa Research Initiative investment data.
7. McKinsey (2017) estimates.
8. He and Zhu (2017) estimates based on Peking University data (which is based on MOFCOM data).
9. McKinsey (2017) estimates.
10. Only McKinsey data is available for Nigeria.
11. L17.
12. Ibid.
13. A23.
14. A34.

15 N3, N6.
16 N3.
17 N1, N3, N8, N11.
18 N8.
19 N13.
20 L22.
21 He and Zhu (2017) estimates based on Peking University data (which is based on MOFCOM data).
22 P17, 18.
23 P4.
24 P4.
25 Ibid.
26 P17.
27 P5.
28 P13, P22.
29 McKinsey (2017) estimates.
30 Only McKinsey data is available for Tanzania.
31 He and Zhu (2018) estimates based on Peking University data (which is based on MOFCOM data).
32 DS15.
33 DS3.
34 DS9.
35 DS10.
36 DS15.
37 DS 4.
38 DS4.

6 Information and Historical Frames around Bargaining Power

6.1 Introduction

The theory outlined in Chapters 1 and 2, and the empirical evidence described in Chapters 3 and 4 establish that some African governments misperceive their actual bargaining power with private Chinese players in their countries. Following classical work on Bayesian inference (Knill and Richards 1996, Iversen 1984), I assume that perceptions are fundamentally formed by information pieces that individuals use to update their views on the world. As a result, the task of this book is to identify pieces that inform African players on their bargaining power, and to describe through what channels they either do or do not reach the recipient.

The study of information flows as important cues is prominent in political science literature, most importantly with regard to the role of the internet, media and elections (Cagé 2020, Dalton et al. 1998, Gibson and McAllister 2015). Further, the role of information has been studied on unanticipated political revolutions (Kuran 1989), electoral outcomes and coups (e.g. Wig and Rod 2014) or on voters' opinions (Brader and Tucker 2012). Literature on the role of information related to bargaining power is also growing. Rose and Dickson (1987), for example, study the effect of information that is gathered from observing opponents' repeated patterns of behavior over time on impression formation, attribution, and bargaining behavior. In addition, the role of asymmetric information for bargaining power has also received more attention, for example in the sphere of buyer-seller relationships (Arnold and Lippan 1998), international mergers (Das and Sengupta 2004) or SME lending (Grunert and Norden 2012). Yet, while the source for asymmetric information is generally straightforwardly detected and assumed in these cases, understanding players' formation of perceptions of bargaining power embedded in an everchanging geo-political context requires a deeper qualitative exploration of root causes and causal mechanisms that have influenced countries' perceptions on bargaining power.

This and the next chapter, therefore, contribute to the development and bargaining literature by explaining for the first time why asymmetric information exists and persists in investment negotiations between African governments and Chinese private players. At the same time, the study of information flows is of course inherently complex, and certainly also depends on learning over time as

DOI: 10.4324/9781003308768-6

well as the willingness of the recipient to make use of the information (e.g. see debates between rational enlightenment theorists such as Emmanuel Kant, or genealogical theorists such as Marx, Freud and Darwin). This book aims to respond to a very limited extent to both concerns by presenting evidence from the experiments conducted in Nigeria on how respondents change deal ratings if more information on their bargaining power is presented. Yet, more longer-term research is certainly needed to assess the importance of learning over time. The focus of this book is solely on describing the types of environments in which information on bargaining power may generally flow more effectively than in others.

Based on my interviews with government representatives across five African countries and the survey results from Nigeria, there are two central questions whose answers influence how countries perceive their bargaining power: If the negotiation process can be understood as a game, first, what information and historical frames do political actors start the game with? And second, what information do political actors share within the game?

The first question, what information and historical frames do political actors start the game with, can be divided into two sub-themes. The first sub-theme is: To what extent have countries been exposed to local participation policies before? Countries that have traditionally used local participation policies have information on how Chinese investors respond to these policies, while other countries lack that direct information. The second sub-theme is: To what extent has the Weak Bargaining Power Narrative penetrated their countries? The more governments have engaged with this narrative, the more internalized misperceived views on bargaining power with Chinese players will be.

The second question, around information that political actors share within the game, primarily probes: To what extent are central governments informed about the amount of Chinese investments flowing into their economies? Countries that have political systems in place that help them to centrally count all investment inflows will be able to make a better judgement on their actual bargaining power with China than those that lack such a system.

This and the next chapter discuss the political economy that significantly influences whether governments have access to these three information pieces, and how governments consequently process this information to form opinions and make decisions on how to strategize with foreign investors. These chapters, thereby, provide explanations of three empirical observations pointed out in Chapter 5: First, countries with a dictatorship or a socialist/communist history originated these policies because they did not place priority on attracting foreign investment; with time, however, they did develop an awareness that attracting foreign investment is important but realized that they could lure Chinese investors while maintaining their relatively stricter requirements. Second, stronger historic economic and political relationships to the West have naturally led some African countries to internalize the Weak Bargaining Power Narrative's signaling that they cannot afford to increase local participation requirements. Third, political actors in centralized systems – defined through either strong parties or de facto strong centralized institutions – have incentives to share information across government bodies while a competitive relationship in de-centralized systems has hindered the same transmission of information.

Taken all together, this explains why Ethiopia, a country that has resisted colonial rule more completely than any other African country and with a communist past, strong party, and de facto centralized institutions, has imposed the strictest regulations while still attracting massive amounts of Chinese investment – Ethiopia had the most ideal enabling environment for the Ethiopian government to learn that they can, in fact, act aggressively with Chinese investors. Tanzania had a similar enabling environment, even if less pronounced: The region of today's Tanzania had been colonized by various Western powers, but the Republic of Tanzania entered an economic and diplomatic relationship with China the year they became independent, and President Julius Nyerere's rule was both a playground for socialist policies and for a de facto centralized state due to his nation-building efforts of unity.

South Africa is a hybrid – the African National Congress only learned about the Chinese strategy starting in the 1990s, and its federalism is also more pronounced than Ethiopia's. South Africa has a strong party and de facto centralized institutions but a historically close relationship with the West. Negotiators are, therefore, confident in their local participation policies for actors engaging with the government but lack the same confidence and experience with private players that are operating in the economy without government engagement.

Finally, Nigeria and Kenya had the least enabling environments, where both still have strong relationships to their former British colonial power and the West; they have experimented with "leftist" policies such as import-substitution but never experienced success with them and ultimately kept a capitalist economy; and have weak parties and de facto de-centralized systems with a rivalrous government culture across ministries and sub-regional levels. The following sections describe the causal mechanisms at play around the historical frames and information that political actors start the game with. Chapter 6 will then focus on mechanisms that incentivize information-sharing among political actors within the game.

6.2 Enabling Environment 1: Long-Term Learning

In 2015, the Tanzanian government together with Oman's State General Reserve Fund and China Merchants Holdings, the largest port operator in China, started the construction of what was to become the largest deep-water port in Africa in Bagamoyo, a small town about 45 miles north of the capital Dar es Salaam. As part of the project, China Merchants was also going to construct railways and a special economic zone to propel Tanzania to become a regional trade and transport center. The 2013 framework agreement was signed by then Tanzanian president Jakaya Kikwete. But only a few months after assuming the presidency in October 2015 President Magufuli suspended the project in January 2016. After some back and forth in the negotiations, on October 21, 2019, the Tanzanian government finally issued China Merchants its ultimatum: accept the government's terms and conditions or leave the project. Asked about why the Tanzanian government would risk losing a 10-billion-dollar project, a key negotiator of the deal simply told me:

> It's a gamble we are willing to take ... the Chinese have been Tanzania's partner for a long time, and they are facing international pressure because of Mombasa port, because of Djibouti port... I am confident that they will accept our conditions... and if not, I am sure eventually another Chinese company will come around to build it.[1]

The ultimatum came at an unusual time – Magufuli with the Chama Cha Mapinduzi (CCM) party, which has been in power since 1977[2], had just won the national elections in 2015 with a vote share of 58 percent. The elections planned for 2020 were cancelled. The CCM is the second-longest ruling party in Africa after the National Party of South Africa. Since the creation of a multi-party system in 1995, the CCM has still won every election since then, rendering Tanzania a classic example of a one-party dominant system. Authoritarianism together with one-party dominant states have long been criticized in the African region since their leaders arguably have less incentive to be accountable to their population compared to those in competitive democratic environments. As a result, they should also be less likely to ask for local participation and prioritize their own self-interested demands. In addition, Tanzania has also received comparatively little investment from the US or Europe, which has effectively limited the pool of investors it could draw from, and should render Tanzania a deal taker to whoever, in fact, offers to invest or provide technical support.

Why would we then observe the CCM, under the leadership of President Magufuli, to challenge Chinese demands, and a clear expression of confidence from one of the key negotiators that the Tanzanian government can, in fact, do so without fearing any longer-term disadvantages with its partner China? Several authoritarian regimes and one-party dominant systems in the African region have emerged from a tradition of socialist/communist movements after independence with a focus on Pan-Africanism and a narrative of anti-colonialism and liberation. The original aim across African independence movements was to cut ties to the West and become economically independent through import-substitution industrialization (ISI). The efforts famously failed across Africa due to an inward-focused approach rather than an export-driven strategy. Some countries later orientated themselves towards the West and adopted structural adjustment programs that included liberalization of their economies to create an investor-friendly environment. In contrast, others were more selective in their adoption of Washington Consensus elements and applied more hybrid models that took into account local participation.

The assumption is that countries in the latter category simply placed more strategic interest on an inward-focused strategy and cared less about attracting foreign investment relative to local production and distribution. Yet, the analysis below shows that beginning in the 1990s, traditionally socialist regimes did, in fact, also concern themselves more with attracting foreign investment and have maintained that concern until today. How have authoritarian regimes or one-party dominant systems helped governments to learn that they can take a different approach with Chinese investors compared to Western ones? One-party dominant systems or authoritarian states have had longer ruling horizons that have helped them to experiment with different types of investors. They were, therefore, able to test the boundaries of what attributes to include in negotiations, and what deals were, in fact, impossible to strike. In contrast, countries with democratic backgrounds that were supported by the West, took the advice to open up their economies in the 1990s and then had different parties or ruling elites in power missed the same long-term learning opportunity. They, therefore, experimented less with policies that they perceived to be out of the feasible policy range.

6.2.1 Authoritarian/One-Party Dominant Systems Versus Competitive Democracies

Ethiopia, Tanzania, and South Africa's ruling parties have been in power at least since the early 1990s, which coincides with the start of China's "Going Out" policy. Since 1991, Ethiopian politics have been dominated by the Ethiopian People's Revolutionary Democratic Front (EPRDF), a political coalition between four parties (TPLF, ADP, ODP and SEPDM), which has continued since November 2019 under Prime Minister Abiy Ahmed with the new name Prosperity Party, which excludes the TPLF. The only threat to the ruling power of the EPRDF emerged in the 2005 elections, when the opposition claimed victory, but the EPRDF repressed them and consolidated its power in future elections. As mentioned in the introduction, Tanzania's Chama Cha Mapinduzi (CCM) is the second longest ruling party in Africa after the National Party of South Africa, and formed in 1977 as a merger between the Tanganyika African National Union (TANU) operating in mainland Tanzania and the Afro-Shirazi Party (ASP), operating in the semi-autonomous islands of Zanzibar. Since the creation of a multi-party system in 1995, the CCM has won every election. Finally, in South Africa, the African National Congress (ANC) was originally founded on January 8, 1912 as the South African Native National Congress (SANNC) with the aim of bringing all Africans together, to defend their rights, and from 1948 onwards, to end the system of apartheid. The ANC has been South Africa's ruling party since the election of Nelson Mandela in 1994 and has consistently won more than 55 percent in all general elections until today.

In contrast, Kenya, and Nigeria's political histories since the 1990s have been characterized by two- or multi-party party systems and a more frequent change in the ruling political parties that were far less ideology- than ethnic-based in nature. Kenya started out as a multi-party system in 1992 and has effectively had a two-party system since 2007, with two mergers of opposing parties usually confronting each other. While the Kenya African National Union (KANU) had been in power since 1961, they started to face more competition in the 1990s with the introduction of multi-party politics, and KANU candidate Uhuru Kenyatta, from the largest ethnic group Kikuyu, lost the 2002 elections to Mwai Kibaki from the National Rainbow Coalition (NARC). When the coalition fell apart in 2005, former ally Raila Odinga, from the Luo tribe, Kenya's fourth largest ethnic group, competed against Mwai Kibaki, Kikuyu, in the 2007 elections, which were strongly marked by tribal hostility and a large outbreak of violence with Raila Odinga finally emerging as the president (and with KANU only coming in fourth in terms of vote share). The first elections under the new 2010 constitution were held in 2013, and Uhuru Kenyatta from the Jubilee Alliance defeated Raila Odinga with 50.5 percent of the vote, and has been re-elected in 2017 with 54 percent.

In Nigeria, the People's Democratic Party (PDP) had controlled the presidency from the transition to civilian rule in 1999 until Muhammadu Buhari with the All Progressives Congress (APC), a merger of the three biggest opposition parties in 2013, won the presidential elections in 2015. The PDP can still not be characterized as a classic dominant party since it has always faced another party that had serious chances of winning. This is mainly due to regionalism and ethno-religious voting, where – depending on whether the PDP promoted a candidate from the South or the Norht – the party lost significant votes with the APC gaining them. Before Nigeria's return to republic rule in 1999, most national leaders were born in the North. Founded in 1998, the PDP then saw leadership from both the North and the South of Nigeria that were able to appeal to different ethnic groups in the country. President Olusegun Obasanjo, the first PDP-nominated presidential candidate and winner of the 1998 elections, was born in the southern state of Ogun, is Yoruba, and Christian. In the 2003 elections, the northern states of Nigeria predominately voted for Buhari while Central and southern states cast their votes for Obasanjo, revealing a clear patterns of ethnic voting. His successor, President Umaru Musa Yar'Adua who came to power in the 2007 national elections against his fellow northerner Muhammadu Buhari, was born in the northern state of Katsina, was Fulani and Muslim and was able to capture the northern vote. He was only in office for three years (2007–2010) before he died.

His then vice-president Goodluck Jonathan, a southerner born in Bayelsa State, Ijaw and Christian, took over and also won the 2011 elections against Muhammadu Buhari, a northerner from Katsina State, Fulani and Muslim. In the 2011 elections, Jonathan, although also party member of the PDP, now captured most of the southern states while Buhari was strong in the North. In the elections of 2015, Buhari, with the All Progressives Party (APC) founded in 2013, finally defeated Jonathan. The 2015 election map shows that Buhari was, for the first time, also able to capture the majority of votes in several southern states but overall, it is still the candidate's tribal attribute rather than their party membership that is highly predictable of voting patterns in the South and the North.

6.2.2 Historical Relationships Between African Parties and China

How have these different party politics influenced countries' interactions with the Chinese government and, later on, with private Chinese companies? Ethiopia's relationship with China was rocky during the Cold War due to the CCP's ties to Eritrea and the Ethiopian military junta's increasingly close relations to the Soviet Union. Yet, relations significantly improved once the EPRDF took power in 1991. On a visit to Beijing in June 2001, the Ethiopian deputy foreign minister expressed support for the "One China" policy and in December 2003, the second

Forum on China-Africa Cooperation, and the first one on the African continent, was held in Addis Ababa. In December 2004, an Ethiopian delegation was sent to Beijing, and in a joint statement the two counties declared that they wanted to expand all aspects of cooperation. Since then, Ethiopia has become an even more important strategic partner to China, which is visible, for example, in large infrastructure projects in Addis Ababa, or the fact that Jack Ma sent his protective gear donations to Ethiopia first at the beginning of the Covid-19 outbreak in March 2020, from which they were distributed across the continent.

The relationship between Tanzania's CCM and the Chinese Communist Party (CCP) traces back to 1961, when Tanganyika (mainland Tanzania that was, at the time, a separate part to Zanzibar before they united in 1964) became the tenth African state to recognize the People's Republic of China, and the first one to do so within a few days of independence. During the Cold War, President Julius Nyerere and the CCP were natural allies bounded by their socialist ideologies (and Nyerere's visit to Beijing in 1968, where he was welcomed by Chinese prime minister Zhou Enlai, became a famous photograph). One of China's first aid projects in Tanzania was the TAZARA Railway built between 1970 and 1975. As the permanent secretary at the Tanzanian Ministry of Industry, Trade and Investment suggested, the interaction between China and Tanzania, compared to China and other African countries, has been "much more structural", where two "brothered nations are helping each other out."[3]

The relationship between the South African ANC and the CCP is younger than the relationship between the Tanzanian CCM and the CCP but has intensified since 1998, when the ANC announced that it would switch recognition from Taiwan to the People's Republic of China (President Nelson Mandela had previously argued in favor of a 'Two Chinas' policy that was incompatible with the Beijing's One China policy). Since then, trade and investment relations between China have skyrocketed. In December 2010, South Africa joined China in the BRICS group of emerging economies and in the 2010 Beijing Declaration, South Africa was upgraded to Strategic Comprehensive Partner by the Chinese government. Relationships between the ANC and the Chinese government deepened further when the ANC started to send party officials for trainings in China and the CCP built the ANC's new political leadership school in Venterskroon, a former gold-mining town south-west of Johannesburg. South Africa was also invited to co-chair the 2018 Forum on Chnia_Africa Cooperation (FOCAC) meeting together with China, right after China had announced a 14.7-billion-dollar investment to South Africa, signaling that China views South Africa as a "brother" on the African continent through which it could penetrate other African markets.

The relationships of Kenya and Nigeria's different ruling parties with China are naturally less consistent due to different presidencies. Every president certainly did sign economic agreements and build diplomatic relations with China. But while Nigeria and Kenya received consistent political and economic support from China, until today, every new presidency has also had to define a new relationship with Chinese players. In Kenya, during the Mao-Kenyatta era, the radical left-wing of the ruling Kenya African National Union (KANU) party led by then KANU vice president and Minister for Home Affairs Jaramogi Oginga Odinga, sought closer relations to China. Yet, the movement found strong resistance from the KANU right wing and later disappeared when Odinga, who, in 1966 formed an explicitly socialist-oriented opposition party, the Kenya People's Union, was arrested and detained.

Daniel arap Moi had accused China of plotting a revolution in Kenya in the 1960s. Yet, once he came to power, he intensified relations to China, with the two countries signing an "economic and technological cooperation" agreement in 1980, and trade between the two countries increased, especially for Chinese imports to Kenya in the second half of the 1990s. Under President Kibaki, the "broad governance and economic reform program" resulted in the longest period of sustained growth (2003–2007) since the roaring Kenyatta years (Chege 2007). Most of the investment spurring the growth was interestingly domestic, with only 50.1 million of US $4.1 billion in gross capital formation in 2006 originating from foreign direct investment. China-Kenya economic relations had first started off with high-level political contacts and a series of agreements. Yet, for the first time, independent operators from Kenya and China were also part of the act, which is reflected, for example in President Kibaki's state visit to China in August 2005, with eleven Kenyan trade- and investment-seeking delegations (Chege 2007). Finally, under President Uhuru Kenyatta, economic relations with China have been further intensified, with Kenyatta, for example, famously using large Chinese-financed prestige infrastructure projects such as the Standard Gauge Railway during his election campaign in 2017 (Kuo 2017).

Like in Kenya, every different Nigerian presidency has also had to newly define their relationship with China up to today. During military rule, 1966–1979, Nigeria established formal diplomatic relations with China in 1971 following the Nigerian Civil War of 1967–1970, where China had expressed its effective support for Biafra. Nigeria was a member of the Frontline States and supported Southern African independence movements, siding with the Soviet-backed People's Movement for the Liberation of Angola (MPLA) while China was supporting the National Liberation Front of Angola (FNLA), backed by the US Under military rule, 1983–1993, General Ibrahim Babangida largely supported the World Bank and IMF's structural adjustment programs. While the PDP had then been in power between 1999 and 2015, the party's relationship to China was still more defined by the individual presidents rather than a shared ideology between the PDP and the CCP as was the case in Ethiopia, Tanzania, and South Africa. In fact, the PDP only entered a formal relationship with the CCP in 2013, when PDP Chairman Bamanga Tukur, on a visit to China, was reported to have asked the CCP to train its political public office holders on party supremacy, governance, and management of the political staff. Interestingly, only three years later in 2016 after Muhammadu Buhari had won the 2015 elections, he announced that the APC would also "enter into partnership with the Communist Party of China" (Seteolu and Oshodi 2017). This signals that President Buhari is interested in maintaining a solid diplomatic relationship with China but there also appears to be no particularly strong party alliance between the CCP and the APC, and both the APC's and PDP's party relationships to the CCP are very young.

6.2.3 "Africa Opening Up"– From an Inward to an Outward Focused Strategy

To be clear, despite the closer political alliances between the CCM, the EPRDF and the ANC with the CCP, Nigeria, Kenya and South Africa have still received more amounts of Western and Chinese investments, while Tanzania and Ethiopia have secured relatively small amounts of foreign capital. In 1996, Tanzania and Ethiopia were also on the World Bank and IMF's list of Highly Indebted Poor Countries (HIPC), which meant that in order to receive debt relief, such countries had to reform their economies. Despite their former alliances with the Soviet Union during the Cold War, starting in the 1990s, Ethiopia and Tanzania did, therefore, also work closely with the World Bank and the IMF to adopt structural adjustment programs to be able to raise their trade and investment volumes.

Pitcher (2012) focuses on explaining different privatization trajectories in 27 African countries based on the degree of democratic quality and the nature of party systems between 1988 and 2005. Her analysis shows that during that time, Tanzania was, in fact, more committed to privatization – one measure for economic reform – than Nigeria or Kenya. Importantly, Tanzania privatized 72 percent of SOEs between 1988 and 2005 and had an agency in place solely tasked with privatization. Certainly, and as Pitcher argues, the CCM had survived the transition to democracy by sheltering its base from the negative effects of privatization while also capturing stakes in the new arrangement. But the degree of privatization and commitment to market reforms was quite impressive. As one opposition leader pointed out in his interview with me,

> The country decided to liberalize the economy first in 1992, and then more actively in 1996 because we had a serious debt problem, we were spending more money than social services covered… so the IMF and the World Bank recommended and forced the further structural adjustment and, from 1997, we knew we needed FDI. and the area that was more lucrative for that was mining…when Mkapa was president, he brought it to parliament to open up the mining sector. So, you saw the first changes in 1998 when the mining law was legislated, and from then we saw massive FDI, five gold mines opened in a period of five years. We saw that the reforms were working.[4]

In contrast, Pitcher (2012) notes that Kenya and Nigeria had, in fact, low commitments to privatization and did not set up institutional "lock-in mechanisms" that would bind them for a longer time. Kenya and Nigeria privatized 45 and 24 percent of SOEs, respectively, between 1988 and 2005. With fragmented party loyalty and a limited democracy, Kenya's private sector developed ad hoc, comparable to Zambia. Nigeria was more comparable to Zimbabwe or Guinea, where governments continued to intervene arbitrarily in strategic sectors.

On South Africa, Pitcher (2012) writes that the privatization process was shaped by two opposing forces. On the one hand, privatization was central to finding a common ground between the state and capital for the expansion of black ownership. On the other hand, concerns over employment equity, preferential procurement, and unemployment forced the state to form parastatals in the early 2000s and in doing so, to abandon the privatization of state assets. South Africa then, unsurprisingly, had only privatized 9 percent of SOEs as the high quality democracy paired with a stable party system led the government to keep commercialized and corporatized parastatals and financed public work projects to appease its supporters.

Due to its undemocratic nature, Ethiopia is not one of the 27 African economies that Pitcher (2012) studied. Ethiopia would certainly rank low for privatization, especially for the period that Pitcher studied (1988–2005). Yet, Ethiopia's motivation to switch to a market-led strategy was arguably even stronger than Tanzania's given the number of reforms that were conducted in the 1990s: Between 1991 and 1999, Ethiopia adopted three phases of IMF/World Bank structural and economic reform programs and subsequent liberalization of trade and a market-led economic strategy; in 1998 an export promotion strategy and support of high value agricultural exports (e.g. horticulture products and meats) and labor-intensive manufacturing products (clothing, textiles, and leather) (Gebreeyesus 2013); and formulated an official Industrial Policy Strategy (IPS). In the words of an employee at the Ethiopian Investment Commission, "Back then we were so poor that we just had to develop, we knew we had to switch to capitalism… it was the only way out of poverty."[5]

6.2.4 Long-Term Learning About Bargaining Power and Policy Options

Interestingly, however, Ethiopia, Tanzania, and South Africa later on retracted reform policies, or never fully opened up in the first place. Two reasons stand out for these developments: First, beginning in the early 2000s and especially after the financial crisis of 2008, Western over-confidence in capitalism famously took a big hit (Kurlanzick 2016), with some countries retracting to models that more closely resemble China's state-capitalism, where the government typically owns firms in strategic industries. This shift also coincided with the (re-)introduction of local participation requirements in countries such as Ethiopia and arguably Tanzania, which had initially signaled that they had subscribed to the capitalist model. Ethiopia's economic reforms in the 1990s and early 2000s were certainly guided by the advice of Western institutions (for example, in 2002/03 to 2004/05, the Sustainable Development and Poverty Reduction Program, providing great emphasis on smallholder agriculture; or in 2005/06 to 2009/10, the Plan of Action for Sustainable Development and Eradication of Poverty, stressing urban and industrial sector development). But the reforms captured in the country's Growth and Transformation Plans I and II in the second decade of the 21st century resembled much more the Chinese and South Korean models. From 2010/11 to 2014/15, the Growth and Transformation Plan I was meant to deepen the stress on urban and industrial sector development, and in 2015/16–2019/20, the Second Growth and Transformation Plan had the goal of improving physical infrastructure through public investment projects and transforming the country into a manufacturing hub, with formal incentives menus and informal expectations of local participation of foreign investors. As one retired Ethiopian party member of the EPRDF, who met with me over coffee, shared:

In the 90s, the EPRDF knew it had to deliver. so, we looked out there in the world and the West offered us a hand... but so did China, we knew they had supported us for a long time. So, we initially listened to what the World Bank had to tell us, and we implemented some of that stuff. But we had also been looking towards the East, and we knew that they had done it differently... if someone develops so fast that they can then put money in your country, that is impressive and we wanted to be like them... we wanted to play [sic!] the East Asian Miracle in Africa [...] Their model was more convincing... and it became more and more clear that the Western model of capitalism wasn't going to be ideal for us.[6]

While I have less concrete evidence from Tanzania, what is perceived as a return to "socialism" by scholars and journalists could, in fact, also be a form of "state capitalism." One of the concerns about John Magufuli's presidency is that he has an inward-focused strategy that discriminates against foreign investors and is actively "kicking them out."[7] Yet, I perceived the opposite on my visit to Dar es Salaam – all ministries and government agencies I interviewed, in fact, expressed exceptional interest in providing a favorable environment for foreign investors. This was visible in direct questions by interviewees on whether I personally knew any investors that Tanzanian interviewees could try to lure to Tanzania; or by the actions of senior economists at ministries who were ready to conduct multiple day interviews with me on Maundy Thursday and Good Friday, in between holding meetings with investors (who I also got to meet). One senior-level interviewee said he had worked until 4.00 am in the morning on Good Friday, went home for an hour to shower, and came back to meet more potential investors and me. Asked why they were so extremely motivated to attract investors, he said: "It is all part of President Magufuli's strategy; we need investment to grow."[8] In addition, articles have emerged where the government is defending its policies and publicly saying that "We're Not Venturing Into State Capitalism", thereby providing indirect evidence that their economic program, in fact, does resemble state capitalism.

Second, and relatedly, public pressure has also certainly led Tanzania and South Africa to implement stricter local participation requirements. Probably the most famous example are South Africa's Broad Based Black Economic Empowerment (B-BBEE) regulations that emerged out of a need to rectify the racial inequalities that apartheid had produced. Or, in Tanzania, After President Mkapa had opened the mining sector to foreign investment in the late 1990s, public grievances emerged around locals not benefiting from the growth. The government eventually responded by implementing an act that places mining rights in the hands of Tanzanian nationals and required mining companies to list with the Dar es Salaam Stock Exchange as well as restricted participation of non-Tanzanians in small scale mining, dealing in minerals, and gemstone operations. Several interviewees confirmed that the Mining Act of 2010 inspired local participation requirements in other sectors (e.g. in 2016, the CCM instituted significant measures on foreign investment to encourage the hiring of Tanzanian citizens over foreigners, and protect/grow local industry).

Yet, what is interesting is that again, contrary to a pure "return to socialism and inward-focused strategy", government officials and opposition leaders displayed a high level of confidence that attracting FDI from Chinese investors was unharmed by their local participation policies. So, rather than facing a tradeoff between local participation requests and attracting FDI, the CCM appears to be confident that Chinese investors would still enter and stay Tanzania under local participation requirements. As one interviewee summarized:

> It was for sure to some extent public pressure… but how could we have implemented these stricter rules if we knew we had no chance of actually keeping that investment? It would have been political suicide in the long-term to have policies that would shy all foreign investors away.[9]

While motivations for reforms differed, the central question for the analysis conducted here is: Why have Nigerian and Kenyan government officials lower perceptions of bargaining power with China despite being the top-receivers of Chinese investments on the continent, and why did the Ethiopian, Tanzanian and, to some extent, the South African governments all carry confidence that they would not deter Chinese investors from entering their economies even if they never fully reformed and opened up their economies or later retracted some economic reforms? The analysis below shows that ruling parties that had longer-standing relations with China observed that Chinese investments had consistently flown into their economies, thereby sending a signal that Chinese private companies would be less sensitive to economic shocks or supposedly unfavorable investment conditions. The CCM, the EPRDF and to some extent the ANC have been politically aligned with China and this political alliance translated into economic benefits during the first two phases of Chinese engagement with Africa even when they were not (yet) economically attractive to China. As a result, now where there are also substantial economic benefits from private Chinese players in the third wave of Chinese engagement, these countries carry more confidence that Chinese investors will come despite relatively strict regulations.

Moreover as Chapter 3 illustrated, China's signaling of its willingness to enter African economies under subpar conditions was not subtle. Bräutigam (2009) also provides two fitting examples on the Tanzanian case. The first one is about a small factory called Tanzansino United Pharmaceuticals (T) Ltd:

> Originally built as a Chinese aid project in the 1970s and set up to produce tropical vaccines and medicines, it was initially operated directly by the Tanzanian military. It was not run successfully, so Chinese managers were asked to come back and a US $3 million joint venture was set up in 1997 between the New Technological Applications Center of northern China's Shanxi province and the Tanzanian Ministry of Defense. The factory was still not profitable until in 2006, a Chinese entrepreneur who had started Holley Pharmaceuticals saw an opportunity to grow Artemisia annua, a plant used as a Malaria medicine, in Tanzania. They invested more than six million dollars to build an Artemisia annua plantation in Tanzania because it was too

expensive to import medicine from China. As the managing director said: 'This creates an opportunity for us to produce locally. And the Tanzanian government gives a 15 percent preference for local products for its medical stores.'

(p. 72)

The second story is about a stadium: In 2000, then President Benjamin Mkapa promised as a departure gift to the population that he would build a 60,000-seat stadium before leaving office in 2005. Yet, since Tanzania was on the list of Highly Indebted Poor Countries (HIPC), the country had to stick to a strict regime of austere spending if it wanted the IMF and the World Bank to cancel some of its debt. As a result, Mkapa turned to the Chinese: The Chinese government agreed to offer a grant of US $20 million which covered half of the costs while Tanzania would pay for the rest. While the stadium turned out to be considerably smaller than first envisioned by President Mkapa, he was still granted his wish. As Bräutigam writes:

> The stadium, and the pharmaceutical factory sitting in its shadow, represented the political side of China's aid (the joint venture with the Ministry of Defense, the stadium [was] a politically important "prestige project"). But the factory is now in its third life: first as a traditional aid project, second as one of the joint ventures that rose in the consolidation experiments of the 1980s, and now part of the wave of Chinese companies going global.

(p. 73)

This gradual evolution of Chinese cooperation with Africa is central to the argument advanced in this book. As mentioned earlier, the CCM is a strong party with party members having to typically serve 29 years[10] before advancing to senior positions within the government. The vast majority of government officials that I interviewed in all three countries have been holding their positions for at least ten years and have been party members for at least 15 years, reflecting the need to demonstrate high party loyalty before anyone could assume higher office, and a low turn-over rate among office holders. As one Tanzanian senior official shared: You actually need to serve more than 29 years to [get my current position] [...] I got promoted here after 13 years [...] but that was exceptional, because I got a PhD in Japan in industrial economics, the government really needed me.[11] Of all the senior officials I interviewed in Tanzania (19), 91 percent had been party members for more than 15 years and 83 percent had held an active position in government for at least 10 years, which outdates the Magufuli administration. Members, therefore, experienced all phases of Chinese expansion that were first politically and then economically motivated. As a result, the CCM had a reason to believe in China's long-term commitment and interest. Several interviewees confirmed this before they had even been asked about it directly. In the words of one respondent: "In the beginning, we were valuable for political reasons. But since the early 2000s, we have been valuable for our economy as well."[12]

The comment of a Tanzanian key negotiator that was mentioned in the introduction of this chapter that probably another Chinese company would come around to build the port appears logical then. As Chapter 4 outlines in detail, I observed a very similar attitude among Tanzanian politicians regarding local participation requirements that have become even stricter under the Magufuli administration. And its former socialist orientation certainly helped build this confidence. In the words of a ministry senior government official:

> Tanzania is proud of its socialist past, and President Magufuli is reminding us and bringing back that past... why would we change policies now? They have been working! We have attracted so much Chinese investment, and Chinese investors value us for our labor, and they know they have to contribute, it isn't an issue.[13]

In Ethiopia, the picture looks similar. Again, of the 21 senior officials I interviewed, 76 percent had been party members for more than 15 years, and 81 percent had been holding an active political position for more than 10 years. Asked about the Ethio-China Polytechnic College, opened in late 2009 and funded by Chinese aid, that I discussed in Chapter 3, and about why the Ethiopian government is negotiating more aggressively around local participation, one government official said:

> We know we have to, and it is being received well with the Chinese. Ethiopia is coming from a tradition where we gave out food to the population, we had food subsidies, housing subsidies... and the government is trying to slowly get away from that to a market economy but we know we have to strike a balance, especially with all this growth, there also comes a lot of inequality, a lot of rising food prices, housing prices, inflation... especially because of our past, we need to ensure that the people benefit from the growth because you see, there is a lot of expectation in the government to provide reliefs... And we invite investors to participate in this tradition, and if you want to be part of it and gain the benefits, you will also contribute. The Chinese have always appreciated, or should I say respected us for our development style [...] Yes, you could certainly say that the EPRDF learned that over time.[14]

Another officer was even more explicit:

> As a country, we have always been experimenting with local content, that's a legacy of our communist past... We know we can ask for it with the Chinese because we already did it in the 80s, in the 90s... there is one lesson I took from back then: If things get harder, American companies are the first to leave, but Chinese companies stay.[15]

In contrast, evidence from Nigeria and Kenya shows that different ruling powers have been working with much shorter time-horizons than in Ethiopia or Tanzania and did not engage in the same learning process about Chinese behavior and their long-term interests in their respective countries. This is not to say that China tried to engage significantly differently in its three-part strategy with Nigeria and Kenya. For example, already in the latest phase of the colonial period, China hosted students from Kenya, Uganda, Malawi, and other colonies that were fighting for independence. And even before colonialism came to an end, Nigeria took out a loan with China for US $80 million for a hydropower dam on the Niger River. In August 1979, the Chinese State Council allowed some Chinese companies to invest abroad, and a Chinese aid team took on construction projects for profit in Nigeria in the same year. Chinese premier Zhou Enlai visited ten newly independent African countries between December 1963 and February 1964, where he committed around US $120 million in aid to Congo-Brazzaville, Ghana, Kenya, Mali, and Tanzania. And as Chapter 2 highlights, since the early 2000s, Nigeria and Kenya have been among the absolute top receivers of Chinese investments (Bräutigam 2009).

Yet, the Chinese strategy was met differently on the receiving end. Due to the two- or multi-party nature and competitive elections in Nigeria and Kenya that were discussed earlier, a change in ruling powers led to a large re-staffing of government offices that was absent in Ethiopia, Tanzania, or Kenya. The reason was that each new president and the ruling elite around them wanted to ensure that they had allies within the government rather than keeping potential non-allies in the inner circle of power that could threaten the ruler. These dynamics arose due to ethnic or regional competition that was not tamed by an overarching national political ideology. As multiple interview partners shared with me, with every new presidency, ministries are almost completely re-staffed, thereby preventing "technocrats" from maintaining their positions for a longer time, learning about the amount of Chinese money flowing into Nigeria, and developing a more aggressive negotiation policy. Out of 45 Nigerian senior officials that I interviewed, only 24 percent had been party members (of one of the parties that merged into the PDP in 2013) for longer than 15 years, and only 36 percent had been holding a political position over the past 10 years. Most were appointed to their current positions under the Buhari administration in 2015.

In the words of a Nigerian senior-level government official:

> You see, in Nigeria, there is no such thing as party loyalty... you can switch from the PDP to the ANC and back to the PDP; many state governors have done that, they first run for the PDP, then the ANC... but in a political system like that you have to watch out for yourself, not the party, you need to form alliances with individuals who have your back... so that means whenever somebody new is elected, you need to get rid of the old administration and bring in someone you can trust, especially when there are so many regional blocks and interests... Jonathan changed everything when he came to power, Buhari changed everything when he came to power, his successor will do the same... it is always the same. There is no such thing as trust or political ideology here period. How can things change?[16]

I did interview a senior official who has been in his position for 23 years, and I asked him how he managed to hold the position for so long. His answer was that he switched party membership and:

> I know 23 years is quite unusual... I guess I got lucky because I used to work for a long time in [named foreign country, omitted here to protect the interviewee's anonymity] since I was the Nigerian appointee for [name of the international organization omitted here to protect the interviewee's anonymity], and they tend to keep employees based abroad for longer than if you were in the country... And then when I got older I managed to get back to this ministry. I knew it was always important to stay close to a few key players. And you have to be loyal and ready to negotiate whatever your new president is asking you to. Otherwise, you are gone.[17]

This re-staffing of political personnel then overall leads to a sporadic rather than a consistent interaction with foreign players, where the relationships need to be defined again from the beginning. This was confirmed by the majority of interviewees. As a Nigerian Foreign Ministry officer told me:

> The PDP was never strategically aligned with China, they sold our country in 2011 and then in opposition they complain about China – look at their Covid response, back in March they were mad when Buhari invited these doctors to help us with the crisis. And it is the same with the APC, obviously they all talk to China, and China is more powerful, so you essentially see the APC and the PDP acting similarly, sign deals that aren't ideal for us. But yes, there was not much information sharing between the different administrations when it comes to the investment deals we discussed or what policies would be the best for the country.[18]

In Kenya, a member of parliament shared a similar sentiment with me:

> If you ask me, Tanzania has an advantage because it was always ruled by the same leadership. Democracy is great but the way we practice it with so many different tribes, it might be inefficient... because you see, we can't rally the nation around one cause, we can't even rally the government around one cause... there is an election and the political landscape, the set-up of each office completely changes... one of our issues is that we are unable to build a bureaucracy that can maintain the knowledge we accumulate over longer time, we always learn from scratch.

When the strategy of the new player China was unclear to governments, the evidence below suggests that governments then defaulted to the narrative of the dominating investors, the Western ones, which had always conveyed that local participation requirements were out of the feasible policy space for African players. Asked why they had never experimented with local participation policies, several Nigerian officials referenced the local participation requirements for oil and gas but said they felt like in any other sector, they would not be helpful for attracting foreign capital. One Nigerian official respondent said: "These policies are not what's feasible for us if we want to grow through investments."[19] As a Kenyan member of parliament said: "Local participation requirements – "We have never tried them. But it's not something that would work here."[20]

As mentioned earlier, in South Africa, perceptions on bargaining power were largely shaped by an interplay of the ANC's relationship with China and the need to address inequalities of apartheid by granting economic privileges to the black population. As Pitcher (2012) describes, South Africa kept a relatively large number of parastatals that serve to fulfill the government's commitment to the BB-EEE. Asked whether Chinese companies in South Africa that are interacting with the parastatals are following the black ownership and employment regulations, a senior-level employee at a South African national development finance institution shared: "Yes, everyone has to. South Africa is very strict here."[21] Yet, when asked whether Chinese companies in South Africa that are private and not interacting with parastatals are following BB-EEE regulations, the person said: "Well… labor costs here are very high, and we have already industrialized… so I would expect them not to follow the regulations… I can imagine it is a tough place for companies that need cheap labor."[22] The sentiment was echoed in several interviews that I conducted with other government offices, where I observed relatively high confidence that Chinese companies would be following the BB-EEE framework if they were of higher-profile while in the purely private sphere, interviewees were doubtful of their bargaining leverage.[23]

One conversation with a senior-level employee at the National Planning Commission was particularly enlightening on why that may be the case:

> The ANC is "young" in the sense that we have only been in power since the end of apartheid… We are still learning how to position ourselves with the West and China. We see with our eyes that the Chinese are okay with BB-EEE regulations, the regulations have definitely helped us there to figure out what we can demand… And that they offer us a lot of money and they also let us co-chair FOCAC… But we don't know about the private sector and the BB-EEE, whether they [the Chinese companies] stick to them or not. How can I know about something that I have not seen with my own eyes or heard with my own ears? Maybe it takes more time for mutual learning to trust that the Chinese are different to our experience with the West… but yes, you are right, they act differently, I have never given it enough thought.[24]

That they have not given it much "thought" was echoed in several other interviews across government bodies.

> I think we are only slowly realizing now what we are worth… with the ascent to becoming a full BRICS-member in 2010, and you say we get so many Chinese investors that are private now… you have raised a good point, there may be more leverage for us than we have realized.[25]

Overall, South African government respondents, therefore, appeared to have confidence in probed methods, and the BB-EEE regulations, but were skeptical about entering new territory with imposing local participation requirements on purely private B2B interactions.

The analysis above suggests that countries with authoritarian rule or one-party dominant systems incrementally moved towards more open economies but were very selective, and also chose to retract some policies later on. In contrast, countries with multiple party systems and short-term horizons were much less likely to implement stricter policy regulations or experiment with them in case-by-case negotiations. This section described how the domestic political dynamics interacted with China's expansionary quest in Africa. The next section addresses countries' historical relationship to the West, and how the Weak Bargaining Power Narrative appears to have penetrated some countries more than others.

6.3 Enabling Environment 2: Countries' Historical Relationship to the West

In 2015, something unusual happened in Kenya. President Kenyatta signed the new Companies Act (2015), which contained language requiring all foreign companies to demonstrate at least 30 percent of shareholding by Kenyan citizens by birth. The move was drastic as this would have been the first time that Kenya placed any ownership restrictions on foreign companies. Yet, while the law was supposed to go into effect on June 15, 2016, United States' business associations, including the American Chamber of Commerce, quickly raised concerns over the bill and pointed out that this could run against Kenya's commitments under the WTO. As one interviewee said:

> We wanted to push this bill through. But from the responses we received, we felt a lot of pressure to abandon the law… a lot of Western companies told us that they would want to exit the country if we went through with it.[26]

Finally, the US government also directly intervened with the Kenyan government until in the end, the clause was repealed the same year.

The story raises larger questions on how countries define their bargaining power through longstanding relationships with the West and China, how countries that have historically been more closely aligned with the West have been exposed to the Weak Bargaining Power Narrative, and through what channels it has informed their understanding of bargaining power with Chinese investors. One causal mechanism could be that countries that have positioned themselves closer to West have naturally also received more aid and investment from the West. They might, therefore, also choose to play by Western capitalist rules regardless of what Chinese investors would offer them under stricter regulations as the absolute amount of Western investment still surpasses Chinese investment. Finally, it also begs the question whether national governments have any bargaining space if the global capitalist regime, through international organizations, still dictates rules. As Ramamurti (2001)'s two-tier bargaining model illustrates, a second causal mechanism could, therefore, be that developing countries may be "locked into" the global capitalist rules without any real space to demand own conditions.

Both arguments assume that deal conditions have to be fixed through formal national policies across all types of investors and that countries know that private Chinese investors would be willing to agree to stricter rules. Yet, the evidence I describe below casts doubt on both assumptions. Based on my interviews, this book instead argues for the validity of a third causal mechanism – that governments generally know that in weak institutional settings, there is both room for case-by-case negotiations with deal conditions that can differ between investor types; but because some governments have so much internalized the Weak Bargaining Power Narrative, they also believe that private Chinese players would not enter, or exit their markets under stricter policy regulations. As a result, they have insufficiently strategized around how to position themselves with formal FDI policies and informal case-by-case deal conditions with private Chinese players.

6.3.1 African Countries' Relationships to the West Since Independence

Kenya, Nigeria, and South Africa have had strong economic and political ties to the West and are naturally also among the top-receivers of Western investment, which is mostly concentrated in five African countries. During the Cold War, both the United States and the Soviet Union expressed a strong interest in Nigeria due to its large reserves of oil, and Nigeria chose a position of non-alignment with a leaning towards the West. Between 1966 and 1977, the United States and Nigeria were conflicted over southern African liberation, the US pro-Biafran stance, and by the US refusal to sell weapons to Nigeria during the civil war. When Jimmy Carter became president in 1977, however, relations between the US and Nigeria suddenly improved since the US started to recognize Nigeria as a stabilizing force in Africa and moved closer to Nigeria's position on southern Africa. Reagan's presidency again led to a diplomatic conflict with Nigeria over southern Africa but Namibia's independence and the opening of debate for eliminating apartheid in South Africa in the early 1990s removed the largest obstacles to closer relations with the US (The Library of Congress Country Studies and the CIA World Factbook) that have been strong until today (e.g. as visible in multiple million dollar trade and investment deals and state-visits).

Kenya and the United States have been close allies since Kenya's independence while its relationships the Soviet Union never fully picked up. Similar to China, Soviet leaders were perhaps the closest to Vice-President Jaramogi Oginga Odinga, when contacts between the Soviets and the more radical elements within the Kenya African National Union had been made immediately before Kenya was granted independence from the United Kingdom. When Odinga was arrested and detained in 1966, relationships broke off. President Moi then sought to further strengthen relations with the United States by joining the US' Rapid Deployment Joint Task Force, thereby inviting US military installations in Kenya. Yet, tensions over human rights issues in 1991 led the United States to join a coalition of other nations who gave financial assistance to Kenya to pressure for reforms, and the US even suspended its aid in 1992. This pressure led to multi-party elections in 1992 and relations significantly improved during Kenya's democratic transition in 2002 and the new president, Mwai Kibaki was honored as the first African head of state to be invited to Washington D.C. for a state visit. Diplomatic relations have been solid until today, as visible in the shared experiences of terrorism (e.g. with the bombing of the US embassy in Nairobi in 1998, or the Westgate Mall Attack in 2013) and an increased trade and investment relationship.

South Africa's white minority was haunted by the fear of communism during the Cold War, and rallied Western support around the idea that any opposition party would overthrow capitalism and nationalize the private sector. As a result, the West was willing to accept institutionalized racism and minority rule government in exchange for keeping commercial and mining investments safe from nationalization. The ANC's relationships to the US improved after the threat of communism was diverted with the fall of the Soviet Union, and South Africa is today the #1 receiver of US investments on the continent, with particularly strong collaboration in the areas of health, education, environment, and digital economy.

6.3.2 The Promise of Western Investments in the 1990s

While Nigeria, Kenya and South Africa are among the top 5 receivers of Western investments, Ethiopia and Tanzania were on the list of heavily indebted poor countries (HIPC) that were not receiving significant amounts of Western investment until today. As a result, it was the relatively more attractive countries that first got to engage with Western investors and that developed policies on FDI based on the Western narrative that they would have to liberalize and privatize in order to receive more FDI. These relatively larger receivers of Western investment in the 1990s clung to the promise that with more investment-friendly policies, more investment would follow. As one Nigerian business elite member shared, before the IMF and the World Bank stepped in,

> We had tasted what Western investment would look like… but Western investors were nervous about political instability and whether returns were really there. But they told us if we well behaved just a bit better and followed their rules, they would start flocking in en masse. But once they were completed, there was still no Western investment.[27]

This experience exacerbated the perception that the added value of each country was small and that governments could impose few requirements regarding human capital and technology transfers on foreign investors if they wanted to grow their economies with the help of foreign capital.

The sentiment appears to have been fundamentally different in countries who were small receivers of Western investment. From the beginning, countries like Ethiopia and Tanzania could not rely on any amount of Western investments. As an officer at an Ethiopian ministry shared with me:

> We started worse off than Nigeria, than Kenya, than South Africa… we had a huge amount of debts, and never had that allyship during the Cold War. So,

we felt like we would have had to wait for another 20 or 30 years to see any investments from the West pour in. So, I think policy makers back then knew they had to look towards what other countries in the East were doing so we had any chance at development.[28]

And in the words of an Ethiopian policy advisor:

> There was no Western investment coming, period. In most African countries, there is no Western investment coming... I know that the media probably tells otherwise, but they are sending no money. But we observed that there was Chinese presence, growing presence, they seemed to be okay with the poor living conditions, the lack of electricity. We saw that at least someone wanted to come. So oddly, our model was working and attractive to someone and so we thought we should keep going with it rather than wait for more promises from the West. We couldn't count on the fact that once we did what the West was telling us, Western investment would actually come, other countries had better chances than us, they had more to offer, like Nigeria, like South Africa, they already received Western money... But there was also a second consideration behind the shift in reforms... you see, China developed 40 years ago, South Korea developed 60 years ago... When did the West develop? How can Western actors still tell us what to do, when there are actors in this world who have just made it happen within the past century? And I think China respects us for what we are doing, "being aggressive as you call it, they respect it because they were aggressive themselves and it paid off."[29]

In Tanzania, a similar sentiment around Western "disengagement" in the 1990s was visible. When asked whether the 1990 reforms were working in attracting Western investment, interviewees generally said yes, but also said that the West could not be counted on as a natural ally as much as China.

> The West came in as a 'father', to tell us what we should do and what we can't do, but to be frank, it was very unreliable... no one knew whether after all the reforms, Western investors would actually decide to suddenly pop up, and there were a lot of threats and conditions involved. But we had always been allies with China, and we knew that China was a brother, they treated us on a more equal level if you will.[30]

These accounts suggest that countries which were relatively small receivers of Western investment in the 1990s were more distrustful of Western promises attached to structural adjustment, and appear to have sought to find a closer engagement with alternative forms of capitalist development, while relatively larger recipients of Western investment tried to gradually improve and kept up hope that they would receive more Western capital thereafter.

6.3.3 Perceptions of Bargaining Power and Deal Flexibility

If deal conditions were fixed through national policies, this might also suggest that countries with closer relationships to the West could have simply chosen to play by Western rules in the 1990s, which has effectively "locked them" into the international capitalist regime with little room to alter conditions today. Yet, in countries with weak formal institutions, deal negotiators do know that in theory, they have room for case-by-case demands. Perhaps one of the most striking examples I encountered was a story that an NIPC officer told me during a group interview: An Algerian[31] company had approached them in the spring of 2019 saying that they would like to open a paper production company in the north of Nigeria and insisted on wanting to work with a local partner through a Joint Venture contract. Yet, as the NIPC officer proudly said: "We explained to them that they can have a 100 percent foreign owned company according to the NIPC Act of 1995. We did not stop arguing with them until they agreed to operate fully 100 percent foreign owned."[32] Asked why they insisted on a weaker deal, he responded: "It is a forced marriage if it is a 60 percent percent–40 percent with a local partner. If you read recommendations by the World Bank, by UNCTAD, you will understand, we regularly get their reports... it makes more sense like this."[33] Asked whether he felt pressured by the World Bank or UNCTAD to implement these policies, he simply said: "No, they wouldn't know about individual deals like these... we just felt like it made sense, we don't want to force marriages, we were worried they would decide in the end not to come."[34]

When I told Kenyan and Nigerian government officials that in Ethiopia, the government has informal expectations of foreign investors to add to local content with the investment, they almost unanimously said that in theory, that would also be possible in their countries, but they choose not to because they felt like it would hurt their overall attractiveness. Asked in Kenya whether it would be possible to have Chinese investors obey different rules, an officer at a ministry tasked with attracting investment said:

> Oh, they already do... when they build the SGR, we had discussions on the costs... they initially wanted to bring in a machine to dig the whole tunnel but then they did not bring in the machine and hired locals... they had the idea, it was more expensive for them but I think they wanted to have a balance, they knew it would look better if they hired locals.[35]

Kenyan officials also signaled that Kenya could have implemented an informal dual strategy through an incentives menu with foreign ownership requirements based on the new Companies Act in 2015, but that President Kenyatta received a lot of pressure from the US not to. Asked whether they knew how the Chinese government reacted to the foreign ownership plans, respondents said they did not know, with one respondent saying:

> I was advising our President at the time [when he signed the Companies Act] ... I know that some Chinese companies were not happy with it but we

didn't hear anything from the Chinese embassy or the Chinese Chamber of Commerce... [...] Because the United States was so against it, we thought it would be the best idea to get rid of the requirement... but yes, you are right, the Chinese would have probably stayed anyways, they really want to be here, they would have made it work... Maybe it was a missed opportunity. We just didn't think of it that way.[36]

6.3.4 Permeation of Ideological, Educational and Intellectual Spheres by the West

This focus on Western needs and preferences compared to a relative absence of information regarding Chinese preferences was very common across the interviews I conducted in Nigeria, Kenya and to a lesser extent in South Africa. While China has emerged as a new trading and investment partner in all the five case studies, the behavior of Chinese companies appears to still be understudied in Nigeria, Kenya, and South Africa compared to Western companies, and therefore, also receives less policy attention. Why is that the case? One reason appears to be that the Western narrative has permeated ideological, educational, and intellectual spheres in Nigeria and Kenya, as well as to some extent, South Africa and that has perpetuated a Western-centric focus, despite China's presence in their countries.

First, where respondents were educated and what development books they have read can be informative of what has influenced their understanding of their own bargaining power. In the Kenyan and Nigerian examples, a slight majority were educated in their own countries while the rest received their education in the United Kingdom or the United States, and one person went to university in another African country. In contrast, in Ethiopia and Tanzania, most respondents were educated in their home countries, one-third were educated in the United Kingdom, and three respondents received an advanced degree in China or Japan. One senior official at a ministry in Tanzania told me that he had always been interested in industrial policy, so he decided to get his doctorate in Japan, which he had heard was the best place to study the subject. "Productivity improvement in manufacturing and the public sector was my dissertation... and when I came back, the government wanted to hire me immediately."[37] While this is just one example, the interviewee holds a senior position in the ministry and enjoys significant power to influence investment deal outcomes. In South Africa, most of the politicians I interviewed were educated in South Africa, probably because South Africa has a disproportionally large number of universities, compared to the rest of the continent.

Second, countries that received biased information on their bargaining power with foreign investors over an extended period of time also continued to predominantly engage with the Western narrative, not the Chinese one. Observations from my interviews shine light on the rationale around this Western-centric focus: First, among Tanzanian and Ethiopian government officials, I observed a surprising level of familiarity with the "Chinese model" that was less visible in Nigeria, Kenya, and South Africa. Asked what development model their country was following, most respondents across countries unsurprisingly replied that their country was not "copy pasting" any one model but trying to learn from development successes around the world. In the words of a Tanzanian interviewee: "For us, we study situations and then we try to localize our needs, we aren't following any country's model... if something is adapted by many countries, you study what's good about it."[38]

Asked, however, what the "Chinese model" meant to them, answers considerably differed across countries: While respondents almost unanimously cited special economic zones to be characteristic of the "Chinese model", only respondents in Tanzania and Ethiopia also listed "industrial policy", "state capitalism", "protection of infant industries" and "gradualism", with two respondents in Ethiopia citing Deng Xiaoping's famous saying: "You cross the river by feeling for the stones."[39] Perhaps the most striking experience I had was when I attended the Financial Times Nigeria Summit 2018 and interviewed a senior-level official in the federal government, who had just recently been tasked with attracting foreign investment. He listed "special economic zones" as emblematic of the "Chinese model" after which I asked whether they would also characterize industrial policy, or gradualism as being part of the Chinese model, noting that, in fact, countries like Ethiopia are experimenting with these two features based on China's approach. He replied: "Yes, we just learned [in a session at the conference] earlier today that Ethiopia was doing that, they have a full industrial policy... we will look into it."[40] Only by attending a Western conference, where the Financial Times chose to address the Ethiopian development model, was he updated about another African country's strategy.

Third, again in Nigeria, where I had time to establish stronger relationships with my interviewees, I observed a correlation between the books my respondents liked, and how they perceived their bargaining power with Chinese investors. For example, I was quite surprised by the intensity with which Jeffrey Sachs' work seems to have penetrated government thinking in Nigeria, with many respondents saying "yes" when I asked whether they found Sachs' work on poverty traps "inspirational" for Nigeria. The only person who found more critical words for Sachs was the director-general of a leading federal government agency, who was also the only one of my interviewees in Nigeria who said they believed Nigeria possessed bargaining power with private Chinese players. He invited me to his house for dinner, and on his bookshelf, I saw famous titles such as: *How Asia Works: Success and Failure in The World's Most Dynamic Region* by Joe Studwell (2014). He later sent me a WhatsApp message with a link to a talk by Jeffrey Sachs on Covid-19 in the African region, with the note: "Not a big fan of Jeffrey Sachs, has done a lot of terrible things for Africa." While this is, of course, only anecdotal, I did find striking that the only person from my interviews who said that they believed Nigeria is underselling its economy due to a misperception of power was also the one who openly criticized Jeffrey Sachs' work.

Finally, what metrics do governments use to assess their "policy fitness"? Interestingly, the World Bank's Ease of Doing Business (EDB) rating was mentioned by two interviewees in Nairobi. One Kenyan official said the government is "working tirelessly on improving the investment climate,"[41] which has indeed witnessed an unprecedented improvement in the World Bank's Ease of Doing Business Index with Kenya's rank moving from 136 in 2014 to 56 in the 2020 ranking. The other interviewee listed Kenya's EDB ranking when I asked what countries Kenya aspired to imitate in their FDI policies. In Nigeria, no one mentioned the EDB index, but government respondents kept referring to "official recommendations" by third party advisors. When I kept asking who these advisors were, I was told the UNDP, AfDB, the World Bank, and the UK's Department for International Development (DFID). In South Africa, when asked about South Africa's EDB ranking, one respondent said:

> Yeah we have fallen a bit behind and this is certainly a concern with foreign investors… We need to be very careful because of the Middle Income Trap, foreign investors won't want to come unless we provide a suitable environment for them… I think they [foreign investors] do check the EDB index.[42]

Interestingly, in Ethiopia and Tanzania – both ranked low on the EDB index – I observed that they were concerned about their performance regarding capacity, for example, rapidness of investment approval by their agencies, which is also captured by the EDB. An interviewee at an Ethiopian ministry shared with me that the Investment Commission is sometimes still struggling to effectively meet promised turnaround timelines for investment approval: "This is certainly a capacity issue, and we know it hurts our attractiveness. We are always striving to become faster, but we do not have the human capital yet to get there today. But tomorrow we will."[43] Yet, I observed very little concern for other areas included in the EDB like minimum capital requirements to open a business.

6.4 Conclusion

Overall, the evidence presented here suggests that government officials from one-party systems or authoritarian regimes that were able to engage with local participation requirements early on learned over time that private Chinese investors would also stay under these stricter regulations. In contrast, government officials from countries more exposed to the Weak Bargaining Power Narrative have also tended to perceive their bargaining power with Chinese investors to be weak, regardless of their actual relative attractiveness to private Chinese investors on the continent. If conceived as a negotiation game, this chapter has highlighted what information and historical frames countries have started the game with – it has described the interplay of domestic and international forces that matters for how governments have experimented with local participation requirements before, how much they were exposed to the Weak Bargaining Power Narrative, and how both forces have influenced how governments perceive their own bargaining power with foreign players. The next chapter focuses on the question: What information do different domestic actors share within the game? It describes different players' incentives to report investment-related information "up" to the central government. These incentives then influence how well governments are able to accurately count private Chinese investment flows into their economies, which in turn also shapes their perceptions of bargaining power.

Notes

1. DS15.
2. In 1977, the Tanganyika African National Union and the Afro-Shirazi Party, which had been the ruling parties in mainland Tanzania and the semi-autonomous islands of Zanzibar respectively, merged into one-party, the CCM.
3. DS14.
4. DS7.
5. AA3.
6. AA4.
7. As Prof. Caroline Elkins suggested in her lecture for the Short-Intensive Program "Africa Rising" at Harvard Business School in January 2020.
8. DS12.
9. DS2.
10. DS19.
11. DS19.
12. DS12.
13. DS5.
14. AA17.
15. AA21.
16. A5.
17. A8.
18. A21.
19. A13.
20. N12.
21. P3.
22. Ibid.
23. e.g. P1, 2, 8, 14, 15.
24. P18.
25. P11.
26. N5.
27. NH1.
28. AA19.
29. AA2.
30. DS14.
31. Country changed to protect the company's anonymity.
32. A3.
33. Ibid.
34. Ibid.
35. N17.
36. N6.
37. DS19.
38. DS13.
39. AA3, 18.
40. L7.
41. N13.
42. P8.
43. AA2.

7 Information-Sharing Incentives around Bargaining Power

7.1 Introduction

In the spring of 2015, business leaders, trade and finance officials of Laikipia County in Kenya, around a four-hour drive to the North of Nairobi, embarked on a one-week trip to visit Liaoning province in China. The journey was only one part of the county government's larger efforts to attract Chinese investment to the region's trade, tourism, infrastructure, cattle, dairy and leather industries. The county government advertises its ambitions online with the hashtags "#Laikipiaonthemove" and "#DestinationLaikipia", and there is a formal investment committee and a one-stop information desk established to assist investors with settling and operating in the county. The government also has ambitious plans for building a 200-hectare airport to facilitate exports and the flow of Chinese tourists coming to visit Laikipia in the future.

The story about Laikipa County is not unique. In March 2018, Oyo State in Nigeria received a four-star rating for its efforts to attract foreign investment to its region in a certification process scored by the Nigerian Investment Promotion Commission (NIPC) and international and domestic consultants. The state was ranked fourth best investor-friendly state in the country. Finally, in 2017, Amahara Region in Ethiopia signed a Memorandum of Understanding (MOU) with the Chinese company Maxter Group for the construction of a special economic zone in the area. The MOU came during the construction of twelve industrial parks throughout the country.

The accounts of Laikipia County, Oyo State and Amhara Region raise important questions about the dynamics within the central government and across sub-divisions in their negotiations with foreign investors. While the introductory chapters have illustrated that there is less need for cross-country competition for Chinese investments, within-country cross-regional and inter-ministerial competition turns out to still be a real concern for perceptions of bargaining power and the resulting quality of investment deals. This is because most private Chinese entrepreneurs either enter African countries through Chinese SOEs or are referred through a friend to a specific location in Africa. Chinese public investments and aid projects that SOEs attend to are often strategically allocated through the diplomatic relationship between the respective African federal government and the

DOI: 10.4324/9781003308768-7

Chinese government. Yet, He and Zhu (2018) and my interviews suggest that private Chinese companies, who have later ventured off from SOEs, often actually have very little knowledge of where to invest within a country, and that private Chinese companies that come directly from China tend to follow the advice of their Chinese friends' who have already established a presence in a particular African country. The respective African ruling government may then not be directly involved in the process, and may have very little information on the amount of private Chinese investment pouring into the economy if clear counting mechanisms that create transparency are not set in place.

I define political centralization as the concentration of a government's power. Centralization emerges either out of strong centralized parties or strong *de facto* centralized institutions. Riker (1975) measures party centralization according to first, whether the party that controls the central government also controls the regional governments and second, the strength of party discipline. In addition, institutions – or in other words, the strength of the centralized "state" itself – matters: Central governments that are strong can either reward or punish local administrations, reducing both the risk of local capture and the scope of competition for rents (Huang, 1998). Yet, if the state and its institutions are weak, the government's power is naturally less concentrated, and more players will be able to capture and compete for rents (Blanchard and Schleifer 2001).

Centralization played a large role in the development trajectories of countries in East and Southeast Asia: In South Korea and Singapore, specialized elite agencies (e.g. the Singapore Economic Development Board or the Korea Trade-Investment Promotion Agency) were tasked with investment promotion and coordinating investment policies for the entire economy. Yet, in sharp contrast, China has employed a more diversified approach (Ang 2016). As Oi (1999) writes, China demonstrates a new variety of developmental state with "*local* [emphasis added] governments in the leading role" (p. 3).

Yet, what both the Chinese, the Singaporean and South Korean strategies have in common is that the central government still had enough power to centrally collect information on how much investment was flowing into the economy and could base their policy decisions on this piece of information. As Ang (2016) writes,

> local investment bureaus in China do not (or did not, depending on location) actually bear sole responsibility for investment work. Instead, *all* party and state offices regardless of nominally assigned functions, are required and rewarded for participating in courting investors. Each agency has to perform its formal functions [...] but at the same time they are all enlisted to prospect for investors for their home states.
>
> (p. 29)

Counties had to track investment targets for county agencies, which then reported up to central officials, and counties that met and exceeded targets received bonuses while others were penalized. The central government consequently had information on how much money was flowing into the economy, and this information directly informed China's Foreign Investment Catalogue that maintained national local participation requirements on foreign investment.

These findings suggest that competition among regions may only be beneficial when the central government is still strong enough to be able to track how much investment is flowing into the economy, and what national policy restrictions are feasible to implement given the overall amount of FDI flows. In other cases, if there are a lot of actors competing for investment, and they generally have incentives not to cooperate and share information and the central government is not able to "force" information sharing through strong parties or centralized institutions, this can lead to a race-to-the-bottom in deal quality when in fact, the country would have the bargaining power to impose stricter regulations.

The same logic holds true for individual central government ministries and agencies. If there are incentives in place to employ a collaborative approach in attracting investment, they are also more likely to share how much investment comes in through their collaborative effort. In contrast, if government bodies have incentives to employ a Machiavellian approach, then they are less likely to share investment-related activities with other government bodies, who are competing in the same environment. This chapter is, therefore, largely about competition between entities that have disincentives to share information on what investment is entering their sub-regional unit. There is, then, a lack of complete information about how much investment the country is making at the central level, which leads to lower perceived bargaining power compared to the actual level.

7.2 Enabling Environment 3: Centralization and Information-Sharing Incentives

As mentioned in the introduction, centralization may emerge either from strong parties or strong *de facto* centralized institutions. Chapter 5 has shown that Ethiopia, Tanzania and South Africa all have strong parties that control the central and regional political spheres and have strong party disciplines (e.g. a clear path from years of membership to higher political positions) compared to Kenya and Nigeria. In the next section, I am therefore focusing on *de jure* and *de facto* centralized institutional systems and strength of the state that determine the overall degree of centralization of each country.

Nigeria, Ethiopia and South Africa are certainly the longest standing and most prominent federal experiments on the African continent. Yet, the discussion below shows that the centralization through the concentration of government power significantly differs between Nigeria on the one hand and Ethiopia and South Africa on the other hand. I then compare these two types of centralization to the political systems in Kenya and Tanzania and afterwards show that the degree of centralization seems to matter for the flow of information between the central government and sub-regions and how competition across central government offices further exacerbates the flow of information on Chinese investments. Finally, I present the case of hidden village industrial parks in Nigeria as one example of how information sharing up to the central government is blocked in a highly de-centralized, competitive environment.

7.2.1 Experiments Around De-Centralization Across Africa

Federalism in South Africa, Ethiopia and Nigeria is all *de jure* present in political (sub-national elections), administrative (decentralization laws) and fiscal dimensions (formula-based transfers) through territorial upper chambers, elected sub-national officials and constitutional protections for sub-national units. Yet, as Dickovick (2014) points out,

> federal dynamics in Africa are complicated by the long-running argument that state power in Africa is paper-thin and that governing authorities are connected to society mainly via informal mechanisms (e.g. patronage and clientelism) rather than well-institutionalized legal-rational structures (cf. Bayart et al. 1993, Chabal and Daloz 1999). Per this argument, federalism may have some implications for identity and for resource division, but it is subordinated as a causal variable. In short, federalism will matter little where institutions themselves have little import.
>
> (p. 555)

At the same time, Dickovick (2014) points out that this impression arises due to a lack of comparative work on African federalism, and points out that there is in fact a clear distinction between South Africa and Ethiopia on the one hand, and Nigeria on the other hand, which resembles the closest other federal countries worldwide. In Ethiopia and South Africa, the "powers of SNGs [sub-national governments] are quite limited *de facto* by fiscal, political and administrative centralism" (p. 561). This centralism plays out through dominant party governance (limiting the political dimension of federalism), state control over expenditures (limiting the administrative dimension), and limited own-source revenues (limiting the fiscal dimension). In contrast, Dickovick argues that *de jure* and *de facto* regulations overlap much more significantly in Nigeria's federalist experiment, where federalism is embodied in a clearer vertical separation of powers and more substantial autonomy of SNGs. I offer a discussion below on the differences between Ethiopian, South African and Nigerian *de facto* federalism that translates into relatively more centralization in Ethiopia and South Africa and a more de-centralized system in Nigeria.

Ethiopia's regional states as well as the lower-level *woredas* (districts) and *kebeles* (localities) effectively have very limited local tax bases (Dickovick 2014). Meanwhile, in South Africa, an obstacle to *de facto* fiscal federalism is the division of tax collection. Provincial tax revenues are mostly concerned with vehicle taxes and limited user fees, while property taxes are the principal source of income for municipalities. Yet provinces are responsible for providing substantial services such as education and health, so they depend on the federal government to fil the expenditure gap.

In addition, as Chapter 5 illustrates, both Ethiopia and South Africa have been ruled by dominant parties since the 1990s, who have been able to extend and manifest their powers to the sub-national levels, which effectively limits political federalism. The strength of parties is also manifested and re-enforced by institutions:

After the 2005 elections, the EPRDF introduced a reform aiming for more "participatory democracy" by increasing the number of candidates who can run in the kebele and woreda councils. As a result, all parties that wanted to run had to register 3.6 million candidates, which only the EPRDF had the capacity to do. The EPRDF then unsurprisingly won almost all seats. As Green (2011) writes, the EPRDF has thereby achieved vertical extension of its power to the local level. In South Africa, the ANC has won all provincial elections in 2019 except one (Western Cape). Naturally then, the National Council of Provinces, one of the two houses of parliament, is also dominated by ANC representatives, and since 1997, the president has also had the power to appoint and dismiss ANC provincial premiers and other officials.

Finally, forces of both fiscal and political centralism in Ethiopia and South Africa also limit *de facto* administrative federalism. *De jure*, sub-national divisions are empowered to choose expenditures according to local demands. Yet, dominant one-party systems and the party penetration of all sub-divisions of governance has led to *de facto* national state control over regional expenditures (see Meheret 2007, Vaughan 2006). One finding from individual woredas suggests that over 90 percent of spending is earmarked for the use on administrative and operational rather than capital expenditures (Dickovick and Gebre-Egziabher 2014, Meheret 2007). In South Africa, when some provinces engaged in overspending after the federation was set in place in the late 1990s, the federal government implemented stronger controls over subnational spending that effectively limited the spending autonomy of provinces (Wehner 2000). These controls include a set of administrative procedures determined by the Finance Ministry and the National Treasury, among other government bodies, to include the Medium-Term Expenditure Framework (MTEF), which requires multi-year budgeting across all public service sectors.

> The availability of this sort of multi-year budget enables the [...] National Treasury [...] to coordinate across sectors and levels of government, and to approve SNG [sub-national governments'] budgets on specific compliance with centrally deter- mined priorities such as pupil-teacher ratios, health care standards, and the like. Central – provincial relations are also regularized through meetings of national and provincial ministers [...], in which the latter communicate provincial needs, but are essentially subordinate to the central minister, since all are typically members of the ANC and provincial officials are fiscally dependent on resources from the centre.
>
> (Dickovick 2014, p. 563)

In contrast, *de jure* federalism has translated into significantly more *de facto* regulations in Nigeria's federalist experiment. First, as Chapter 5 illustrates, there is far less pronounced national party dominance that would be able to permeate subnational units. The PDP's influence has been much more contingent than the one of the EPRDF or the ANC, with a real possibility of losing elections to the APC. The PDP was in power between 1999 to 2015 but was replaced by the APC in the 2015 elections. The PDP currently controls 15 out of 36 states, and there is a clear North-South division, with the North consistently voting for the PDP and the

South usually electing the APC. Overall, this creates a degree of electoral competitiveness that has important effects on the practice of federal governance.

In addition, state divisions of the PDP or APC are more independent of the national party compared to Ethiopia or South Africa. For example, against the concerns of the national government and state governments in the South, Sharia law has constituted a main body of civil and criminal law in nine Muslim-majority states, and in some parts of three Muslim-plurality states since 1999, when then-Zamfara state governor Ahmad Sani Yerima began to advocate for the institution of Sharia at the state level of government. Consequently,

> although it lacks many of the regional autonomy features of the Ethiopian constitution, the Nigerian federation appears to exhibit greater political decentralization because of the benign nature of PDP dominance of the federation in comparison to EPRDF hegemony in Ethiopia.
> (Suberu 2001, p. 85f)

Second, Nigerian states have a higher local tax base compared to those in South Africa and Ethiopia since they are able to collect taxes on land, land registration, estates and licenses combined with a favorable fiscal federal dispensation. Third, they also enjoy less top down control on state expenditures due to federal institutions and clientelistic politics:

> With regard to spending intergovernmental transfers, substantial portions of the Federal Account are used for capital expenditure and sub-national personnel at the discretion of the state. With regard to clientelism, the prevalence of rent-seeking in Nigeria by sub-national politicians itself suggests a degree of autonomy from central government oversight a[t] least as traditionally defined.
> (Dickovick 2014, p. 565)

Overall, centralizing forces that balance out *de jure* federalism are therefore significantly less present in Nigeria compared to Ethiopia and South Africa.

How do these different realities of centralization in the three case studies compare to Tanzania and Kenya? With the advent of independence, the United Republic of Tanzania (formerly United Republic of Tanganyika and Zanzibar) started off as a two-sided federalist system under the union of Tanganyika and Zanzibar. Tanzania can today still be classified as an example of a centralized country with a strong presidency and a dominant party that exercises centralized control. For administrative purposes, mainland Tanzania is divided into regions. Each region is administered by a commissioner who is appointed by the central government. At district, division, and ward levels, there are popularly elected councils with appointed executive officers.

Kenya experienced a highly federal-like system – also often referred to as "*majimbo*", with seven regions with certain autonomy in the run up to independence from 1960–1963. The 1964 constitution then established a Unitary Republic Kenya that had some elements of federalism that became less *de facto* exercised in the 1990s and 2000s (Negussie 2016). Kenya again started to experiment more seriously with majimbo in 2010, where the new constitution devolved power from the central government to 47 new elected county governments. Kenya's federalism, compared to the Nigerian one, is certainly more limited (e.g. in land administration functions) and much younger, where county governments are still in the process of building capacity. Even so, the new constitution did establish Parliament with two Houses: the National Assembly responsible for national concerns, and the Senate of 47 county representatives with special powers in relation to the allocation of a fair share of resources to county governments. The World Bank (2019) has described Kenya's developments "as among the most rapid and ambitious devolution processes going on in the world", with countries like Senegal or Mozambique using it as an example case for its own devolution processes.

Interestingly but perhaps not surprisingly, the degree of centralization across the case studies also overlaps with how collaborative or competitive investment-related federal government bodies (e.g. ministries or investment commissions) are in relation to each other. The reason is probably again the closest related to party strength that I describe in Chapter 5: If individuals' career is linked to how long they have been party members, competing against each other is less needed. In contrast, if anyone who happens to be aligned with the president is able to get a political position, there will be more competition with other "newcomers" who try to cut in. A more detailed description of these mechanisms and how they relate to the flow of investment information is offered below.

7.2.2 Information Flows in Centralized Versus De-Centralized Systems

How does de-centralization hinder information flows on the amount of Chinese investment up to the central government? If ministries compete for funding and loyalty from the president to stay in power, they are less likely to collaborate and share information about investment deals. In contrast, if ministries are rallied under a shared party ideology and longevity of party membership determines pay-offs, they are more likely to cooperate and share information. In addition, *de facto* political de-centralism stalls information sharing because it lessens the trust among government officials who would otherwise be working towards a shared goal. If politicians are frequently competing in sub-national elections in a multi-party system, they gain legitimacy "from below" over the unit they govern. In contrast, if there is one strong party that also dominates local elections, politicians gain legitimacy "from above" through trust and party loyalty.

Finally, *de facto* administrative and fiscal de-centralism are also an obstacle to information flows because they decrease the need for assistance from the central government. If sub-national units are able to raise their own revenues and are not dependent on central government directions for spending, they are also less likely to be transparent about their revenue inflows. In contrast, if sub-regional units need funds from the central government, they will be more likely to ask the central government for assistance and share information on their revenues and investment inflows. Elements of all three forces were visible in the interview responses that I collected and are presented below.

7.2.2.1 Inter-Ministerial Competition and Information Flows

Nigeria's and Kenya's inter-governmental agencies at the federal level compete for funding and loyalty of the president, which appears to have serious implications for information-sharing incentives around foreign investments. In Nigeria, the Nigerian Investment Promotion Commission (NIPC), the Ministry of Budget and National Planning (MBNP), the Ministry of Industry, Trade and Investment (MITI), and the Ministry of Foreign Affairs (MFA) perform formal facilitating roles in attracting FDI, and several industry-specific ministries are directly approached by investors or later pulled in to sign investment deals if it concerns their department. Individuals considering investment in Nigeria are free to address all government offices and ministries but are generally met with a non-standardized approach to facilitating the investment deal.[1]

This is because in practice, alliances within the government seem to have led government offices to try to capture investors without pulling in other government offices. The NIPC was founded in 1995 to encourage, promote and co-ordinate investments and as a parastate directly reports to the Vice-President of Nigeria. One senior employee shared with me that the NIPC views itself as:

> the private sector in government. Specifically to Nigeria we have government institutions that are not receptive to investors, they are not aware of the value of investment…so they put in all bottom necks, they don't understand what FDI does to the country… Investors approach different ministries separately and yes, there certainly is an inter-agency rivalry… we want to make it as easy as possible to make business and we make other offices obsolete, we give tax wavers etc., so we compete… all these ministries see our organization as counterproductive… but all deals, permits and licenses are done through us.[2]

The NIPC and the MPNP generally operate as a block because they are both under the direct supervision of Yemi Osinbajo, the Vice-President of Nigeria.[3] As an officer at NIPC told me: "The NIPC has the last say on all investment matters as it reports to the office of the VP."[4]

Yet, other ministries that are not part of this alliance appear to have a strikingly different view on the role and importance of the NIPC. When I asked about the relationship between MITI and NIPC, a senior officer at the MITI responded:

> The ministry makes policy while the agencies implement policies, the NIPC is effectively only an agency under our ministry. They think they are special because they do not technically report to a ministry but the vice-president. But if you look at NIPC, they are only reporting to the President's Office because the person who headed NIPC then was once a minister of this ministry [MITI], and when he then was about to head the NIPC, he just wasn't comfortable reporting to another minister.[5]

I asked interviewees to draw an organogram of the government bodies tasked with attracting foreign investment, and interestingly, the NIPC respondents unanimously drew the President's Office and the NIPC next to it, with all the federal ministries below. In contrast, the majority of the ministry respondents drew the President's Office on top, below the ministries (four interviewees drew their ministry significantly larger than the others), and again below the NIPC, with only one interviewee drawing the NIPC on the same level as the ministries.

When asked to list the government offices that they had worked together with on the last investment deal they were involved in, the majority of interviewees implied or directly confirmed that generally, they set up deals as a ministry without necessarily pulling in or sharing information with the NIPC or the MITI, and that the key negotiators were always from their ministry. This seemed to be partially sector-specific: For example for oil and gas related matters, President Buhari, who appointed himself as the Minister of Petroleum Resources, seems to send communiqués to the NIPC but does not formally invite them to sit on the table or offer background expertise while the MITI is more frequently asked to send an advisor.[6] For agricultural matters, the NIPC and the MITI are sometimes asked to advise with background information at the Ministry of Agriculture and Rural Development.[7] And at the Ministry of Foreign Affairs, I was told that they are the ones "making the larger deals"[8] while the NIPC is responsible for the "execution of smaller deals with maximum 1 million dollars",[9] so their "spheres do not overlap and we don't really engage."[10] Nigeria does not have its own ministry on industrialization, a gap which the NIPC appears to want to fill. Asked whether there are any other ministries highly invested in industrialization, they mentioned the Ministry of Labor and Employment and the Nigeria Export Processing Zones authority but even then, they did not collectively attempt to count the amount of manufacturing that has entered Nigeria:

> We attempt our best but it is very de-centralized, because companies aren't required to sign up with us, we can help them but only if they reach out… so we are alone in this quest of trying to have a good database of foreign manufacturers in Nigeria.[11]

Asked why they felt the need to compete and not pull in other ministries, one respondent laughed and said:

> This is Nigeria. There are a lot of people who will want to take credit for your work… and there are also many alliances within the government… Osinbajo is from the South… but many people in government are from the North… you need to pick your alliances right and show that your ministry is performing… we are all out for ourselves.[12]

Asked whether party loyalty and longevity of party membership mattered at all, another respondent said:

> No, you need to be good with the President's Office, they give you funding, they determine your political career, regardless of how long you have been a

party member. So ministers naturally want to take credit for whatever investment deals they can get.[13]

I mentioned to interviewees at other ministries that I heard this answer in one interview, and the sentiment was confirmed by several other respondents.[14]

In Kenya, responses looked quite similar. Asked who usually sits on the negotiation table with foreign investors, a former employee at KenInvest said: "Most of the time, we have different ministries negotiating different deals and we weren't really pulled in [...] because each ministry has a different project and it is so specific to their field of operations"[15] and that "investors can come to Kenya through us but they don't really have to… we have a list of investors who are registered with us, but of course that is not all investors in Kenya."[16] At the Ministry of Foreign Affairs, I was told that they were in fact the ones primarily responsible for setting up business deals.

> KenInvest is being contacted if investors want to have some extra assistance… but it is us who organize the delegation visits to China, who work with the Chambers of Commerce in Kenya, the embassies… We work the closest with the President's Office and making sure we attract investments, that is one of our main tasks, and we co-ordinate the ministries and who gets to negotiate what.[17]

Yet, at the Ministry of Industry, Trade & Co-operatives, I was told: "No, the Ministry of Foreign Affairs is not involved in getting us investments, we usually are being approached by investors themselves, or we send someone from our ministry to China."[18] And on KenInvest: "I think they act more as an advisory role, if investors have any problems, they can go there."[19] When asked whether party loyalty and longevity of party membership mattered at all, most respondents said that you had to be a party member but it did not matter how many years you had been a member, and that you could rise quickly by performing well,[20] with one interviewee saying:

> This is an environment where you can become minister in one day and they kick you out the next one if something happens [...] no, there are no particular rewards for working together as ministries, I think every ministry is trying to do their best and attracting investment deals to show to the President's Office… yes you can say they are competing and that's sort of it.[21]

When asked to draw organograms of the ministry constellation for attracting and negotiating investment deals, most interviewees drew ministries next to each other, in same sizes or their ministry in bigger size, but with KenInvest below them. This shows that like Nigeria's approach, Kenya's strategy to attract investment also appears to be rather de-centralized.

The fact (discussed in Chapter 5) that ministries were largely re-staffed with the rise of a new ruling party is also relevant for the argument advanced here. While Chapter 5 highlights that the re-staffing led to sporadic rather than consistent interactions with foreign players, where relationships need to be defined again from the beginning and the African side is *learning* again "from scratch" about the Chinese strategy, re-staffing is also hindering information sharing *incentives* between different opposing ruling powers. For example, I received the opportunity to talk at a café in Nairobi to a senior officer who used to work at a ministry under former President Mwai Kibaki. He was part of the negotiation committee that signed a Memorandum of Understanding in 2011 with the China Road and Bridge Corporation to build a standard-gauge railway between Mombasa and Nairobi, the largest infrastructure project in Kenya since independence.

Asked how the transition of the project to the Kenyatta administration went, he said:

> This was a deal negotiated by us, under President Kibaki, it was our win. And then it was handed over to the Kenyatta administration, handed over the official paperwork, and we left… Kenyatta is getting a lot of political praise for this but this was essentially our win.

Asked whether any new staff had asked them for advice on how they negotiated, and how to approach China as a negotiation partner, he said:

> I was personally never approached… Kenyatta had his own new staff, his own allies… and I am proud of the work I have done with the Chinese but I would not have wanted it to be used by Kenyatta's administration.

Asked whether generally, ministries were re-staffed, he replied: "Yes, absolutely."

In contrast, Tanzania and Ethiopia's ministries efforts around investment promotion and facilitation appears to be more collaborative due to party loyalty that needs to be demonstrated in years. In Tanzania, the Tanzania Investment Centre, the Ministry of Industry, Trade and Investment and the Ministry of Foreign Affairs and East African Cooperation are all formally tasked to attract investors. While the NIPC and the KenInvest offices I visited were empty, when I stepped into to the Tanzania Investment Centre for the interviews, it was full of applicants. "If you want to open a business in Tanzania, you have to go through us, we are the first stop,"[22] as one senior employee at the Investment Center told me. This was confirmed by a senior officer at the Ministry of Industries, Trade and Investment who asked me at the beginning of the interview whether I had been to the Investment Center since they "will also have all the information for me."[23]

At the Ministry of Foreign Affairs and East African Cooperation, I was also first told that I should go to Investment Centre.[24] Asked how different ministries negotiate with foreign investors, all three agencies told me the same set-up, that investors would first have to approach the Investment Centre, which, if necessary (usually for larger investments), then invites different ministries to the negotiation table.[25] If investors happen to address a federal ministry first before the Investment Centre, the ministry is supposed to inform the Investment Centre, which then coordinates pulling in ministries for the negotiations.[26] Asked why there appears to exist such a high amount of collaboration and a clear structure on negotiations, one interviewee said that President Magufuli had just sent out another communiqué to all government offices the week prior to the interview reaffirming that "we talk as one government, that is one of the principles of his presidency but really the CCM's strength in general."[27] I also asked whether ministers would be able to gain credit for striking deals with investors and then report their work to the President's Office, and how the President's Office assesses ministry performance in general. I was told: "I don't understand your question... I don't know why a ministry would want to negotiate by itself if you can ask the Investment Centre, the Ministry of Industries for help"[28] and that

> you have to be a party member for a long time, to show that you can be trusted with a more senior role... and once you are the minister, you are still part of the whole CCM apparatus. The expectation is that you collaborate, the president does not like if a minister does their own thing... it is not viewed well.[29]

When asked to draw organograms of the ministry constellation tasked to negotiate investment deals, the vast majority of respondents interestingly drew the ministries next to each other in a circle around the President's Office, and then an extra circle ("where they all meet"[30]), the Tanzania Investment Centre, right next to the Ministry of Industry, Trade and Investment, with the Ministry in a larger size than the Centre. Compared to the organogram drawings from Nigeria and Kenya, these ones showed a "center" where negotiations took place and "information was collected."[31]

In Ethiopia, the Ethiopian Investment Commission is an autonomous government institution accountable to the country's Investment Board, which is chaired by the Prime Minister, and mainly responsible for attracting and facilitating investment, including handling permits, business licenses, and technology transfer agreements, among other functions. Like in Tanzania, all investors must register with the Commission. When I visited the Commission, there were fewer applicants present than in Tanzania, perhaps because applications can also be submitted online. Like the Tanzania Investment Center, the Ethiopian Investment Commission views itself as a "one-stop shop"[32] that is the main organ responsible for investor-related issues in Ethiopia.

I also interviewed individuals at The Ministry of Foreign Affairs, Ministry of Finance and the Ministry of Trade and Industry to better understand the *de facto* role of the Commission, and individuals at all three ministries confirmed that the Investment Commission is the first point of entry to Ethiopia.[33] I asked all interviewees to draw an organogram if they had to describe the investment negotiation landscape, and they all either placed the Investment Commission on top of the sheet, with the ministries below, lined up next to each other, or the ministries and the Investment Commission all next to each other, with arrows pointing to and from each ministry to the Investment Commission. Asked why the arrow also leads from the Ministry of Foreign Affairs to the Investment Commission, a senior officer at the Ministry of Foreign Affairs did say that sometimes investors, especially larger ones sent by the Chinese government, would approach them first, or a diplomatic delegation from Ethiopia would involve the Ministry of Foreign Affairs in investment deals before the Commission. Yet, he also said that even if they happen to be the first point of entry, "we will involve the [Investment] Commission."[34] Asked whether competition might also arise for funding or prestige with the government, I was told: "we have clear performance targets, and it is easier to fulfill these targets if we work together… you also get credit if you help set up a deal."[35] Party loyalty and longevity of party membership again appear to significantly matter:

> Yes, you need to demonstrate that you support the government's development agenda, and it is mostly long party members that get to fill higher positions… that is necessary if you want to ensure that we are implementing the Growth and Transformation Plan as a government.[36]

In South Africa, responses were somewhat similar to Ethiopia and Tanzania, where ministries did not appear to actively compete. At the same time, there seems to be no central organ that would deal with investment-related matters, especially for smaller, private investors. I was told that under the Jacob Zuma administration (2009–2018), the President's Office often directly negotiated large loan and investment deals with the Chinese government.[37] Yet, when Cyril Ramaphosa came to power in 2018, he actively started to pursue a slightly more de-centralized model, where he tasked South African parastatals to negotiate large loan deals with Chinese banks, including the billion dollar deals promised by China for South Africa in 2018.[38] As one officer at one of the parastatals shared with me: "We are trying this new model, mostly because of Zuma's corruption history… Ramaphosa wants more checks and balances, and to move negotiations away from the traditional beneficiaries of these deals."[39] Asked whether there is oversight on the amount of investments entering South Africa, he said:

> Yes, certainly, because it always goes through the President's Office first… they are then the ones delegating it then for the actual negotiations but they always keep an oversight and check in with what and how much money is being discussed.[40]

Asked whether the B-EE regulations have always been successfully enforced with foreign investors, or whether the government makes concessions depending on the size of the deal, interviewees at the President's Office, two parastatals and the South African Department of Trade, Industry, and Competition (DTIC) confirmed that B-EE regulations were "not up for negotiations"[41] since they are "so engrained in South Africa's institutions."[42]

At the same time, negotiations with small, private investors appear to be highly de-centralized, and there seems to be no office that would count the amount of private investment in South Africa. InvestSA is a division of the South African Department of Trade, Industry, and Competition (DTIC) and tasked with the attraction and facilitation of investment in South Africa, with one stop shops in Western Cape, KwaZulu Natal and Gauteng. Yet, several interviewees confirmed that many private companies in South Africa are not registered with InvestSA.[43] "You are only on the government's radar if you do business with the government."[44] I also asked whether private South African companies doing business with Chinese investors would enforce B-BBEE regulations, a professor at a South African University told me: "No, if it is B2B relations, and not business to government, no business has to care about B-BBEE. All they care about is profits, and it isn't properly enforced."[45] What is central to the argument advanced here is that while larger loan and investment deals are becoming slightly more-decentralized, information is still being reported up and down between the ministries, parastatals and the President's Office, which keeps an oversight of investment amounts. In contrast, there appears to be no central collection of information regarding private investments.

The discussion above shows that in Nigeria and Kenya, federal government offices tend to compete while their interactions in Tanzania, Ethiopia and South Africa tend to be more collaborative. How do these interactions then influence what information the central government is able to collect on Chinese investment inflows? I asked all government officials where they generally receive their information on Chinese investments, and respondents significantly differed between the "centralized" and the "de-centralized" systems. In Nigeria, the vast majority of interviewees said that they either received information on Chinese investments "from Nigerian newspapers" (42 out of 45), from deals they are directly involved in (45 out of 45), or their own ministry (39 out of 45).

The NIPC also sends out an almost-daily newsletter on its activities, for which anyone can sign up – six interviewees (four of them NIPC employees) said that they are receiving the emails while 39 said that they had not heard of any NIPC newsletter. I tracked for Chinese-investment related news between May 20, 2019 and May 20, 2020, and 46 emails included Chinese investments, of which 39 addressed an investment of a Chinese SOEs in the raw material or industry sector (with five emails on the Lekki FTZ). These deals were again mostly set up with Chinese SOEs, not with private companies.

In Kenya, most respondents said that they receive information on Chinese investments "from Kenyan newspapers" (21 out of 23) from deals that they are directly involved in (23 out of 23), and their ministry (20 out of 23). These deals were again reportedly mostly set up with Chinese SOEs, not with private companies. What is particularly worth highlighting here is that in both countries, the vast majority of respondents indicated that they receive their information from newspapers or their own ministry, not internal government communiqués or from other ministries.

In Tanzania and Ethiopia, only three and five interviewees respectively reported that they would consult the newspaper for information on Chinese investments while the majority referred to deals they are directly involved in, their own ministry, and internal newsletters that are being sent out by the prime minister and presidents' offices as well as the investment centers (17 out of 23 interviewees in Tanzania and 19 out of 21 interviewees in Ethiopia) and from other ministries (18 out of 23 interviewees in Tanzania and 20 out of 21 interviewees in Ethiopia). In South Africa, the majority of interviewees said that they receive information on

Chinese investments from "South African newspapers" (14 out of 19 interviewees), deals they are directly involved in and their ministry (19 out of 19 interviewees), and the national development plan (10 out of 19 interviewees).

Finally, and most importantly, I asked the key ministries tasked with formulating investment laws what investment-related information they receive from other ministries to base their recommendations to the legislature on. Respondents at the Nigerian Ministry of Industry, Trade and Investment and at the Kenyan Ministry of Industry, Trade and Cooperatives shared with me that other ministries do not send them information on investment amounts. I asked why they have not set up a system where they would track and share information across ministries and the Nigerian response was: "We have been trying to ask them to send us information but it is really up to the ministers how they want to engage with us."[46] And in Kenya, KenInvest said: "We tried to come up with something more central in 2017, my boss was the lead initiator behind this… but he ran against walls. We are asking for information that ministries don't like to share."[47] In contrast, at the Ethiopian Ministry of Trade and Industry and at the Tanzanian Ministry of Industry, Trade and Investment I was told that they did have central systems in place that track investments that also capture smaller investors. "Yes, we have tasked the Investment Center and the Export Processing Zone Authority with collecting information for us that is vital. We receive a lot of small companies."[48]

I wanted to test the claim that the Export Processing Zone Authority is collecting information for the central government. So, I randomly selected one of the export zones in Dar es Salaam and interviewed the managing director. What was the most puzzling was that, without me even asking, he pulled out a document with statistics on all the firms operating in the zone, and said: "The government takes this information very seriously."[49] Overall, these responses suggest that how ministries and other federal government bodies interact with each other influences what information is being shared on the inflow of foreign and Chinese investments. The next section focuses on information flows between the central government and sub-regional units that differ between de-centralized and more centralized government systems.

7.2.2.2 Communication between Central Government and Sub-Regional Units

Responses in Nigeria and Kenya show that regional electoral competition and more independence in raising revenues has led states and counties to engage separately in attracting foreign investors while both forces are less present in Tanzania, Ethiopia and South Africa. Competition among Nigerian states is a famous concern with nation-building efforts. As a senior aid to the Lagos State Governor shared with me:

> The North always receives government support, extra money, and where does it go? The North is in a worse economic state than 50 years ago. Meanwhile, we in Lagos raise our own funds, domestic and foreign, we create own growth. The North should just separate, we would be better off.[50]

An Ogun State official shared a similar sentiment with me: "Effectively, Ogun State has to compete for investment all by itself, we send delegations to China, we try to make them come here [...] A mutual strategy? We can do it ourselves, and probably better."[51]

In this environment, some states then become very entrepreneurial. For example, Edo State in South Nigeria set up a full website to attract investors and also has an Edo State Investment Office. Governor Godwin Nogheghase Obaseki, a businessman who has for a long time worked in investment banking and also founded AfriInvest (a large investment banking firm), is a PDP member. One of his employees shared with me during a visit to Lagos that the county's relationship to the APC as the federal ruling party is difficult.

> We can't count on receiving support from the APC... the Governor is very skilled in investments, so he took on the task to lead investments to Edo State, otherwise we might be left out. He is a very smart man and he was elected on the promise to bring in more money to the state.[52]

Asked whether they are working together with any federal government agency, he said that they take advice from the NIPC. Interestingly, as mentioned before, the NIPC is also associated with Vice President Osinbajo, a Southerner, so the trust of the Edo State Governor in the NIPC might be higher than in the MITI. Asked whether governors are supposed to submit investment reports to the federal government, representatives of Lagos, Ogun and Edo State told me that they need to submit "revenue reports" and that investments are sometimes captured there but that there are no checks on accuracy or completeness. "No, you do not need to keep count of state investments... yes, the NIPC technically tracks it but we don't really submit anything detailed... I wouldn't trust the other states' numbers, Edo State is doing really well."[53]

Asked about in what capacity Kenyan counties collaborate with KenInvest, the KenInvest representative said that if counties want, they can work with KenInvest but that counties also host their separate events and that he has heard that some counties are now starting to attract investments in "blocks."[54] Due to time constraints, I was unable to do more sub-national research in Kenya but the fact that a senior official at KenInvest apparently knew very little about these blocks suggests that there is little cooperation between the federal and the county level.

Asked whether KenInvest helps to match investors with counties, one officer said: "Well they are responsible for their own investments... since 2010, counties have more responsibilities there. they are elected to raise their own revenues, and investments are part of that." Interestingly, the Governor of Laikipia County mentioned in the introduction of this chapter used to work as Assistant Minister for Industrialization under the Kibaki administration between 2007–2013, where he was involved in reforms to improve the business environment through policy incentives. He ran as an independent candidate for the Laikipia county elections and is therefore not affiliated with the Jubilee Party, the current ruling party at the federal level. While I do not have direct evidence, Laikipia County's exceptional quest to directly attract investment resembles the story of Edo State, where the

Governor is from a different party to the federal government, has an investment (policy) background and is implementing an entrepreneurial approach to attracting investment to their region.

In contrast, in Tanzania and Ethiopia, regional elections are dominated by one party, and sub-regional units are also significantly less able to raise their own revenues, which tends to lead to a more centralized effort to attract investors. As the senior economist at the Tanzanian Ministry of Industry, Trade and Investment told me:

> The Investment Centre gives investors suggestions on where to go, we have regional quotas to fill…the quotas ensure that each commissioner gets investments for their region… and our investment activities depend on the five year development plans, and all ministries and sub-regional units are supposed to work towards that… or it is the same with the SDGs, we have a very similar approach there.[55]

I also asked why different Tanzanian regions do not simply venture off to attract investments themselves: "They simply can't, you have to know that some regions are very poor… and so they rely on the government to distribute investment."[56]

In Ethiopia, the government has also been driving industrialization very centrally through the Growth and Transformation Plans. As mentioned in the introduction, in 2017, Amahara Region in Ethiopia signed a Memorandum of Understanding with the Chinese company Maxter Group for the set-up of a special economic zone in the area. The MOU came during the construction of twelve industrial parks throughout the country, including Bahir Dar, Gonder, Jimma, and Mekele. Asked why the central government is so involved in re-distributing investments across the country and what role kebele and woreda governments play in attracting investors, one interviewee was confused and said: "There is just one government",[57] probably alluding to the fact that the EPRDF was also ruling in most local councils. Another respondent said that the central government is so involved in attracting foreign investment "because they [local councils] can't do it themselves, some regions are very poor and it is the task of the government to help out with funding."[58] His response confirms Djockovic (2014) that some regions are too poor to raise funds themselves.

Finally, in South Africa, there appears to be a counting system in place that captures the amount of official Chinese investment, promised by the Chinese government, and private Chinese companies that settle in special economic zones across the country. National, provincial or municipal authorities or Public Private Partnerships (PPP) need to formally apply and meet defined criteria for recommendation by the Special Economic Zones Advisory Board to the Minister of the Department for Trade, Industry and Competition.[59] "All business is done with the government",[60] I was told by a professor of a South African university.

But what about private companies that are not procuring to the government or are not located inside a special economic zone? He said that as a company,

> once you have ventured off, there is no agency that would have any oversight, we don't have a classic mandatory one-stop-shop system like in Ethiopia,

InvestSA has fewer mandates... they are only starting to learn now to set up counting systems in the provinces... before, they thought there wasn't any private money coming in but you are right, there are a lot of companies in the provinces that we all need to know more about.

South Africa therefore appears to be a more nuanced case, where information on larger C2G deals is being collected by the President's Office but where awareness around the magnitude of private Chinese investments is developing slower, and provinces or InvestSA have not been tasked to pay particular attention to this relatively new type of investor.

In countries where sub-regional units have incentives not to share information "up" to the federal level, the central government will have less information on what sub-regional units attract what kind of investments. When I told respondents at the Nigerian Ministry of Industry, Trade and Investment that the NIPC gives out star-ratings to Nigerian states based on how much investment they attract, they all seemed surprised and said that they would like to see the states' rankings, and that they had no similar system in place.[61] I also asked about the rating at the NIPC and what numbers they base their rankings on. I was told that the NIPC had to include international and domestic consultants for the project because "we had to get independent figures... otherwise, states would just tell you any numbers... we had to make sure these estimates are somewhat reasonable."[62] In Kenya, I also asked for county-specific investment numbers but all interviewees told me that they do not know whether such a database exists, and they could not tell me what counties except to Nairobi attracted the largest amount of manufacturing and service investors.[63]

If government officials receive biased or incomplete information on the amount of Chinese investment flows, they will misperceive what sectors companies have invested in and overstress the importance of SOEs that also may get more attention through the high-profile diplomatic relationship between the respective African country and China. As Chapter 4 describes in detail, Nigerian and Kenyan respondents indeed largely underreported the amount of small and medium Chinese companies in manufacturing and the service sector in their economies. Interestingly, those offices that reported to hear about Chinese investments through the newspaper also tended to conflate Chinese official investments, done through SOEs, and smaller private investments under the umbrella term "Chinese investments." When I asked interviewees in Nigeria, Kenya and South Africa whether they perceive any differences between official Chinese investments, decided by the Chinese government, and smaller private Chinese investors, the vast majority told me that they did not really know what the difference was, and that there is predominantly Chinese official investment in their respective country while they estimated the amount of private Chinese investors to be very small.

In contrast, the interview responses presented in Chapter 4 show that there is significantly more awareness around the presence of private Chinese investment in Ethiopia and Tanzania. This is probably because all types of investors are required to sign up with the investment centers, which then report to the ministries. While

I was waiting in the lobby of the Investment Centre in Tanzania, I chatted with a few applicants. Their companies ranged from small kettle businesses to ceramics factories, indicating that also smaller, private businesses did indeed go to register with the government. At the Ministry of Industry, Trade and Investment, I also got a chance to talk to two investors who wanted to build a global supply chain for nuts and fruit from Tanzania. The senior economist met directly with them (and me) but they also told me that they had registered with the Investment Center and are now trying to see if the senior economist can help with additional business contacts and suggestions on where to invest.

Overall, the analysis above demonstrates that more centralized systems may be able to more effectively collect information on small, private Chinese investments compared to de-centralized systems. At the same time, the described experiences in Tanzania, Ethiopia and South Africa are of course not supposed to imply that investment data collection is always working perfectly across the three cases. I was only able to interview Chinese companies located in or around the capitals and in highly urban areas across all cases. What supports the theory advanced here is that of the 38 Chinese companies I interviewed in Lagos, Ogun and Oyo State in Nigeria, only five responded they had registered with the NIPC. In Kenya, of the 15 Chinese companies I interviewed around Nairobi, two had registered with KenInvest. In Ethiopia, of the 13 Chinese companies I interviewed around Addis Ababa, twelve said that they had registered with the Ethiopian Investment Commission. In Tanzania, of the 16 Chinese companies I interviewed around Dar es Salaam, 14 reported that they had registered with the Investment Centre. Finally, in South Africa, of the two Chinese companies that I interviewed around Johannesburg that had interacted with the government in some capacity, both were registered with Invest SA. In contrast, of the three private Chinese companies I interviewed around Johannesburg, none told me that they had registered with InvestSA.

At the same time, capacity constraints are certainly an issue, and it was outside of the scope of this book to study more rural regions, where realities of actual service delivery could be substantially different. In Ethiopia, for example, one interviewee at the Investment Commission told me: "It is a mess sometimes... licenses still come late, or they use wrong addresses... We are still learning how to improve our services and build capacity."[64] My interviews do reveal, however, a clear difference across the structural set up around investment promotion and facilitation across the five studies cases that does seem to lead to different information inflows that influence perceptions on bargaining power. Chapter 4 shows that respondents in countries with a central organ tasked to track investment flows and a collaborative government culture provided significantly more accurate estimates on the amount and type of private Chinese investments in their countries, compared to the ones with de-centralized structures. As a result, I conclude that while investment-related institutions do not always have the full capacity to track all investment inflows, they appear to be able to track "enough" inflows to provide governments with a good enough idea of the magnitude of private investments that in turn influences perceptions on bargaining power.

7.3 "Hidden" Village Chinese Industrial Parks – Sub-National Evidence From Nigeria

The aim of this study is to explain cross-national variation in perceptions of bargaining power across five African countries. But in the context of federal political systems, it is also important to ask how de-centralized systems feed federal, state and traditional leaders with different cues about bargaining power that then influence views of the federal governments. I received the opportunity to visit "hidden" village Chinese industrial parks in Nigeria after an interviewee in Lagos State had shared with me that a private Chinese businessman had set up an industrial park in his village in Ogun State,[65] of which the federal government was not aware. I was able to visit the village for two days and to conduct interviews with seven Chinese businesses (out of 17 fully operating), 10 villagers as well as the king and his ruling family. I was then also able to interview two members of two other villages with Chinese parks in the same state, who are now based in Lagos.

First evidence from these "hidden" village Chinese industrial parks in Nigeria suggests that players at different government levels do have different perceptions of bargaining power, but they have few incentives to share their information "up" with other government bodies, which overall results in low perceptions of bargaining power at the federal level. These findings further support the theory advanced in the first chapter but also shine first light on sub-national variation in bargaining power and open a new avenue for future comparative research on the topic.

When I visited the interviewee's village in March 2019, the village king kindly invited me to his palace to have tea, and he told me the following story that was also confirmed by several villagers and Chinese company managers operating in the village: In 1992,[66] a private Chinese man came to this specific village because it had a pond, "and the man was interested in fishing",[67] and because it is located on a road that is conveniently connecting the South with the North. The Chinese businessman talked to the village king, who seized the opportunity and asked the Chinese man to build him two additional houses to his palace in exchange for allowing him to use some of the village land. The Chinese man agreed to the deal, opened up a foam (mattress) company and soon brought more Chinese companies (foam, shoes, ceramics and fishing) from China.

What are some of the motivations of these Chinese companies to settle in the village industrial park? This industrial park is completely independent from the official Chinese industrial parks in Nigeria (Lekki Free Trade Zone and Ogun Guangdong Free Trade Zone (OFTFZ) and offers different incentives. OGFTZ spans an area of 10,000 hectares and the land is leased for 99 years. As a joint venture between the China African Investment Company (CAIC, under the control of the Chinese Guangdong Province, 82 percent ownership) and the Ogun State Government (18 percent ownership), the CAIC has 100 percent management control of the zone (although the zone had undergone different phases of state-owned and private Chinese management that had led to conflict in the past).

When asked why they preferred to operate in this village and not in OGFTZ, the Chinese companies in the village park told me that they would have to pay management fees in the official free trade zones, that they also received tax incentives here, that they liked the close relationship to the king, the little bureaucracy and that their complaints were attended to quickly, and that they also liked to be located on the road that connects the North and the South. I also carefully mentioned the conflict over management in the OGFTZ and the Chinese government's final rule to reinstate state-owned management after a private Chinese company had led the zone for a few years. Six out of seven Chinese managers said they did not know what I was referring to. When I hinted at it, they said they were not worried that this would happen to them because the Chinese government is not involved with their park. One Chinese interviewee hinted that they are too small, so the Chinese government effectively does not care.[68]

Certainly, the companies also had complaints about electricity shortages and water supply, and especially about the high rate of kidnapping in their area. "Last week, a Chinese man in a different village was kidnapped",[69] one manager told me, "many Chinese now have policemen that go with them."[70] But when I asked whether they would consider leaving the region because of the safety issues, she said: "No.... I have heard of the ones kidnapped, they often pack their bags and go on the next plane back to China [laughs]... but most Chinese stay."[71] Asked why they would stay, she said: "This just happens, it's part of life, we just go back to work."[72]

What are the concrete conditions under which these companies are allowed to operate in the village? I asked the king how he is able to keep attracting Chinese companies. He said that he convinced the Ogun State Government not to tax the small, growing Chinese companies but to make them pay once they are already bigger. "That was really attracting a lot of companies."[73] At the same time, he said he is very strict around local contributions. "They have to help us in the village, they have to employ the people, they have to build wells, they have to help fixing what's broken."[74] Asked how readily the Chinese are complying with the demands and whether there were any complaints, he said: "No, no complaints, they know it is expected, and it is natural in our relationship... we give them land, they give us help."[75]

What about competition from other villages? After all, there is plenty of land in Ogun State, with different village kings that could simply engage in a "race-to-the-bottom" in luring in companies. At least the kings in the three villages that I studied do not appear to feel pressure to compete against each other because each one has their own Chinese company community in China that, through existing Chinese contacts in the Nigerian villages, picked theirs.[76] The other two village industrial parks are located 67 km and 122 km, respectively away from the first one. Their first point of contact with Chinese companies was also through adventurous, entrepreneurial Chinese businessmen.[77] I asked about inter-village competition but as the interviewee who had shared the location of the first village with me said:

> No the trust and the relationship is everything... Chinese don't know anything about Nigeria when they first come here, so they will go to wherever their friend is. And once they are here you build relationships with them, too. But they usually don't go to a village that they don't know, they are very careful.[78]

Why are the three village chiefs that I studied able to negotiate local participation with the Chinese companies? Like at the national level, several explanations stand out as to why the village chiefs would negotiate strong deals with Chinese business owners. In Chapter 4, the experiment results suggest that at the federal level, electoral incentives did not influence government respondents' willingness to sign deals, probably because there is very little transparency around these deals in media. At the same time, at the local level, electoral, party, or social incentives may certainly still influence whether people seek out broadly public benefits or aim for private payoffs. For example, chiefs' embeddedness in local communities may encourage them to cut better deals than elected officials. Baldwin (2015) famously calls such individuals "development brokers," who help their communities resolve collective action problems and make sure they have access to development projects such as improved roads, clinics, schools and water wells.

These factors certainly play a role. After all, the king did first ask for improvements of his personal home. He also then later ensured that his village was benefitting from the Chinese presence by ordering local participation in the Chinese factories. Yet, the central point put forward by this book is that the village king *was aware* that he could ask for local participation in the first place. In particular, he was surprisingly very aware about the policy attributes that Chinese companies were sensitive to (taxes), and the ones around which he could be more aggressive (local participation) without deterring valuable Chinese capital. The king had realized that his village had bargaining power due to its cheap land and location, and he is using it to ask for personal and village benefits. While we were drinking tea at his palace, I asked him why he thinks he can ask the Chinese company community to contribute to his village's development. He seemed surprised that this would even be a question, and he confidently said: "They want to use our land, so we can set the rules."[79]

The reasons as to why the kings had high perceptions of bargaining power can again be related to the three variables pointed out to matter also for the federal level. Baldwin (2015) argues that the long-time horizons of chiefs and the repeated nature of their interactions with local society lead to different incentives compared to those of elected politicians. She writes that

> traditional leaders have a unique ability to organize community contributions to these projects... because they expect to rule for life and thus have an incentive to make up-front investments in institutions that will improve the ability of their communities to act collectively over the long-term.
>
> (p. 10)

This book argues that, similarly, the long-time horizons of the three chiefs that I studied and the repeated nature of their interactions with Chinese companies helped them to learn over time that they do possess bargaining power around local participation and that they can in fact ask for these up-front investments from Chinese companies, which has led them to set up institutions that will improve the ability of their communities to act collectively in negotiations with the Chinese over the long-term. The village chief therefore provides a contrasting example to the replacements and re-staffing happening at more central levels of government in Nigeria.

As one prince in the first village shared with me:

> My father has seen continued interest of the Chinese coming since the 90s, so he set up a whole committee of us to talk to them... sometimes it's him who does the talks, sometimes it's us... but we are ready as the next generation to take over.[80]

That long-term learning has been taking place since the 1990s is visible in the quality of deals that appears to have become stronger over time.

> Yes, in the beginning I didn't ask the Chinese man for much, the two houses for my palace, then he would get some land... when he brought in more companies, the conditions changed, I started to ask more for the village, repairs, some material... and then when we saw even more coming, I started to ask them to employ people. And it's the same with taxes, for now some have tax holidays but once they are bigger, we will ask them to pay state taxes.[81]

In addition, the villages' relative isolation from Western influences may have also been beneficial for the confidence in the value of their land. The first village king used to work in marketing for Heineken Nigeria but has otherwise no reported connection to Western thought. Asked what he learned at Heineken, he said: "If you do it right, you can make a lot of business in Nigeria, and I wanted the same for my village."[82] I asked whether Ogun State government has ever sent advisors on how to negotiate with the Chinese companies, which he negated. I also asked whether he had taken any inspiration from the "Chinese model" of development, and he said no, he just saw the interest and that he could make money off of the companies. The other two village kings apparently have lived their whole lives in their villages and have also mostly only interacted with the state government (and not with the federal one).[83] They were therefore probably also relatively more isolated from the Weak Bargaining Power Narrative compared to politicians at the federal level.

Finally, the villages themselves are very small and centralized under the king's rule. I also asked whether it had occurred that any villagers had set up "side deals" with the Chinese companies, or whether there is any competition for cooperation with Chinese companies in the village. The prince responded: "It wouldn't be possible or in the interest of villagers to set up side deals, and also for the [Chinese] companies."[84] The other two villages are even smaller than the first one, and I received very similar responses to my questions on centralization, where both interviewees said that due to size and power of the king's family, it would not be possible for villagers to set up separate side deals with companies.[85]

As a result, this again appears to be a story about one dominant ruler in power for a long time, who was able to test out different deal conditions with Chinese companies while having small exposure to the Weak Bargaining Power Narrative. In addition, it is also a story about a very centralized system, where power rests in the king and it was very transparent how many Chinese companies were in fact operating in the village. The reported experiences from the three villages are certainly not enough to draw larger inferences about the universe of villages in Southern Nigeria, let alone the negotiation rationales of traditional rulers in the African region more broadly. Yet, there may exist an important comparison between incentives of traditional rulers and (elected) politicians in authoritarian or one-party dominant state with communist/socialist histories that lead to different incentives and to more awareness around bargaining power that would be interesting to study in the future.

7.4 Conclusion

The findings described in this chapter suggest that information around investment flows may be captured more effectively in political environments that have a high degree of centralization. Federalist experiments are often touted to lead to more democracy and accountability, and to reduce the risk of one single agency abusing political power for their own purposes. Yet, the findings in this chapter suggest that federal experiments should be carefully designed to prevent competition between sub-regional units if this competition hinders information sharing up to the federal government. This may only be possible in systems with strong parties or strong institutions that are able to extend their control to all regions of the state. If parties or institutions are weak, the federal government will be underinformed on the amount of investment flowing into the country. They may then underperceive their actual bargaining power with foreign investors, which is then harmful to the quality of deals that political actors would otherwise collectively be able to negotiate.

Notes

1. As confirmed by e.g. A3, 4, 10, 11.
2. A11.
3. A2, 4, 11, 12, 14.
4. A12.
5. A16.
6. A21, 22.
7. A14, A21.
8. A31.
9. Ibid.
10. Ibid.
11. A11, 12.
12. A12.
13. A16.
14. A17, A22, A31.
15. N1.
16. Ibid.
17. N8.
18. N6.
19. Ibid.
20. E.g. N1, 2, 7, 8, 15, 19.
21. N19.

22 DS2.
23 DS3.
24 DS12.
25 DS1, 2, 3, 12, 13.
26 DS12.
27 DS10.
28 DS3.
29 DS12.
30 DS12.
31 DS14.
32 AA5.
33 AA7, 14, 16.
34 AA19.
35 AA18.
36 AA12.
37 P4.
38 Ibid.
39 P6.
40 Ibid.
41 P8.
42 Ibid.
43 P1, 2, 4, 5, 11.
44 P4.
45 P10.
46 A11.
47 N1.
48 DS4.
49 DS18.
50 L13.
51 L22.
52 L14.
53 L14.
54 N2.
55 DS5.
56 Ibid.
57 AA15.
58 AA4.
59 P5.
60 P10.
61 A16, 17.
62 A4.
63 E.g. N2, 5, 6, 9, 16.
64 AA3.
65 L5.
66 Year changed to keep the village's anonymity.
67 VA2.
68 VA15.
69 VA1.
70 Ibid.
71 Ibid.
72 Ibid.
73 VA17.
74 Ibid.
75 Ibid.
76 VA17, VB1, VC1.

77 VB1, VC1.
78 VB1.
79 VA17.
80 VA18.
81 VA17.
82 Ibid.
83 VB1, VC1.
84 VA2.
85 VB1, VC1.

8 African Bargaining Power, Foreign Investment and Development
A Conclusion

8.1 Main Findings

This project was motivated by an empirical puzzle: That some African governments with relatively lower bargaining power – with bargaining power defined here by economic and political structural variables that are less replaceable by exit options for the investor – ask private Chinese investors to contribute more to developing local content than some African governments with relatively higher bargaining power, and that private Chinese investors are, in fact, willing to accept these stronger deals around local participation.

The Weak Bargaining Power Narrative, supported by the traditional development schools, suggests that African countries should act as deal takers and is unable to explain the second part of the empirical observation described above, that private Chinese investors are, in fact, willing to accept these stronger deals. As a result, this project developed a new explanation, the Power of Weak Economies Theory in Chapters 1 and 2. I posited that due to a shift in the global economic and political landscape, private Chinese investors are attracted to the African region and, perhaps surprisingly, are willing to comply with local participation regulations in exchange for large prospective returns.

The empirical evidence provided in Chapter 3 is inconsistent with the Weak Bargaining Power Narrative and supportive of the Power of Weak Economies Theory. Total and private Chinese investments are widespread across the continent, and uncorrelated with the strength of local participation requirements. The analysis suggests that there is indeed space for counties to negotiate more aggressively with Chinese investors, and with private investors in particular.

Chapter 4 tested this proposition more directly by comparing the results of two complementary conjoint experiments conducted with technical advisors and key investment negotiators to the Nigerian government, as well as Chinese companies in Lagos and Ogun States. Both government and company respondents were presented with hypothetical deals with randomized policy attributes that they were asked to rate for attractiveness. By highlighting a statistically significant gap between what the government believed they could ask for regarding local participation (ownership and employment), and what Chinese companies would, in fact, be willing to give, these results also supported the Power of Weak Economies Theory. Chapter 5 extended the experimental findings from Nigeria to observational

DOI: 10.4324/9781003308768-8

evidence from additional four African countries (Kenya, Ethiopia, South Africa, and Tanzania) and described interview results highlighting perceptions of low bargaining power in Kenya and Nigeria, perceptions of medium bargaining power in South Africa, and perceptions of strong bargaining power in Ethiopia and Tanzania.

Chapters 4 and 5 established that a gap exists between perceptions and actual bargaining power in some African countries while Chapters 6 and 7 then dived into why the gap exists and persists. If countries possess bargaining power with Chinese investors regarding local participation, why would some choose to use this power while others would not? I established that what information political actors start the game out with, and what incentives actors have to share information within the game largely determines perceptions of countries' bargaining power. Chapter 6 homed in on the historical relationships between the selected countries and the West, as well as with China. It highlighted that cases with authoritarian or one-state dominant systems and a socialist past have learned over time that Chinese investors stay, even under stricter local participation regulations. In contrast, such regulations were seemingly always out of any feasible policy range for countries with closer relations to the West and competitive multi-party systems that – with every new party in power – led to information-erasing, constant new learning and re-defining of a relationship to the West and the East.

Chapter 7 then showed that centralized political systems – that either emerge from strong parties or strong de facto centralized institutions – encourage political actors to share information on Chinese investment flows, while de-centralized systems with high levels of political competition and clientelism tend to disincentivize politicians at various sub-levels to share information on Chinese investment flows "up" to the central government. Overall, out of the cases studied, it is, therefore, governments of authoritarian or one-party dominant systems with a longer-term ruling party, like Ethiopia or Tanzania, who are very confident in their bargaining power with private Chinese investors, while governments in competitive democracies, like Nigeria or Kenya, lack the same confidence.

The main contribution of this piece is the finding that several African governments can, in fact, act as price setters in local participation with private Chinese investors, and that perceptions of bargaining power – that are shaped through both historical frames and incentives to share information with other political actors – fundamentally matter for investment deal outcomes. With the crisis in the West, which started with the financial crash in 2008, China stepped in to "fill the void" that the West had left behind in Africa, and has been increasing its presence until today. Since then, China–Africa studies have asked many questions around the Chinese strategy in Africa. For example, is China only interested in oil and other natural resources? Is China directly supporting authoritarian regimes such as Sudan and Zimbabwe? Is China hurting efforts to promote democracy and human rights? Or, is China making corruption worse? This one-sided perspective in the literature may have given the impression that the African region is one passive unit that is essentially a price taker of global economic and political power dynamics. After all, the whole strand of literature is called "China–Africa studies", not "Africa–China studies", although the phenomenon is taking place on the African continent.

This project strongly questions this perspective and shows that questions such as: "Will China develop or exploit Africa?" are the wrong ones to ask. I have provided evidence that whether the rising Chinese presence in Africa leads to positive or negative development outcomes fundamentally depends on the development strategies that individual African governments decide on. As a result, this project calls for a shift in the China–Africa literature to pose fewer absolute questions that assume that one China–Africa story exists on the continent, and to instead study different China–Africa stories that may vary depending on host countries' strategies.

8.2 Policy Implications

This book started with a roundtable discussion of four development experts, who were discussing how African countries could not only attract larger amounts of foreign investments, but also request more local benefits from investors for their economies. The evidence presented here shows that African governments could be implementing stricter local content policies with private Chinese investors. But governments are, of course, dealing with a multitude of foreign investors, whose sensitivity around local ownership and employment may substantially differ. After all, the analysis of policy shocks across countries in Chapter 1 showed that US investors would, in fact, exit African markets under stricter policy regulations. And while Chinese investments on the continent have been growing the fastest over the past two decades, Western investment still accounts for by far the largest share of foreign investment in the African region. How can policy makers then meaningfully use the findings of this book to implement laws that both attract the maximum number of investors while also ensuring that those willing to contribute to local content, in fact, do so?

The surprisingly simple solution could be "policy menus" that allow for maximum buy-in from both Western and Chinese investors. The Ethiopian government is already implementing a policy menu around minimum investment and local content, where foreigners can choose between investing a higher or lower minimum capital, depending on whether the investment is jointly made with a domestic investor. Yet, the regulation is not fully effective as bigger companies who are also able to invest larger amounts would have more capacity to benefit from economies of scale around training for more employees, but they are the ones that can opt out of the local content requirement. Instead, it is smaller companies who invest less who are incentivized to find a domestic partner, and whose impact on human capital development will be more limited.

Instead, policy menus that offer a trade-off between tax and local content restrictions would be more effective. An example would be the following:

Tax and Local Content Regulations:
Foreign investors are required to pay a corporate income tax of:

- *30 percent for a wholly foreign owned enterprise, or*
- *25 percent if at least half of the company management is local, or*
- *20 percent if set up with a domestic investor under a Joint-Venture Agreement*

Such a policy menu would benefit both investors and governments. Western investors, who appear to be more sensitive around local content policies, may choose to pay higher taxes and employ foreign personnel, while – as the results from two conjoint experiments in Nigeria have also shown – Chinese investors may opt for local content over higher taxes.

Both taxes and local content should contribute to human capital development. Companies either: pay taxes, through which the government can finance education programs, or, companies finance training themselves, thereby transferring skills to locals. Incentivizing companies to train internally may have several benefits in environments like Nigeria, where the number of unemployed university graduates was estimated to be between 20 and 25 million in 2019, yet where development organizations have been pouring money into building more universities. What Nigeria needs is targeted vocational training that matches the needs of industry. And asking foreign companies to help "getting the job done" would be beneficial. Other countries such as Rwanda or Ethiopia have already done so: As Bräutigam (2011) writes, the

> Ethiopian government asked China to establish a college that would focus on construction and industrial skills. The fully-equipped Ethio-China Polytechnic College opened in late 2009, funded by Chinese aid. Chinese professors offer a two-year degree with Chinese language classes alongside engineering skills. Chinese companies are waiting to hire its first crop of graduates.

On the flip side, are there also benefits for investors to local content in the African context? First, in the search for specialized vocational skills, it often makes sense for foreign companies to institutionalize training of local employees. In Ethiopia, several Chinese companies shared with me that although they had hired locals who had graduated from vocational schools, they ended up having to re-train them.

Second, the third assumption for the theory advanced here was that governments have credible commitment issues with foreign investors, and that foreign investors want to minimize re-negotiation risks, which can both be solved by creating mutual dependencies, such as through local participation. This sparks two questions: As governments, how can you provide enough commitment to foreign investors so that they would enter, but not too much that they have a free hand to do as they please? And as investors, how do you negotiate deals to minimize the re-negotiation risk, that is, that the government does not later decide to open up negotiations again once capital has already been moved to the country?

By creating mutual dependencies through ownership or employment requirements, both issues can be mediated. For example, establishing a Joint-Venture between a local and a foreign firm with 50:50 ownership creates more mutual dependencies than a 40:60 division, where the partner with 60 percent ownership maintains the upper hand.

Steven Chapman, group vice-president at Cummins, a multinational engine producer, summarized in a lecture[1] at the School of Management at Yale University in 2018, that when Cummins entered China soon after its economic opening in 1978, he knew his company should focus on engine production, while local truckers should remain responsible for distribution, where both sides need and depend on each other.

In addition, for companies to be perceived as "local" may also shield against political risks. During the 2016 State of Emergency in Ethiopia, protestors burnt down factories perceived as "foreign". As one South African interviewee shared with me, in Ethiopia, the South African Industrial Development Cooperation (IDC), together with PPC South Africa built a cement plant in Ethiopia that was located right next to Dangote's plant. During the state of emergency, locals burnt down factories around Addis Ababa to protest against foreign investment with few benefits for the population. Interestingly, protestors marched around the PPC South Africa plant to attack Dangote's plant, which, according to a senior level employee at the IDC, had one reason: the PPC plant has 17,000 local shareholders and is, therefore, perceived as a local project which has significantly reduced the risk of the project. In his conversations with the Chinese investors, the IDC officer shares this story and stresses that if they do not involve locals in their projects, they will be "viewed as an external player, and with that comes risk". When I asked how the Chinese generally respond, he continued:

> The Chinese reception was pretty positive... they saw the importance but at the same time, the Chinese only know Chinese... when you tell them things like this, they accept it logically... but in their heart, I am not sure, it will take time for them to understand the benefits.

The Algerian company mentioned in Chapter 5, who told the NIPC that they would, in fact, be happy to include a local partner, was, therefore, probably acting out of self-interest because they had understood that incorporating someone local may help to mediate political risks.

8.3 The Future of African Economic and Political Development

I have shown that African governments have space to strategize around private Chinese investments in their economies. What should these governments use this space for? There are three variables that are key to both economic and institutional development: first, economic growth; second, economic diversification; and third, an export-oriented focus. There are numerous reasons as to why countries should focus on these three variables. First, manufacturing generates more economic activity per dollar of production than any other sector in the economy (IFC 2020). Empirical evidence shows that without building a path of industrialization, very limited long-term economic development will follow (e.g. Haraguchi et al. 2017). Second, while literature can still say surprisingly little about the advent of democratization, Przeworski et al. (2000) show that democracies are more likely to survive with a per capita income of $14,300 (2019) and a diversified economy. Also, in places where politics is usually the only sector to earn a significant amount of money such as Nigeria, a diversified economy suddenly offers lucrative exit options to ruling politicians in the private economy. In turn, this creates room in the political sphere for individuals motivated by other factors that are less monetary in nature.

So, investing in growth and diversification should stabilize existing democratic states in the African region.

Third and finally, one of the major flaws of import substitution industrialization starting in the 1950s was that it was not export-focused, which should be set in place now together with a more Pan-African view towards development. An export focus is important especially for developing nations as they can strategize around manufacturing products for a global consumer market, rather than being limited by the often low purchasing power of their own population and insufficient supply channels due to high transportation costs. In addition, exports also serve the purpose of earning foreign currency.

When assessing the longer term economic and political development in the African region, we, therefore, generally need to ask whether – based on the theory advanced here – different African countries are likely to set in place policies to grow and diversify from agriculture and raw material to more sophisticated forms of agriculture and manufacturing that are export-oriented.

Literature suggests that democracy fosters growth by improving the accumulation of human capital, and by lowering inflation and income inequality (e.g. Doucouliagos and Ulubaşoğlu 2008, Tavares and Wacziarg 2001). But, in environments with little transparency, ethnic voting, and weak institutions, the promoted benefits of democracies may have less room to come into play. In addition, I show that at least the democracies studied here have strong historical relationships to the West, which has promoted the view that local content requirements, supposed to foster additional human capital transfers, are out of the feasible policy range for many African countries. Further, the de-centralized nature of these democracies may constitute an additional disadvantage in which information sharing is inhibited. It is then, perhaps surprisingly, one-party dominant systems or authoritarian countries that have looked toward the East and implemented more state-led models that also include human capital transfer requirements.

At the same time, Rodrik's (1997) findings that democracies yield more predictable long-run growth rates; that they produce greater stability in economic performance; and that they handle adverse shocks better, as well as pay higher wages certainly, also produces important questions on the long-term viability of countries' political regimes and development strategies studied here. It is beyond the scope of this project to study or make claims about general long-term viability of democratic versus authoritarian systems for development prospects in the African region, which is certainly mediated by the de facto strength of democratic institutions in Africa in the first place. But, there are still important lessons to be learned from the theory advanced here on growth and diversification and the survival of political regimes that may provide us with an indication about the future of economic and political environment in the selected cases, and on the continent more generally.

8.3.1 Growth and Diversification

I have shown that background conditions in countries like Ethiopia and Tanzania have so far been more conducive to building an FDI policy ecosystem that allows for local human capital and technology transfers that help to grow the economy and to diversify toward industry. In contrast, countries like Nigeria and Kenya have been held back by their legacies of close relations to the West and de-centralization. Notably, Nigeria does not even have a stand-alone industrialization plan. At the same time, any path-dependent theory needs to account for waning over time. So, we need to analyze how Western influence in these countries, and the dynamics of competition across ministries and sub-units may be changing for the discussed country cases. Based on the theory advanced here, will countries like Nigeria and Kenya start to utilize this space more in the near future? And will governments like those of Tanzania and Ethiopia continue to substantially benefit from the more aggressive stance that they have taken with private Chinese players?

The analysis of US and Chinese investment patterns around policy shocks across six African countries in Chapter 2 suggested that US firms may be significantly less willing to provide local transfers compared to Chinese firms. And as my interviews show, the Western narrative is still highly visible in the ideological, educational, and intellectual spheres in Nigeria and Kenya. At US $2.2 billion in 2017, Nigeria is still the second largest US export destination in Africa, closely followed by Kenya. An example of continued Western influence is the plastic industry, with plastic being the biggest US export source to Kenya with sales totaling Sh 6.21 billion (around 60 million US dollars) last year. The country banned plastic bags in 2018 but has recently been considering lifting these policies amidst new trade talks with the United States in 2020. The US is now pushing for relaxed policies through the American Chemistry Council (ACC), a trade association with members such as Shell, Exxon, and Total, as it would enable them to build a platform for expanding exports to new growth markets across sub-Saharan Africa (Olingo 2020).

Yet, with the rapid rise of Chinese businesses and investments in both countries, there certainly is a possibility that this Western influence will slowly wane. For example, Kenya and Nigeria have started to become more aggressive now about raising tax revenues. In July 2020, both countries announced that they would begin taxing Silicon Valley's global tech companies Facebook, Google, or Uber in their economies (Kazeem 2020).

Another example is that China had notably sent a team of medical experts to Nigeria in April 2020 during the first Covid-19-induced lockdown while a Western response to the virus outbreak in Africa was missing (certainly also because the West was dealing with their own domestic outbreaks). Kenya has also publicly praised the support it received from China to combat the Covid-19 crisis. These developments stand out as interesting, since it had traditionally been the United States that had provided fast humanitarian assistance and, with that, achieved soft power influence that China now appears to want to be taking over.

Certainly, the relationship between Nigeria and China has also been complicated by the maltreatment of Nigerians in China during the outbreak, where Nigerians were evicted from their houses out of fear that they were carrying the virus. Or, in Kenya, where a racial slur by a Chinese businessman against his employees in 2018 was widely covered by the media and resulted in his public deportation from Kenya. Then again, in early April 2020, right after the announcement of the hard Covid-19-induced lockdown in Nigeria, the company Enterprise

Limited (LPLEL) received an infusion of US $221,047,248 (N83.997 billion) equity funding from China Harbour Engineering Company (CHEC) for the Lekki Free Trade Zone Port. Or, in Kenya, also amidst the Covid-19 outbreak in August 2020, both governments hosted a China–Kenya online Investment and Cooperation Dialogue on the healthcare and light manufacturing sectors (XinhuaNet 2020). All these events may be signals that the Chinese government is pushing its expansionary investment quest, despite the recent downturn of its domestic economy.

The discussion above shows that Nigeria and Kenya are two of the most important strategic investment destinations for both private and state investment on the African continent, so we may observe more economic rivalries between the US and China in these two countries soon. At the same time, there are no clear signals that the lack of cooperation across ministries and states (in Nigeria) and counties (in Kenya) will wane any time soon. Both countries would need to solve their issues of unifying countries that are still largely split by ethnic (and religious in Nigeria) identities that hinder information-sharing incentives between political actors. The countries would also need to invest more financial resources in building stronger centralized institutions that are able to keep oversight of investment inflows beyond the immediate reach of influence.

On the other extreme of the spectrum, Ethiopia and Tanzania appear to have been reaffirmed in their development strategies by their high growth rates over the past 20 years. Their economic success has equipped them with the confidence to carry on with their more state-centric development models. For example, the Ethiopian ambassador to China, Teshome Toga Chanaka, announced at the end of April 2020 that his country would be pursuing even closer relations with China after the Covid-19 outbreak, and that its Belt and Road projects (including the Addis Ababa-Djibouti Railway, the economic corridor, and the development of industrial parks) would be slowed, but would still be brought to completion. In Tanzania, President Magafuli, during his election campaign in 2020, battled against Canadian mining giant Barrick Gold Corp for a 60 percent share for the government in three of its gold mines to end the "exploitation" of Tanzania's resources. He eventually settled for 16 percent but also canceled two Chinese infrastructure projects, the building of Tanzania's first electric railway line linking the main commercial city Dar es Salaam to the capital Dodoma, and the construction of East Africa's biggest port in Bagamoyo at a cost of $10bn. He stated in local news that only a "madman" would accept the financial conditions offered in the deals. So, overall, it is likely that the Ethiopian and Tanzanian development strategies will be reinforced and strengthened by their strong parties and unitary states although it remains to be seen how experiments such as in Tanzania, where President Magafuli is testing out Chinese investors, will eventually play out.

These trajectories, then, also have different implications for growth and diversification, which in turn influence economic and political development. The Ethiopian and Tanzanian governments have noticed the Chinese interest in manufacturing, and are using local participation policies to force technology spillovers and human capital development that are needed in order to create multiplier effects for industrialization. In contrast, a study conducted by Johns-Hopkins University's

194 A Conclusion

China–Africa Initiative on Chinese manufacturing in Nigeria shows limited technology transfers due to a lack of a "more coherent strategy…to leverage this new, growing source of capital and the potential resources it brings." (Chen et al. 2016, p. 1) Together with other forces (for example that the Nigerian economy is also largely dependent on oil and, therefore, exposed to the risk of the oil curse), growth and diversification appear more likely in countries such as Ethiopia and Tanzania in the near future. Similarly, with little growth and diversification, the survival of democratic regimes seems to also not be directly fostered through Chinese and foreign investment in Kenya or Nigeria.

8.3.2 Survival of Authoritarian Regimes

While growth and diversification can provide us with insights on economic development and the survival of democratic regimes, what can the theory offered here tell us about the future of authoritarian regimes? China is often accused of actively pursuing an expansionary political mission where it is supporting authoritarian regimes and making democratic transitions less likely. The argument here shows that the incentives of at least the small and medium private Chinese players in Africa are non-political in nature, and that these firms are also small enough to eschew the direct control of the Chinese government. I have argued that the influence of these firms on political regimes is, therefore, more indirect, and again driven by the respective development strategies advanced by individual African governments. This is because, as modernization theory suggests, growth in itself can be an inherent threat to the survival of authoritarian regimes: Growth may lead to socio-economic changes (e.g. the formation and organization of a middle class) that is conducive to democratic change. At the same time, and as China has also shown, the government's ability to suppress as well as their performance legitimacy also play a role. Since growth and inequality move in opposite directions at early stages of development, governments may then have to perform a balancing act between growth and distribution in order to stay in power.

The one authoritarian example studied here is Ethiopia. Many of my interviewees told me that as a result of the rapid annual growth rate of around 10 percent between 2007 and 2018 (compared to a regional average of 5.4 percent),[2] the government is dealing with inflation that brings about rising food and housing prices. Emerging from a socialist tradition, where the government used to provide food and housing subsidies, the attempted switch towards a more market-led strategy has created winners and losers that in theory may pose a threat to the rule of the current government. At the same time, the mechanisms pointed out in Chapters 5 and 6 that determine how Ethiopia strategizes around foreign investment are also at play for the government's ability to strategize around other policy areas, and to quickly adapt to new economic realities that require a political response. Many interviewees shared with me that they look towards South Korea's and China's development models, which are famous for their exceptional policy agility around economic and social changes. For example, the government is holding monthly meetings with different stakeholder groups in industries and labor unions in order to gauge sentiments from the population and special interest groups.

The survival of the Prosperity Party (former EPRDF but excluding the TPLF) as the ruling power in Ethiopia, therefore, certainly depends on how the party manages different domestic interests and ethnic groups (and tensions are certainly visible, for example. in the recent Tigray conflict in November 2020), but the outlined favorable background conditions around centralization may render its survival more likely in the near future.

8.4 Implications for Other African Recipients of Chinese Investments

How far do the results travel from the five case studies across the African continent? This study deliberately focused on African countries with strong or very strong bargaining power with private Chinese investors, who are the top recipients of Chinese investments. Yet, an important caveat to the theory developed here is that I included Ethiopia, Nigeria, and South Africa in my sample, who are continent's most famous examples of de-centralization. While other African countries have also been experimenting with devolution, there are no cases that would match the extent of de-centralization executed in Nigeria or Kenya. As a result, centralization plays an important role for my sample but has less of an explanatory power beyond.

Still, the theory in this book predicts that among the top receivers of Chinese investments in Africa, the ones with authoritarian or one-party dominant systems will negotiate stronger deals than those with competitive democracies. And a country comparison reveals that this is indeed the case: the average polity IV score for countries negotiating aggressive deals (Deal quality score > 10) is 1.43 (qualifying as anocracy), while the score for countries negotiating more investor-friendly scores is 6.43 (qualifying as democracy). Three outliers are Algeria and Mozambique, whose democracy scores are high for their aggressive investment policies (2 and 5, respectively), while Egypt's democracy score is low for its lax investment policies. But deeper analysis shows that again, countries' relationships to China and the West as well as party competition have largely influenced leaders' learning about the feasible policy range around local participation policies, which has ultimately influenced countries' approach toward foreign and Chinese investors.

The Democratic Republic of Congo was governed for nearly two decades by President Joseph Kabila before the election of Félix Tshisekedi in 2019, rendering it a classic case of a ruling government with long-policy horizons that has had historically close ties to China. A symbol of the close relationship is that in July 2019, UN ambassadors of 37 countries, including the DRC, signed a joint letter to the UNHRC defending China's treatment of Uyghurs and other Muslim ethnic minorities. Meanwhile, the United States actively supported Zairian president Mobutu Sese Seko during the Cold War to prevent the spread of Marxism. But with the fall of the Soviet Union, the relationship has since centered on economic objectives, humanitarian efforts, and democratization.

Similarly in Angola, the Chinese government has been scolded by the international community for offering multi-billion-dollar resource backed loans (Bräutigam 2009) to the People's Movement for the Liberation of Angola, which has ruled Angola since the country's independence from Portugal in 1975. During the Cold War, the party was linked to the European and Soviet communist parties, and is now a member of the Socialist International grouping of social democratic parties. And business ties to China are also close: Already, back in 2008, Huawei established a training facility in Angola, and in 2020 created a partnership with the government to train university students and state workers on new information technologies.

Zimbabwe was ruled by Robert Mugabe for 29 years, and his Zimbabwe African National Union (ZANU) was actively supported by communist powers during the Cold War, and itself with Maoism versus Marxist-Leninism. Zimbabwe's close ties to China have persisted since, with Russia and China, for example, vetoing UN Zimbabwe sanctions pushed by Britain and the US after election results were withheld in March 2008.

The Mozambique Liberation Front (FRELIMO) was officially Marxist-Leninist during the Cold War and has ruled the country since independence in 1975, and social democratic today, rendering it a classic one-party dominant state. Algeria is classified as an open anocracy, mostly because military and intelligence services effectively limit democracy. Algeria's fight for independence from France in the 1950s was also characterized by the emergence of socialist political thought in contrast to liberal-capitalist France, and the CCP has been supporting the Front de Libération Nation, Algeria's dominating party, since independence.

Meanwhile, Zambia, Ghana, and Mauritius all had frequent changes in political rulers and a closer relationship to the West. Egypt is an outlier in the group of "investor-friendly deals" as it classifies as an anocracy. The key difference to countries negotiating strong deals is that Egypt has never experimented with socialist policies, and has received large aid packages from the US in exchange for its liberal economic reforms. After the death of President Gamal Abdel Nasser, Egypt switched its Cold War allegiance to the United States and launched multiple economic reforms to encourage foreign investment that President Mubarak has continued to pursue since 1991, with IMF assistance.

I deliberately leave out countries with weak or medium bargaining power. Although I do not have enough data from other African countries, and more systematic research needs to reach conclusive evidence, an analysis of general trends suggests that smaller receivers are also allocated an investment pie from China that is dependent on economic and diplomatic factors but, importantly, is independent of countries' local participation policies. As a result, there is also room for some of these countries to strategize more around private Chinese investment projects.

This is also relevant to Francophone West Africa, a region where the term "Françafrique" is still commonly used to describe the sphere of France's influence over its former colonies in Africa. What may be surprising, though, is that China has, in fact, already displaced France as the leading exporter to most of these countries. Beijing has explicitly supported Senegal as the "gateway to West Africa", with President Xi visiting the country in 2018, baptizing it a Comprehensive Strategic Partner and the first West African state to join the Belt and Road Initiative, and selecting it as the first Francophone and West African country to host the FOCAC Summit (held in Dakar in 2021). Private Chinese investors are more concentrated in West African countries with natural resources endowments, but are also present in those without (Chen et al. 2018), and have entered sectors that have traditionally been occupied by French firms, such as civil engineering, extractives, and telecoms.

How is Francophone West Africa responding to these shifting dynamics with such a strong historical relationship to France? Soulé (2019) is one of the first scholars to focus on the relationship between the Francophone West African region and China, which has received relatively less attention in China–Africa studies. She analyzed infrastructure deals in West Africa and put forward four recommendations to governments on how to negotiate better deals around local participation ("1. involve everyone, 2. empower the negotiators, 3. keep the public onside, 4. increase knowledge"). While these recommendations are applaudable, this project has argued that we first need to understand the driving forces of weak deals, and that countries' strategies could also still be heavily influenced by the French narrative. A more systematic study on perceptions of bargaining power and drivers of weak deals in the Francophone African region would, therefore, be very valuable.

Other smaller players on the African continent are also coming up with strategies around private Chinese investors. Rwanda, a small landlocked country with limited natural resources, is a fitting example. In 2013, the Rwandan government adopted an Economic Development and Poverty Reduction Strategy II (2013–2018), which aimed to increase "export orientation of firms in Rwanda's manufacturing" under a "Made in Rwanda" push into global textiles. As part of the plan, Rwanda, together with the East African Community, proposed a plan to ban the import of secondhand clothes from the United States in 2015. Yet in 2017, Kenya, Uganda, and Tanzania backed out amidst threats from the US government to withdraw their status from selling clothes to the US duty free under the African Growth and Opportunity Act (AGOA). Rwanda's President Paul Kagame remained firm:

> This is the choice we find that we have to make. As far as I am concerned, making the choice is simple [although] we might suffer consequences [...] Rwanda and other countries in the region that are part of AGOA, [sic] have to do other things – we have to grow and establish our industries.
>
> (Africanews 2017)

Kenya's benefits from the AGOA are certainly considerably more important than Rwanda's: Exports from Kenya to the US amounted to nearly $600 m (£450 m) in 2017, compared to just $43 m (£32 m) for Rwanda. At the same time, this offers smaller countries like Rwanda an opportunity to build a strong local manufacturing base and to grow their relative industrial importance in clothes, from which to export to markets in Europe or Asia. My interviews reveal that with the Covid-19 crisis in 2020, Chinese companies in Nigeria have been considering, even more loudly now, moving manufacturing out of China, and building more resilient supply chains. So, the current crisis may also offer an opportunity to smaller countries like Rwanda to attract more Chinese investments, to specialize in one industry, and also to emphasize local content.

Similar to the Chinese Polytech School in Ethiopia, Rwanda is currently building a Luban Workshop, a vocational skill training center, a pledge made by Xi Jinping during the Forum on China–Africa Cooperation in 2018. Evidence like this suggests that the Rwandan government is aware of its bargaining power with China, and actively using it to accomplish its "Made in Rwanda" plan. The reasons for the high awareness can again be traced back to the causal mechanisms outlined in Chapters 5 and 6: Rwanda's relationship to the West was severely stained by the lack of Western response to the Rwandan genocide in 1994. While the United States and Europe have since then paid arguably disproportionately high attention to Rwanda given its small size and landlocked position, Paul Kagame has sought a development course that more resembles China's developmental state and state-directed capitalism. The strongly centralized nature of the state certainly helped him to rally political representatives around advancing the agenda; and to gain information from across regions in a comparably very small country. Overall, the Rwandan example, therefore, appear to be supporting the theory advanced here. Yet, more research is certainly needed to substantiate these claims with more empirical evidence.

8.5 Future Research Areas

I have, on purpose, focused only on small and medium private Chinese investors as the incentives on the investor side can be isolated from political incentives in a rather clean fashion. Certainly, Chinese private investments are only a small part of Chinese engagement in Africa, and there is definitely much more to learn from how African players behave around other types of Chinese engagement (loans, trade, and aid). Fraser (2010) made an important start by analyzing the aid negotiations of African governments with international donors against economic, political, ideological, and the institutional conditions under which these negotiations occur. Swedlund (2017) also shared insights on Chinese aid negotiations by focusing on the presence or absence of credible commitments from both donor agencies and recipient governments for successful aid delivery over the long term. Once we have insights from different types of negotiations (trade, investment, loans, and aid), we can then pull together how these negotiations are interlinked.

Since the Chinese banks that provide loans to African players are large, based in China and under strong political control of the Chinese government, the CCP's political aspirations are certainly significantly more present in loan and aid negotiations. I, therefore, expect the bargaining space around loans and aid to be smaller, relative to the one around investments, although there are clear and recent examples, where governments have successfully re-negotiated loan conditions with China. This includes Ethiopia's successful requests for the extensions of loan payback time for a multitude of Belt and Road projects that should be studied in more detail in the future.

Overall, I show for the first time that there is substantial space on the African side to influence the "China–Africa" story and call for a shift in China–Africa literature towards a more Africa-focused perspective. While studies often compare and contrast African development models with either Western or East Asian approaches, there is also a striking lack of focus among scholars and policy makers on what African countries could be learning from each other. In particular, my interviews with African government officials revealed a significant lack of comparison within the continent. The majority of respondents listed Western capitalist thought, or Chinese and South Korean development models as inspirational to their countries' own development trajectory, but few mentioned inspirational examples coming from within the African continent itself. Specifically, some Nigerian government officials were surprised to hear about Ethiopia's industrialization policy, or that countries like Ethiopia, Rwanda, or Cote d'Ivoire were among the fastest growing countries in the world. Scholars and practitioners should, therefore, place more emphasis on African success stories in a comparative perspective on the continent, and study the lessons that could be useful for, and applied to, a broader set of countries in the region.

8.6 Conclusion

Development literature tends to take a pessimistic view on the bargaining space of African countries. And even if governments had space to negotiate stronger deals for their countries, debates around poor governance dominate research and suggest that corruption is the first hurdle to overcome if African countries want to develop. The findings presented here challenge the assumption that governments are always aware of their bargaining power with different investors. The project instead highlights that some countries in the African region may have an "image problem" that perpetuates perceptions of weak bargaining power both externally (Western thought and perceptions of the regions), and internally (perceptions of African leaders themselves).

As mentioned in the introduction, China's image in the world has changed dramatically over the past 40 years. When Western companies first started to invest in China, products manufactured in China had a reputation of being cheap in price and rather poor in quality. Yet, fast forward to today, and China is actively competing with the United States' high-tech industry, and even triggering a trade war. Interestingly, the literature on China's development is not called "The West in China." We instead use terms such as "China Rising", "China's Growth Miracle", or "China's Development Model" to describe China's impressive economic transformation over the past 40 years.

Similarly, the findings here show that what we should not only ask questions about China's strategy in Africa. Instead, the "China–Africa" story is fundamentally about how several African countries strategize around the changing international political and economic order, and its impact on domestic and foreign investment (of which Chinese investment is one part), in order to grow, diversify, export, and ultimately develop in the long term. What we have learned from other successful development stories over past 40 years is that having one national strategy is paramount to this success. Countries are better equipped to come up with such a strategy if they are able to overcome coordination problems across ministries and sub-regional units, as well as if they can detach themselves from the narrative imposed by traditional development thought about the region. In view of the rise of a new global player, it is time for the African region to adopt new strategies that respond to the new global geopolitical dynamics and emphasize growth, diversification, and export-orientation. It is the hope that we can then talk about a "Nigerian", "Ethiopian", "Kenyan", "Tanzanian", "South African", "Rwandan" – or more broadly, a "Pan-African" – stand-alone development model, that will hopefully lead to sustainable growth and long-term prosperity in the region.

Notes

1 As part of Professor Ian Shapiro and Professor Mushfiq Mobarak's course: "State and Society".
2 World Bank estimates.

Appendix
Survey Material

Government Survey

| Survey number: | Investment Deal Numbers (4): | Interviewer: | Ministry/ Office: | Date: |

Please introduce yourself using the following script:

> Good morning/Good afternoon, my name is [insert research team member's name] and I am from the Public and Private Development Center, a Nigerian NGO. We are working together with Christina Seyfried, a PhD candidate at Yale University, on a research project concerning the attractiveness of Nigeria's investment policies to foreign companies.
>
> Participation will involve answering some questions about your experience operating in Nigeria's foreign investment policy environment and rating some hypothetical investment deals. You are not obliged to answer any questions you would prefer not to, and your involvement would require 20 minutes of your time.
>
> There are no known or anticipated risks to you for participating. The answers are completely confidential, anonymous, and will only serve the research project. Your responses will be handwritten and not shared with third parties.
>
> The anonymous survey forms will be stored in a locked cabinet and will be immediately destroyed once the study is completed.
>
> Participation in this study is completely voluntary. You are free to decline to participate, to end participation at any time for any reason, or to refuse to answer any individual question. Your decision whether or not to participate in this study will not affect your relationship with PPDC or Yale. We hope that the results will help us to learn more about the role of effective policies to attract foreign businesses.

If you have any questions about this study, you may contact the investigator, Christina Seyfried, christina.seyfried@yale.edu.

If you would like to talk with someone other than the researchers to discuss problems or concerns, to discuss situations in the event that a member of the research team is not available, or to discuss your rights as a research participant, you may contact the Yale University Human Subjects Committee, 203-785-4688, human.subjects@yale.edu. Additional information is available at: https://your.yale.edu/research-support/human-research/research-participants/rights-research-participant

Do you have any questions at this time? Would you like to participate in the study?

Note: The person must give his or her informed consent by answering positively. If participation is refused, walk away and record this here –

Reasons for Unsuccessful Meeting:

_____

If consent was given, please proceed to the questionnaire. If a respondent firmly refuses to answer any question, write "refused" in the answer space and continue to the next question.

Background Questions:

INTERVIEWER: Let's begin by recording a few facts about yourself.

1. What region in Nigeria do you come from? (please circle what is applicable)
   North Central
   North East
   North West
   South East
   South South
   South West
2. Did you also go to school there, or somewhere else?
3. What is your specific role here at [name the ministry/office that you are visiting]?
4. How long have you been working here? Did you work at any other government offices before? If yes, where?
5. Have you advised on investment or trade deals before, or any other deals? If yes, in what capacity?

6   (Only if Q5 was answered with "yes") Could you please tell us a bit about the negotiation processes?
    - Who are the actors usually involved?
    - How do you usually hear about the investor? Who does the investor approach first?
    - How does the decision-making progress work and what is your role as an advisor in the negotiations?

PLEASE DO NOT ASK THE FOLLOWING QUESTIONS DIRECTLY BUT WRITE DOWN AND ESTIMATE BASED ON YOUR PERCEPTION:

7   Age:
8   Gender:

INTERVIEWER: **Ok, thank you. Let's briefly talk about your opinions on the following. Please answer all the questions based on what you have experienced in your day-to-day work.**

1   Have voters in the past asked your office about the conditions specified in the deals? If yes, what were they interested in? (please circle one and take notes if answered with "yes")
    Yes
    No
2   Judging from your past experience, what are important drivers of voters' decision-making during elections?
    (If not mentioned in the list above) Are investment deals an important driver of voters' decision-making during elections? (If respondent says no) – Why not? (Please circle one and take notes if answered with "no")
    Yes
    No
3   Judging from your past experience, have Nigerian businessmen asked your office about investment deals set up by your government office with foreign investors? If yes, what were they interested in? (Please circle one and take notes if answered with "yes")
    Yes
    No
4   Do you believe that the government should generally follow economic deregulation? Can you elaborate on why you think so? (Please circle one and take notes)
    Fully agree
    Somewhat agree
    Somewhat disagree
    Strongly disagree
5   Do you believe that the government should generally follow privatization policies? (Please circle one and take notes)
    Fully agree

Somewhat agree
Somewhat disagree
Strongly disagree
6   Do you think Nigeria should participate as much as possible in open trade? (Please circle one and take notes)
Fully agree
Somewhat agree
Somewhat disagree
Strongly disagree
7   Do you believe the individuals negotiating on behalf of Nigeria with foreign investors are generally skilled negotiators?
Yes
No
8   What makes you believe so, and what could be some challenges?
9   Do you think they are generally experienced negotiators?
Yes
No
10 What makes you believe so, and what could be some challenges?
11 Do Nigerian actors coordinate across relevant government bodies when negotiating with foreign investors?
Yes
No
12 If yes, how does that work? Do you find it effective? If not, how could it be improved?
13 In your opinion, does Nigeria receive little, the same, or a lot of Western money compared to the rest of the African continent? Why do you think so?
Little
Same
A lot
14 In your opinion, does Nigeria receive little, the same, or a lot of Chinese money compared to the rest of the African continent? Why do you think so?
Little
Same
A lot
15 Does Nigeria have no, a few, or a lot of competitors for foreign investment on the continent? Who are they?
A few
A lot
16 Which of the following statements do you think are true? (Please show them the list, printed on a separate document, and let them circle what is appropriate to them. Please attach the form to this survey at the end of the interview)

a. It is easier to negotiate with Western investors than with Chinese ones.
b. It is easier to negotiate with Chinese investors than with Western investors.
c. Nigeria and the West are equal partners.
d. Nigeria and China are equal partners.
e. Nigeria offers land, labor, or raw materials, but foreign investors bring the money. So, foreign investors should have most of the say in investment negotiations.
f. Nigeria is a dwarf and China is a giant.
g. Nigeria has little say in investment deals with the West.
h. Nigeria has little say in investment deals with China.
i. The Chinese are everywhere in Africa, and very aggressive, they will not come to your country if they don't get their way, so you can't negotiate with them.

Conjoint Experiment:

INTERVIEWER: **I am going to read two investment scenarios to you, you can also look at them yourselves after. I would like to hear your opinion on these two deals afterwards.**
(Please read both scenarios, then hand them over to the respondent.)
INTERVIEWER: **Please take as much time as you need to look at these two investment scenarios.**
Time needed to read through the deal pairs: _____
(Once the interviewer looks up)
INTERVIEWER: **Do you have any questions? (Pause) Let's proceed to a few questions regarding your opinion on these two deals.**

1. You want to **maximize the chance of an agreement between the government and the company**. If you were confronted with one of these two deals in your daily work, which one do you think would both the state government and the Chinese company be more likely to sign?
   1
   2
2. In scenario 1, how likely do you think the government and the company would be to both sign the deal?
3. Why?
4. In scenario 2, how likely do you think the government and the company would be to both sign the deal?
5. Why?
6. Given your experience, which deal would the government be likely to prefer?
   1
   2

8   Why?
9   How likely on a scale from 0–3 are you to recommend to the state governor to push Deal 1 forward?
    0
    1
    2
    3
10 Why?
11 How likely on a scale from 0–3 are you to recommend to the state governor to push Deal 2 forward?
    0
    1
    2
    3
12 Why?
13 Do you think the company would sign Deal 1?
    Yes
    No
14 If yes, why? If no, why not?
15 Do you think the company would sign Deal 2?
    Yes
    No
16 If yes, why? If no, why not?
17 How many of the following changes would you make to maximize the chances of the company side signing Deal 1?
    a. Get rid of local participation requirements
    b. Offer more tax incentives
    c. Get rid of license fees
    d. Offer more attractive property rights regulations
    e. Reduce facilitation payments
    f. Reduce environmental regulations
    g. Offer no change in terms for a more extended period of time
18 How many of the following changes would you make to maximize the chances of the company side signing Deal 2?
    a. Get rid of local participation requirements
    b. Offer more tax incentives
    c. Get rid of license fees
    d. Offer more attractive property rights regulations
    e. Reduce facilitation payments
    f. Reduce environmental regulations
    g. Offer no change in terms for a more extended period of time
19 Do you think the government would sign Deal 1?
    Yes
    No
20 If yes, why? If no, why not?

21 Do you think the government would sign Deal 2?
    Yes
    No
22 If yes, why? If no, why not?

INTERVIEWER: **Thank you. Now I am going to read two other investment scenarios to you, again you will can also look at them yourselves after. I would like to hear your opinion on these two deals afterwards.**
(Please read both scenarios, then hand them over to the respondent.)
INTERVIEWER: **Please take as much time as you need to look at these two investment scenarios.**
Time needed to read through the deal pairs: _____
(Once the interviewer looks up)
INTERVIEWER: **Do you have any questions? (Pause) Let's proceed to a few questions regarding your opinions on these two deals.**

1   You want to **maximize the chance of an agreement between the government and the company.** If you were confronted with one of these two deals in your daily work, which one do you think would both the state government and the Chinese company be more likely to sign?
    3
    4
2   In scenario 3, how likely do you think would the government and the company be to both sign the deal?
3   Why?
4   In scenario 4, how likely do you think would the government and the company be to both sign the deal?
5   Why?
6   Given your experience, which deal would the government be likely to prefer?
    3
    4
7   Why?
8   How likely on a scale from 0–3 are you to recommend to the state governor to push Deal 3 forward?
    0
    1
    2
    3
9   Why?
10 How likely on a scale from 0–3 are you to recommend to the state governor to push Deal 4 forward?
    0
    1
    2
    3

11 Why?
12 Do you think the company would sign Deal 3?
    Yes
    No
13 If yes, why? If no, why not?
14 Do you think the company would sign Deal 4?
    Yes
    No
15 If yes, why? If no, why not?
16 How many of the following changes would you make to maximize the chances of the company side signing Deal 3?
    a. Get rid of local participation requirements
    b. Offer more tax incentives
    c. Get rid of license fees
    d. Offer more attractive property rights regulations
    e. Reduce facilitation payments
    f. Reduce environmental regulations
    g. Offer no change in terms for a more extended period of time
17 How many of the following changes would you make to maximize the chances of the company side signing Deal 4?
    a. Get rid of local participation requirements
    b. Offer more tax incentives
    c. Get rid of license fees
    d. Offer more attractive property rights regulations
    e. Reduce facilitation payments
    f. Reduce environmental regulations
    g. Offer no change in terms for a more extended period of time
18 Do you think the government would sign Deal 3?
    Yes
    No
19 If yes, why? If no, why not?
20 Do you think the government would sign Deal 4?
    Yes
    No
21 If yes, why? If no, why not?

(INTERVIEWER: Please read the following text to the respondent and show them the graph attached to this survey package. Please then take notes on the interviewee's response)

Appendix 209

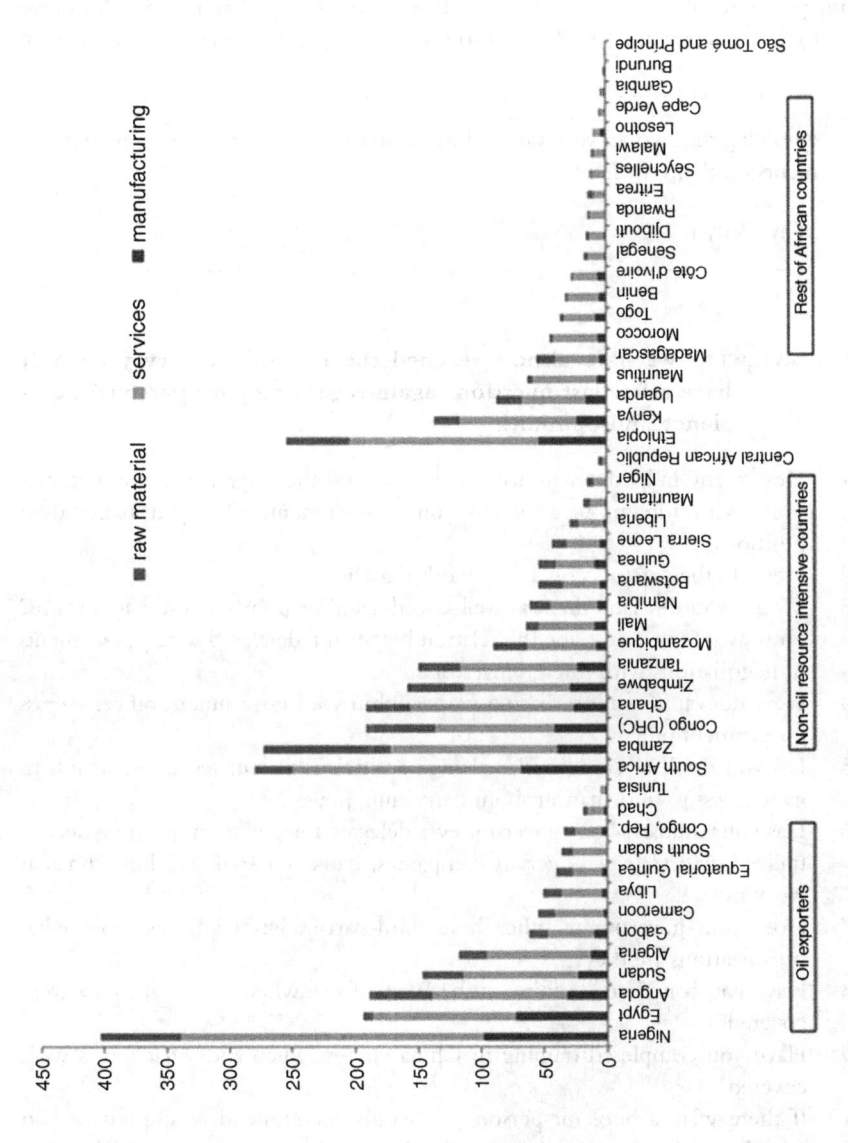

Figure S1.1 Distribution of Chinese ODI Projects by Country and Sector.

Source: Author.

Studies show that Nigeria is the #1 investment destination on the continent for small and medium private Chinese firms. Chinese firms like the cheap land, labor, and the large market size in Nigeria that is unparalleled on the continent. Naturally, the most common response in a survey conducted by us among Chinese manufacturers in Nigeria was along the lines of "Labor is so cheap here, I would stay under any policy regulations". (+show graph below from Chen et al. (2015) This shows that Chinese companies really want to invest and operate in the Nigerian market.

> Knowing this, would you want to impose stricter local participation requirements on them, or not?
>
> Why/Why not?

INTERVIEWER: **We have almost reached the end of the survey an only have a few last questions again regarding your personal experience and opinions.**

1. How many individuals are usually involved on the Nigerian side in negotiations with foreign investors in your government? Can you name their positions?
2. How do these actors concretely work together?
3. Would you describe them as well-coordinated or poorly-coordinated teams? How would you describe the relation between federal and state governments in negotiations with foreign investors?
4. How does information sharing work within your government office? Across government offices?
5. Do you think electoral cycles change politicians' incentives and demands to gain access to information about bargaining power?
6. Has your minister/state governor ever delegated negotiations to more decentralized actors? (e.g. Nigerian companies, banks etc.)? If yes, how did that work out?
7. Does your government office have third-party advisors? If yes, from what organizations are they?
8. Have you completed training in the West? If yes, when and what topics were covered?
9. Have you completed training in China? If yes, when and what topics were covered?
10. If there were a book or person you would recommend whose advice you found inspiring for Nigeria's own development path, what/who would it be?
11. What country, if there is one, do you think Nigeria should aspire to imitate in their development approach?
12. How would you describe the attributes of a "skilled" negotiator?

13 How would you describe the attributes of an "experienced" negotiator?
14 "How do you think have falling oil prices and the devaluation of the naira affected Nigeria's relations with China? With the rest of the world?"
15 "How, if at all, has the Covid-19 outbreak changed your image of China?"

INTERVIEWER: **"Thank you very much for your time!"**

Chinese Company Survey

(All interviewees were shown a Mandarin Chinese version):

Survey number:	Investment Deal Numbers (4):	Interviewer:	Date:

Please introduce yourself using the following script:

> Good morning/Good afternoon, my name is [insert research team member's name] and I am from CitronTechGlobal, a Nigerian consultancy company for Chinese businesses. We are working together with Christina Seyfried, a PhD candidate affiliated with Yale University on a research project concerning the needs and preferences of foreign companies that are running a business in Nigeria.
>
> Participation will involve answering some questions about your experience in Nigeria and rating some hypothetical investment deals. You are not obliged to answer any questions you would prefer not to, and your involvement would require 20 minutes of your time. The results of this survey will only be used for Ms. Seyfried's PhD dissertation.
>
> There are no known or anticipated risks to you for participating. The answers are completely confidential, anonymous and will only serve the research project. No personal or company names will be recorded. Your responses will be handwritten [if conducted via Whatsapp or WeChat – will be written down on a piece of paper and all chats will be deleted immediately after the chat ends] and not shared with third parties.
>
> The anonymous survey forms will be stored in a locked cabinet and will be immediately destroyed once the study is completed.
>
> Participation in this study is completely voluntary. You are free to decline to participate, to end participation at any time for any reason, or to refuse to answer any individual question. Your decision whether or not to participate in this study will not affect your relationship with CitroTechGlobal or Yale. We hope that the results will help us to learn more about the role of effective policies to attract foreign businesses.
>
> If you have any questions about this study, you may contact the investigator, Christina Seyfried, christina.seyfried@yale.edu.
>
> If you would like to talk with someone other than the researchers to discuss problems or concerns, to discuss situations in the event that a

member of the research team is not available, or to discuss your rights as a research participant, you may contact the Yale University Human Subjects Committee, 203-785-4688, human.subjects@yale.edu. Additional information is available at https://your.yale.edu/research-support/human-research/research-participants/rights-research-participant

Do you have any questions at this time? Would you like to participate in the study?

Note: The person must give his or her informed consent by answering positively. If participation is refused, walk away and record this here:

Reasons for Unsuccessful Meeting:

If consent was given, please proceed to the questionnaire. If a respondent firmly refuses to answer any question, write "refused" in the answer space and continue to the next question.

Survey: (Background)

<u>INTERVIEWER:</u> **Let's begin by recording a few background characteristics about your company.**

1. Is your company a private of state-owned enterprise? (please circle one)
   Private
   State-owned enterprise
2. What sector are you working in?
3. What industry are you working in?
4. Would you describe your industry as very competitive (there are a lot of competitors in the same market), or are you one of the only players?
5. How many employees does the company have?
6. How many years has your company been operating in Nigeria?

<u>INTERVIEWER:</u> **Thank you. I am going to read two investment scenarios to you, you can also look at them yourselves after. I would like to hear your opinion on these two deals afterwards.**
(Please read both scenarios, then hand them over to the respondent)

<u>INTERVIEWER:</u> **Please take as much time as you need to look at these two investment scenarios.**
Time needed to read through the deal pairs: _____
(Once the interviewer looks up)

<u>INTERVIEWER:</u> **Do you have any questions? (Pause) Let's proceed to a few questions regarding your opinions on these two deals.**

1. Which one of the two deals presented above would you prefer to sign?
   1
   2
2. How likely on a scale from 0–3 are you to sign deal 1 (0 = definitely not sign, 3 = definitely sign)?
   0
   1
   2
   3
3. Why?
4. What would you like to change about deal 1 if you could?
   a. Get rid of local participation requirements
   b. Offer more tax incentives
   c. Reduce license fees
   d. Reduce facilitation payments
   e. Offer more attractive property rights regulations
   f. Reduce environmental regulations
   g. Offer more assistance in setting up and running the business in Nigeria
   h. Offer no change in terms for a more extended period of time
5. How likely do you think the government would be to agree with your changes and sign the new deal?
6. How likely on a scale from 0–3 are you to sign deal 2?
   0
   1
   2
   3
7. Why?
8. What would you like to change about deal 2 if you could?
   a. Get rid of local participation requirements
   b. Offer more tax incentives
   c. Reduce license fees
   d. Reduce facilitation payments
   e. Offer more attractive property rights regulations
   f. Reduce environmental regulations
   g. Offer more assistance in setting up and running the business in Nigeria
   h. Offer no change in terms for a more extended period of time
9. How likely do you think the government would be to agree with your changes and sign the new deal?
10. (Only ask if they ranked deal 1 and/or deal 2 low) – If you are very unlikely to sign deal 1/2 and you can't operate in Nigeria, where else are you going to go where you think business operations will be better? In Africa? In the world?

INTERVIEWER: Now I am going to read two other investment scenarios to you, you will can also look at them yourselves after. I would like to hear your opinion on these two deals afterwards.

(Please read both scenarios, then hand them over to the respondent)

INTERVIEWER: Please take as much time as you need to look at these two investment scenarios.

Time needed to read through the deal pairs: _____

(Once the interviewer looks up)

INTERVIEWER: Do you have any questions? (Pause) Let's proceed to a few questions regarding your opinion on these two deals.

1. Which one of the two deals presented above would you prefer to sign?
   3
   4
2. How likely on a scale from 0–3 are you to sign deal 3 (0 = definitely not sign, 3 = definitely sign)?
   0
   1
   2
   3
3. Why?
4. What would you like to change about deal 3 if you could?
5. How likely on a scale from 0–3 are you to sign deal 4?
   0
   1
   2
   3
6. Why?
7. What would you like to change about deal 4 if you could?
8. How likely do you think the government would be to agree with your changes and sign the new deal?
9. (Only ask if they ranked deal 3 and/or deal 4 low) – If you are very unlikely to sign deal 3 or 4 and you can't operate in Nigeria, where else are you going to go where you think business operations will be better? In Africa? In the world?

INTERVIEWER: We have almost reached the end of the survey an only have a few last questions again regarding your personal opinions.

1. How many employees work for the company, and how many of them are Chinese?
2. What kinds of roles do your Chinese employees have within the company?
3. What made you come to Nigeria? Did you come from China or another African market?

4   (Only if the respondent came directly from China) Why did you decide to come to Nigeria?
5   (Only if the respondent lived in another African country first): What did you do there, and why did you decide to leave and come to Nigeria?
6   How important was Lagos as a business location for you?
7   Can you imagine running the same business outside of Lagos? For example in North Central? What about in the North East? Why? Why not?
8   How did you open a company here? What was the process?
10 What did your interaction with government offices look like?
11 Were you asked to make facilitation payments?
12 Were you asked to contribute to any local community projects, or hire locals?
13 Did the Chinese embassy assist you in the process?
14 What do you find the most attractive about the Nigerian environment for your business operations?
15 What do you find the least attractive about the Nigerian environment for your business operations?
16 What solutions have you come up with to solve these issues, or at least to make them more bearable?
17 On a scale from 0–10, how important were taxes/tax incentives for your decision to enter and stay in the Nigerian market?
    0
    1
    2
    3
    4
    5
    6
    7
    8
    9
    10
18 On a scale from 0–10, how important were local participation requirements for your decision to enter and stay in the Nigerian market?
    0
    1
    2
    3
    4
    5
    6
    7
    8
    9
    10

19 On a scale from 0–10, how important were license agreements for your decision to enter and stay in the Nigerian market?
   0
   1
   2
   3
   4
   5
   6
   7
   8
   9
   10
20 On a scale from 0–10, how important were facilitation payments for your decision to enter and stay in the Nigerian market?
   0
   1
   2
   3
   4
   5
   6
   7
   8
   9
   10
21 On a scale from 0–10, how important were environmental regulations for your decision to enter and stay in the Nigerian market?
   0
   1
   2
   3
   4
   5
   6
   7
   8
   9
   10
22 On a scale from 0–10, how important were land right regulations for your decision to enter and stay in the Nigerian market?
   0
   1
   2
   3

      4
      5
      6
      7
      8
      9
     10
23 Are there no, a few or a lot of competitors in the market that your company is operating in?
24 Does the presence of a competitor affect your willingness to comply with stricter government rules, or are you indifferent about it?
25 Are you concerned about political risk for your business and personal safety? If yes, how have you tried to mitigate these risks?
26 Are there any markets you considered before entering Nigeria? If yes, which ones and for what reasons?
27 What would have to happen so that you take the decision to leave Nigeria; and where else would you go?
28 How, if at all, has the Covid-19 outbreak affected your business in Nigeria?
29 Do you consider changing anything about your business operations in response to the Covid-19 outbreak?

INTERVIEWER: Thank you very much for your time!

References

Abotsi, Anselm Komla. 2015. Foreign Ownership of Firms and Corruption in Africa. *International Journal of Economics and Financial Issues*, Vol. 5, Issue 3: 647–655.

Adida, Claire; Ferree, Karen; Posner, Daniel and Robinson, Amanda. 2016. Who's Asking? Interviewer Coethnicity Effects in African Survey Data. *Comparative Political Studies*, Vol. 49, Issue 12: 1630–1660.

Africanews. 2017. Rwanda's Kagame Sticks to Used Clothes Ban Despite U.S. Threats. By Ismail Akwei (Retrieved October 20, 2020: https://www.africanews.com/2017/06/27/rwanda-s-kagame-sticks-to-used-clothes-ban-despite-us-threats/)

Akamatsu, Kaname. 1935. Waga kuni yomo kogyohin no boueki susei. *Shogyo Keizai Ronso*, Vol. 13: 129–212.

Akamatsu, Kaname. 1937. Waga kuni keizai hatten no sougou bensyoho. *Shogyo Keizai Ronso*, Vol. 15: 179–210.

Akamatsu, Kaname. 1962. Historical Pattern of Economic Growth in Developing Countries. *The Developing Economies*, Vol. 1: 3–25.

Ang, Yueng. 2016. *How China Escaped the Poverty Trap*. Cornell University Press.

Anyanwu, John C. and Yameogo, Nadege Desiree. 2015. What Drives Foreign Direct Investments Into West Africa? An Empirical Investigation. *Conference: ASSA 2015*.

Arnold, Michael A. and Lippan, Steven A. 1998. Posted Prices versus Bargaining in Markets with Asymmetric Information. *Economic Inquiry*, Vol. 36, Issue 3: 450–457.

Asiedu, Elizabeth. 2005. Foreign Direct Investment in Africa: The Role of Natural Resources, Market Size, Government Policy, Institutions and Political Instability. WIDER Research Paper, No. 2005/24.

Baldwin, Katharine. 2015. *The Paradox of Traditional Chiefs in Democratic Africa*. Cambridge University Press.

Ballard-Rosa, Cameron; Martin, Lucy and Scheve, Kenneth. 2017. The Structure of American Income Tax Policy Preferences. *The Journal of Politics*, Vol. 79, Issue 1: 1–16.

Banerjee, Abhijit and Duflo, Ester. 2011. *Poor Economics: A Radical Rethinking of the Way to Fight Global Poverty*. Public Affairs.

Bates, Robert. 1981. *Markets and States in Tropical Africa*. The Political Basis of Agricultural Policies. University of California Press.

Bende-Nabende, Anthony. 2002. Foreign Direct Investment Determinants in Sub-Saharan Africa: A Co-integration Analysis. *Economics Bulletin, Access Econ*, Vol. 6, Issue 4: 1–19.

Berge, Tarald and Øyvind, Stiansen. 2016. Negotiating BITs with Models: The Power of Expertise. PluriCourts Research Paper No. 16-13.

Besley, Timothy; Persson, Torsten and Sturm, Daniel. 2008. *Political Competition, Policy and Growth: Theory and Evidence from the US*. Oxford University Press.

Bizzarro, Fernando; Gerring, John; Knutsen, Carl Henrik; Hicken, Allen; Bernhard, Michael; Skaaning, Svend-Erik; Coppedge, Michael and Lindberg, Staffan I. 2018. Party Strength and Economic Growth. *World Politics*, Vol. 70, Issue 2: 275–320.

Blair, Robert A. and Roessler, Philip. 2018. The Effects of Chinese Aid on State Legitimacy in Africa: Cross-National and Sub-National Evidence from Surveys, Survey Experiments, and Behavioral Games. *AidData Working Paper #59*. AidData at William & Mary.

Blanchard, Olivier and Shleifer, Andrei. 2001. Federalism with and without Political Centralization: China versus Russia. *IMF Staff Papers*, Vol. 48, Issue 4: 1–8.

Blaydes, Lisa and Gillum, Rachel. 2013. Religiosity-of-Interviewer Effects: Assessing the Impact of Veiled Enumerators on Survey Response in Egypt. *Politics & Religion* Vol. 6, Issue 3: 459–485.

Blomström, M.; Globerman, S. and Kokko, A. 2001. The Determinants of Host Country Spillovers from Foreign Direct Investment, in N. Pain (ed), *Inward Investment, Technological Change and Growth*. Palgrave, 34–65.

Boddewyn, Jean and Brewer, Thomas. 1994. International-Business Political Behavior: New Theoretical Directions. *Academy of Management Review*, Vol. 19, Issue 1: 119–143.

Bokpin, Godfred A.; Mensah, Lord and Asamoah, Michael E. 2015. Foreign Direct Investment and Natural Resources in Africa. *Journal of Economic Studies*, Vol. 42, Issue 4: 608–621.

Brader, Ted and Joshua, A. Tucker. 2012. Following the Party's Lead: Party Cues, Policy Opinion, and the Power of Partisanship in Three Multiparty Systems. *Comparative Politics*, Vol. 44, Issue 4: 403–420.

Bräutigam, Deborah. 2009. *The Dragon's Gift: The Real Story about China in Africa*. Oxford University Press.

Bräutigam, Deborah. 2011. Ethiopia's Partnership with China. *The Guardian*, December 30, 2011.

Bräutigam, Deborah; Diao, Xinshen; McMillan, Margaret and Silve, Jed. 2015. Chinese Investment in Africa. How Much Do We Know? PEDL Synthesis Series, No. 2.

Bräutigam, Deborah; McMillan, Margaret and Tang, Xiaoyang. 2014. Flying Geese in Ethiopia's Leather Cluster? Understanding Asian/Chinese Impact. PEDL Research Note-ERG Project 106.

Bräutigam, Deborah; Tang, Xiaoyang and Xia, Ying. 2018. What Kinds of Chinese 'Geese' Are Flying to Africa? Evidence from Chinese Manufacturing Firms. *Journal of African Economies*, Vol. 27: i29–i51.

Brewer, Thomas. 1992. An Issue Area Approach to the Analysis of MNE-Government Relations. *Journal of International Business Studies*, Vol. 23: 295–309.

Broich, Tobias. 2017. Do Authoritarian Regimes Receive More Chinese Development Finance than Democratic Ones? Empirical Evidence for Africa. MERIT Working Papers 2017-011, United Nations University - Maastricht Economic and Social Research Institute on Innovation and Technology (MERIT).

Brown, William and Harman, Sophie. 2013. *African Agency in International Politics*. Taylor and Francis Group.

Bruton, Henry J. 1998. A Reconsideration of Import Substitution. *Journal of Economic Literature*, Vol. 36, Issue 2: 903–936.

Buelens, Frans and Marysse, Stefaan. 2006. Returns on Investments during the Colonial Era: The Case of Congo. IOB Discussion Papers 2006.07, Universiteit Antwerpen, Institute of Development Policy (IOB).

Cagé, Julia. 2020. Media Competition, Information Provision and Political Participation: Evidence from French Local Newspapers And Elections, 1944–2014. *Journal of Public Economics*, Vol. 185: 104077.

Calvo, Guillermo A.; Leiderman, Leonardo and Reinhart, Carmen M. 1993. Capital Inflows and Real Exchange Rate Appreciation in Latin America: The Role of External Factors. *Staff Papers, International Monetary Fund*, Vol. 40, Issue1: 108–151.

Campbell, Bruce. 1981. Race-of-Interviewer Effects among Southern Adolescents. *Public Opinion Quarterly*, Vol. 45, Issue 2: 231–244.

Chege, Michael. 2007. *Economic Relations Between Kenya and China, 1963–2007.* Center for Strategic and International Studies.

Chen, Guangzhe; Geiger, Michael and Fu, Minghui. 2015. *Manufacturing FDI in Sub-Saharan Africa: Trend, Determinants, and Impact.* World Bank.

Chen, Wenji; Dollar, David and Tang, Heiwai. 2018. Why Is China Investing in Africa? Evidence from the Firm Level. *The World Bank Economic Review*, Vol. 32, Issue 3: 610–632.

Chen, Yunnan. 2020. "Africa's China": Chinese Manufacturing Investment in Nigeria in The Post-Oil Boom Era and Channels for Technology Transfer. CARI Working Paper 36/April 2020.

Chen, Yunnan; Sun, Irene; Yuan, Ukaejiofo; Rex, Uzonna; Tang, Xiaoyang and Brautigam, Deborah. 2016. Learning from China? Manufacturing Investment and Technology Transfer in Nigeria, SAIS-CARI Working Paper 02/January 2016.

Child, John and Rodrigues, Suzanna. 2005. The Internationalization of Chinese Firms: A Case for Theoretical Extension. *Management and Organization Review*, Vol. 1, Issue 3: 381–410.

Corkin, L. 2016. *Uncovering African Agency: Angola's Management of China's Credit Lines.* Routledge.

Cotula, Lorenzo; Vermeulen, Sonja; Leonard, Rebeca and Keeley, James. 2009. *Land Grab or Development Opportunity? Agricultural Investment and International Land Deals in Africa.* IIED.

Cotula, Lorenzo; Weng, Xiaoxue; Ma, Qianru and Ren, Peng. 2016. *China-Africa Investment Treaties: Do They Work?* International Institute for Environment and Development (UK).

Crawford, Gordon and Hartmann, Christof. 2008. *Decentralisation in Africa: A Pathway Out of Poverty and Conflict?* Amsterdam University Press.

Crawford, Young Merwin. 1982. *Ideology and Development in Africa.* Yale University Press.

Dahl, Robert A. 1971. *Polyarchy: Participation and Opposition.* Yale University Press.

Das, Satya P. and Sengupta, Sarbajit. 2004. Asymmetric Information, Bargaining, and International Mergers. *Journal of Economics and Management Strategy*, Vol. 10, Issue 4: 565–590.

De Oliveira, Ricardo Soares. 2007. *Oil and Politics in the Gulf of Guinea.* Hurst.

Deaton, Angus. 2013. *The Great Escape. Health, Wealth and the Origins of Inequality.* Princeton University Press.

Dickovick, Tyler. 2014. Federalism in Africa: Origins, Operation and (In)Significance, Regional & Federal Studies, Vol. 24, Issue 5: 553–570.

Dickovick, J. Tyler and Gebre-Egziabher, Tegegne. 2014. Ethiopia: Ethnic Federalism and Centripetal Forces, in J. Tyler Dickovick and James Wunsch (eds), *Decentralization in Africa: The Paradox of State Strength*, 69–89. Lynne Rienner Publishers.

Doucouliagos, Hristos and Ulubaşoğlu, Mehmet Ali. 2008. Democracy and Economic Growth: A Meta-Analysis. *American Journal of Political Science*, Vol. 52, Issue 1: 61–83.

Drahos, Peter. 2003. When the Weak Bargain with the Strong: Negotiations in the World Trade Organization. *International Negotiation*, Vol. 8, Issue1: 79–109.

Dreher, Axel and Fuchs, Andreas. 2011. Rogue Aid? The Determinants of China's Aid Allocation. CESifo Working Paper Series No. 3581.

Dumitru, Hayat. 2015. *Sub-Saharan Africa: Politically More Stable, But Still Fragile.* Economic Research (KEO), Rabobank.

Dunning, John. 2007. An Overview of Relations with National Governments Journal. *New Political Economy*, Vol. 3, Issue 2: 280–284.

Dupasquier, Chantal and Osakwe, Patrick. 2006. Foreign Direct Investment in Africa: Performance, Challenges, and Responsibilities. *Journal of Asian Economics*, Vol. 17, Issue 2: 241–260.

Easterly, William. 2006. The Big Push Déjà Vu: A Review of Jeffrey Sachs's The End of Poverty: Economic Possibilities for Our Time. *Journal of Economic Literature*, Vol. 44, Issue 1: 96–105.

Eden, Lorraine; Lenway, Stefanie and Schuler, Douglas. 2004. From the Obsolescing Bargain to the Political Bargaining Model. For presentation at the *Annual Meetings of the Academy of International Business in the Session*, "International Business & Government Relations in the 21st Century".

Eden, Lorraine and Molot, Maureen. 2002. Insiders, Outsiders and Host Country Bargains. *Journal of International Management*, Vol. 8, Issue 4: 359–433.

Ernst and Young. 2019. Africa Attractiveness Report. (Retrieved July 3, 2020: https://www.brookings.edu/blog/africa-in-focus/2019/10/09/figure-of-the-week-foreign-direct-investment-in-africa/)

Fagre & Wells. 1982, June. Bargaining Power of Multinationals and Host Governments. *Journal of International Business Studies*, Vol. 13, Issue 2: 9–23.

Fedderke, J. W. and Romm, A. T. 2006. Growth Impact and Determinants of Foreign Direct Investment into South Africa, 1956–2003. *Economic Modelling*, Vol. 23, Issue 5: 738–760.

Feng, Emily and Pilling, David. 2019. The Other Side of Chinese Investment in Africa. *Financial Times*, March 27, 2019.

Fisher and Ury. 1981. *Getting to Yes. Negotiating an Agreement without Giving In*. Penguin Group.

Folashadé, Soulé. 2019. *African Governments Need to Negotiate Better Deals with China. Here's How They Can Do It*. China-Africa Project Podcast.

Fombad, Charles and Steytler, Nico (eds). 2019. *Decentralization and Constitutionalism in Africa*. Stellenbosch Handbooks in African Constitutional Law.

Franchino, Fabio and Zucchini, Francesco. 2014. *Voting in a Multi-dimensional Space: A Conjoint Analysis Employing Valence and Ideology Attributes of Candidates*. Cambridge University Press.

Francis, Suzanne; Onapajo, Hakeem and Okeke, Ufo. 2015. Oil Corrupts Elections: The Political Economy of Vote-Buying in Nigeria. *African Studies Quarterly*, Vol. 15, Issue 2.

Fraser, Lindsey. 2010. Negotiating Aid: The Structural Conditions Shaping the Negotiating Strategies of African Governments. *International Negotiation*, Vol. 15: 341–366.

Gadzala, A. (ed). 2015. *Africa and China: How Africans and Their Governments Are Shaping Relations with China*. Rowman and Littlefield.

Gebreeyesus, M. 2013. Industrial Policy and Development in Ethiopia: Evolution and Present Experimentation. Working Paper No. 6. Africa Growth Initiative, African Development Bank Group, UNU-WIDER.

Gerschenkron, Alexander. 1962. Economic Backwardness in Historical Perspective, in B. Hoselitz (ed) *From the Progress of Underdeveloped Countries*. Chicago University Press.

Gibson, R. K. and McAllister, I. 2015. New Media, Elections and the Political Knowledge Gap in Australia. *Journal of Sociology*, Vol. 51, Issue 2: 337–353.

Globerman, S. and Shapiro, D. 1999. The Impact of Government Policies on Foreign Direct Investment: The Canadian Experience. *Journal of International Business Studies*, Vol. 30, Issue 13: 513–532.

Green, Donald and Shapiro, Ian. 1994. *Pathologies of Rational Choice Theory: A Critique of Applications in Political Science.* Yale University Press.

Green, Eliott. 2011. Decentralization and Political Opposition in Contemporary Africa: Evidence from Sudan and Ethiopia. *Democratization*, Vol. 18, Issue 5: 1087–1105.

Grosse, Robert. 1996. The Bargaining Relationship between Foreign MNEs and Host Governments in Latin America. *The International Trade Journal* 10: 467–499.

Grosse, Robert and Behrman, Jack N.. 1992. Theory in International Business. *Transnational Corporations*, Vol. 1: 93–126.

Grossman, Gene and Helpman, Elhanan. 1996. Electoral Competition and Special Interest Politics. *Review of Economic Studies*, Vol. 63, Issue2: 265–286.

Grunert, Jens and Norden Lars. 2012. Bargaining Power and Information in SME Lending. *Small Business Economics*, 39: 401–417.

Guthrie, D. 2005. Organizational Learning and Productivity: State Structure and Foreign Investment in the Rise of Chinese Corporation. *Management and Organization Review*, Vol. 1: 165–195.

Hainmueller, Jens; Hopkins, J. Daniel and Yamamoto, Teppei. 2013. Causal Inference in Conjoint Analysis: Understanding Multidimensional Choices via Stated Preference Experiments. *Political Analysis*, Vol. 22: 1–30.

Hainmueller, Jens and Hopkins, J. Daniel. 2014. Public Attitudes Toward Immigration. *Annual Review of Political Science*, Vol. 17: 225–249.

Hanson, Stephanie. 2009. *Corruption in Sub-Saharan Africa*. Backgrounder. Council on Foreign Relations.

Haraguchi, Nobuya; Cheng, Charles; Fang, Chin and Smeets, Eveline. 2017. The Importance of Manufacturing in Economic Development: Has This Changed? *World Development*, Vol. 93, Issue C, 293–315.

He, Canfei and Zhu, Shengjun. 2018. China's Foreign Direct Investment into Africa, in *The State of African Cities. The Geography of African Investment*. UN Habitat.

Hirschman, Albert O. 1958. *The Strategy of Economic Development.* Yale University Press.

Huang, Y., 1998. The Industrial Organization of Chinese Government. Working Paper 99-076. Cambridge, MA: Harvard Business School.

Hurt, S. 2012. The EU–SADC Economic Partnership Agreement Negotiations: 'Locking in' The Neoliberal Development Model in Southern Africa? *Third World Quarterly*, Vol. 33, Issue 3: 495–510.

Hymer, Steven. 1960. *The International Operations of National Firms: A Study of Direct Foreign Investment.* MIT Press.

IFC. 2020. Manufacturing. (Retrieved November 4, 2020: https://www.ifc.org/wps/wcm/connect/industry_ext_content/ifc_external_corporate_site/manufacturing)

International Monetary Fund. 2003. Foreign Direct Investment Trends and Statistics: A Summary; Definition of FDI Can Be Found in the Footnote on pg. 1. (Retrieved June 22, 2020: https://www.imf.org/External/np/sta/fdi/eng/2003/102803s1.pdf)

Isaksson, A. and Kotsadam, A. 2016. Chinese Aid and Local Corruption. *AidData Working Paper*, Vol. 33.

Jalata, Asafa. 2016. *Colonial Terrorism and the Incorporation of Africa into the Capitalist World System.* Palgrave Macmillan.

John, Tara. 2020. How the US and Rwanda Have Fallen Out Over Second-Hand Clothes. (Retrieved November 4, 2020: https://www.bbc.com/news/world-africa-44252655).

Johns, Leslie and Wellhausen, Rachel. 2017. The Price of Doing Business: How Upfront Costs Deter Political Risk. Prepared for the 2017 International Political Economy Society.

Kaplinsky, Raphael and Morris, Mike. 2009. Chinese FDI in Sub-Saharan Africa: Engaging with Large Dragons. *European Journal of Development Research*, Vol. 21: 551–569.

Kazeem, Yomi. 2020. Kenya and Nigeria are Leading Africa's Push to Start Taxing Silicon Valley's Global Tech Giants. *Quartz Africa* (Retrieved November 4, 2020: https://qz.com/africa/1881964/kenya-nigeria-pass-new-laws-to-tax-global-tech-giants/?fbclid=IwAR1tV696-uGELSwZ8uhThfIDPbO0kh5QvQZSpf6RxAFZYymC5Pu1Di_zK7I)

Keefer, Philip; Knack, Stephen and Olson, Mancur. 1996. Property and Contract Rights in Autocracies and Democracies. *Journal of Economic Growth*, Vol. 1, Issue 2: 243–276.

King, K. 2013. *China's Aid and Soft Power in Africa: The Case of Education and Training*. Boydell and Brewer.

Kishi, R and Raleigh, C. 2015. *Chinese Aid and Africa's Pariah States*. University of Sussex (draft).

Kobrin, Stephen. 1987. Testing the Bargaining Hypothesis in the Manufacturing Sector in Developing Countries. *International Organization*, Vol. 41: 609–638.

Kumar, V. and Gaeth, Gary. 1991. Attribute Order and Product Familiarity Effects in Decision Tasks Using Conjoint Analysis. *International Journal of Research in Marketing*. Vol. 8, Issue 2: 113–124.

Kuo, Lily. 2017. A Chinese-Built Bridge Collapsed in Kenya Two Weeks after It Was Inspected by the President. *Quartz Africa* (Retrieved March 30, 2020: https://qz.com/africa/1015554/a-chinese-built-bridge-collapsed-in-kenya-two-weeks-after-it-was-inspected-by-the-president/)

Kuran, Timur. 2016. *Sparks and Prairie Fires: A Theory of Unanticipated Political Revolution*. Public Choice.

Kurlanzick, Joshua. 2016. *State Capitalism*. Oxford University Press.

Landau, Alice. 2013. *The International Trading System*. Routledge.

Lauria, Valeria. 2020. Agency Distribution in the Ethiopian Infrastructure Sector (Dissertation Chapter).

Lee, Ching-Kwan. 2018. *The Spectre of Global China: Politics, Labour and Foreign Investment in Africa*. University of Chicago Press.

Li, Jing; Newenham-Kahindi, Aloyisius; Shapiro, Daniel and Chen, Victor. 2013. The Two-Tier Bargaining Model Revisited: Theory and Evidence from China's Natural Resource Investments in Africa. *Global Strategy Journal*, Vol. 3, Issue 4: 300–321.

Lim, Ewe-Ghee. 2001. Determinants of and Relation between Foreign Direct Investment and Growth: A Summary of Recent Literature. IMF Working Paper WP/01/175.

Lipset, Seymour Martin. 1959. Some Social Requisites of Democracy: Economic Development and Political Legitimacy. *The American Political Science Review*, Vol. 53, Issue 1: 69–105.

Lipset, Seymour Martin. 1983. *Political Man: The Social Bases of Politics* (2nd ed.). Heinemann.

Locke, John. 1689. *An Essay Concerning the True Original, Extent and End of Civil Government*.

Lucas, Robert. 1988. On the Mechanics of Economic Development. *Journal of Monetary Economics*, Vol. 22, Issue 1: 3–42.

McKinsey. 2017. Dance of the Lions and Dragons. How Are Africa and China Engaging, and How Will the Partnership Evolve?

Meheret, Aneyew. 2007. A Rapid Assessment of Wereda Decentralization in Ethiopia, in Taye Assefa and Tegegne Gebre-Egziabher (eds), *Decentralization in Ethiopia*. Forum for Social Studies, 69–102.

Mijiyawa, Abdoul' Ganiou. 2015. What Drives Foreign Direct Investment in Africa? An Empirical Investigation with Panel Data. *African Development Review*, Vol. 27, Issue 4: 392–402.

Mohan, Giles and Lampert, Ben. 2013. Negotiating China: Reinserting African Agency into China–Africa Relations. *African Affairs*, Vol 112, Issue 446: 92–110.

Montinola, Gabriella; Qian, Yinqui and Weingast, Barry R. 1995. Federalism, Chinese Style: The Political Basis for Economic Success in China. *World Politics*, Vol. 48, Issue 1: 50–81.

Moura, Rui and Forte, Rosa 2009. The Effects of Foreign Direct Investment on the Host Country Economic Growth - Theory and Empirical Evidence. Submitted to the *11th ETSG Annual Conference*. Preliminary Version.

Moyo, Dambisa. 2009. *Dead Aid: Why Aid Is not Working and How There is a Better Way for Africa*. Penguin Books.

Nalebuff, Barry and Brandenburger, Adam. [sForthcoming]. The Illusion of Power in Negotiation. Draft for comments.

Nebus, James and Rufin, Carlos. 2010. Extending the Bargaining Power Model: Explaining Bargaining Outcomes among Nations, MNEs, and NGOs. *Journal of International Business Studies*, Vol. 41, Issue 6: 996–1015.

Negussie, Solomon. 2016. Fiscal Federalism and Decentralization in Selected IGAD Member Countries. Africa Portal. South African Institute of International Affairs. *New Political Economy*, Vol. 3, Issue 2.

Newman, Carol; Rand, John; Talbot, Theodore and Tarp, Finn. 2015. Technology Transfers, Foreign Investment and Productivity Spillovers. *European Economic Review*, Vol. 76: 168–187.

OECD. 2002a. *The Economics of International Investment Incentives*. OECD.

OECD. 2002b. *Foreign Direct Investment for Development. Maximizing Benefits, Minimising Costs*. OECD.

OECD. 2003. China Ahead in Foreign Direct Investment. OECD Observer. OECD.

Oi, Jean C. 1992. Fiscal Reform and the Economic Foundations of Local State Corporatism in China. *World Politics*, Vol. 45, Issue 1: 99–126.

Oi, Jean C. 1999. *Rural China Takes Off: Institutional Foundations of Economic Reform*. University of California Press.

Olayode, Kehinde. 2015. Ethno-Regional Cleavages and Voting Behaviour in the 2015 General Elections: Issues and Challenges for Democratisation and Nation Building. Paper Presented at a *Two-Day National Conference on "The 2015 General Elections in Nigeria: The Real Issues"*.

Olingo, Allan. 2020. *Kenya: Plastics Ban Glitch for U.S.-Kenya Trade Talks*. AllAfrica.

Olson, Mancur. 2000. *Power and Prosperity: Outgrowing Communist and Capitalist Dictatorship*. Basic Books.

Oqubay, Arkebe and Lin, Justin Yifu (eds). 2019. *China-Africa and Economic Transformation*, Oxford University Press.

Ortigueira, Salvador and Santos, Samuel. 1997. On the Speed of Convergence in Endogenous Growth Models. *American Economic Review*, Vol. 87, Issue 3: 383–399.

Osabutey, Ellis. 2013. Exploring Foreign Direct Investment and Technology and Knowledge Transfer Issues in Africa, in *The Changing Geography of International Business*. Palgrave Macmillan, 222–238.

Owusu, Francis. 2003. Pragmatism and the Gradual Shift from Dependency to Neoliberalism: The World Bank, African Leaders and Development Policy in Africa. *World Development*, Vol. 31, Issue 10: 1655–1672.

Pehnelt, Gernot. 2007. The Political Economy of China's Aid Policy in Africa. Jena Economic Research Paper No. 2007-051.

Pitcher, Anne. 2012. *Party Politics and Economic Reform in Africa's Democracies*. Cambridge University Press.

Prebisch, Raul. 1949. The Economic Development of Latin America and Its Principal Problems. *ECLA Conference*.

Przeworski, Adam; Alvarez, Michael E.; Cheibub, Jose Antonio and Limongi, Fernando. 2000. *Democracy and Development: Political Institutions and Well-Being in the World, 1950–1990*. Cambridge University Press.

Putnman, R. 1988. Diplomacy and Domestic Politics: The Logic of Two-Level Games. *International Organization*, Vol. 42, Issue 3: 427–460.

Ramamurti, Ravi. 2001, March. The Obsolescing 'Bargaining Model'? MNC-Host Developing Country Relations Revisited. *Journal of International Business Studies*, Vol. 32, Issue 1: 23–39.

Rebelo, Sergio. 1991. Long-Run Policy Analysis and Long-Run Growth. *Journal of Political Economy*, Vol. 99: 500–521.

Riker, W. 1975. Federalism, in Fred Greenstein and Nelson Polsby (eds), *Handbook of Political Science*, Vol 5, 93–172. Addison-Wesley.

Rodney, Walter. 1972. *How Europe Underdeveloped Africa*. Bogle-L'Ouverture Publications.

Rodrik, Dani. 1997. Goodbye Washington Consensus, Hello Washington Confusion? A Review of the World Bank's "Economic Growth in the 1990s: Learning from a Decade of Reform". *Journal of Economic Literature*, Vol. 44, Issue4: 973–987.

Romer, Paul. 1986. Increasing Returns and Long-Run Growth. *Journal of Political Economy*, Vol. 94, Issue 5: 1002–1037.

Romer, Paul M. 1994. The Origins of Endogenous Growth. *Journal of Economic Perspectives*, Vol. 8, Issue 1: 3–22.

Rose, Randall L. and Dickson, Peter R. 1987. Says No, but Does He Really Mean It? Bargaining Behavior, Cue Consistency, and Attribution. *Advances in Consumer Research*, Vol. 14: 382–386.

Rosenbluth, Frances and Shapiro, Ian. 2018. *Responsible Parties: Saving Democracy from Itself*. Yale University Press.

Sachs, Jeffrey; McArthur, John; Schmidt-Traub, Guido; Kruk, Margaret; Bahadur, Chandrika; Faye, Michael and McCord, Gordon. 2004. *Ending Africa's Poverty Trap*. Columbia University and UN Millennium Project.

Samy, Yiagadeesen. 2010. China's Aid Policies in Africa: Opportunities and Challenges. *The Commonwealth Journal of International Affairs*, Vol. 99, Issue 406: 75–90.

Scissors, Derek. 2020. China's Global Investment in 2019. *Going Out Goes Small*. (Retrieved July 3, 2020: https://www.aei.org/wp-content/uploads/2020/01/Chinas-global-investment-in-2019-1.pdf)

Sender, John and Smith, Sheila. 1986. *The Development of Capitalism in Africa*. Routledge.

Seteolu, Dele and Oshodi, Tobi. 2017. Oscillation of Two Giants: Sino-Nigeria Relations and the Global South. *Journal of Chinese Political Science*, Vol. 23, Issue 2: 257–285.

Simmons, Joel. 2016. *The Politics of Technological Progress: Parties, Time Horizons and Long-term Economic Development*. Cambridge University Press.

Singer, Hans. 1949. *Post-War Price Relations in Trade between Under-Developed and Industrialized Countries*. UN Economic and Social Council.

Soskice, David and Hall, Peter A. 2001. *Varieties of Capitalism*. Oxford University Press.

Stopford, J., and Strange, S. 1991. *Rival States, Rival Firms: Competition for World Market Shares*. Cambridge University Press.

Stratfor. 2019. Tanzania Takes Another Swipe at Chinese Investment (Retrieved May 15, 2020: https://worldview.stratfor.com/article/tanzania-takes-another-swipe-chinese-investment-foriegn-business-africa)

Suberu, Rotimi. 2001. *Federalism and Ethnic Conflict in Nigeria*. United States Institute for Peace.

Sun, Irene. 2017. The World's Next Great Manufacturing Center. *Harvard Business Review*, May–June 2017 Issue.

Swedlund, Haley. 2017. *The Development Dance. How Donors and Recipients Negotiate the Delivery of Foreign Aid*. Cornell University Press.

Tang, Xiaoyan. 2021. *Coevolutionary Pragmatism: Approaches and Impacts of China-Africa Cooperation*. Cambridge University Press.

Tavares, José and Wacziarg, Romain. 2001. How Democracy Affects Growth. *European Economic Review*, Vol. 45, Issue 8: 1341–1378.

UNCTAD. 1995. *World Investment Report 1995 - Transnational Corporations and Competitiveness*. United Nations Conference on *Trade and Development Division on Transnational Corporations and Investment*.

UNCTAD. 2000. *World Investment Report 2000*. Cross-Border Mergers and Acquisitions and Development. United Nations Conference on *Trade and Development Division on Transnational Corporations and Investment*.

UNCTAD. 2012. *World Investment Report: Towards a New Generation of Investment Policies*.

U.S. Department of State Investment Climate Statements. 2017. 2017 Investment Climate Statements: Angola. (Retrieved September 20, 2020: https://www.state.gov/reports/2017-investment-climate-statements/angola/)

Van Reenen, John and Yueh. 2012. Why Has China Grown So Fast? The Role of International Technology Transfer, CEP Discussion Papers dp1121, Centre for Economic Performance, LSE.

Vaughan, Sarah. 2006. Responses to Ethnic Federalism is Ethiopia's Southern Region, in David Turton (ed), *Ethnic Federalism: the Ethiopian Experience in Comparative Perspective*. James Currey, 181–207.

Vernon, Raymond. 1971. *Sovereignty at Bay: The Multinational Spread of US Enterprises*. Basic Books.

Vernon, Raymond. 1977. *Storm Over the Multinationals: The Real Issues*. Harvard University Press.

Vernon, Raymond. 1998. *In the Hurricane's Eye: The Troubled Prospects of Multinational Enterprises*. Harvard University Press.

Vogel, Christopher. 2011. *Are There Varieties of Capitalism in African Political Economies? The Impact of Colonialism and Globalization on the Emergence of National Economies in Uganda and DR Congo*. GRIN.

Vreeland, James R. 1999. The IMF: Lender of Last Resort or Scapegoat? Presented at the *International Studies Association Conference*, Washington DC.

Wallerstein, Immanuel. 1974. The Rise and Future Demise of the World Capitalist System: Concepts for Comparative Analysis. *Comparative Studies in Society and History*, Vol. 16, Issue 4: 387–415.

Weigel, Dale R.; Gregory, Neil F. and Wagle, Dileep M. 1997. *Foreign Direct Investment*. Lessons of Experience Series; No. 5. World Bank.

Weinhardt, Clara and Moerland, Anke 2017. (Mis)Perceptions in Two- and Three-Level Games: Detachment in Economic Partnership Agreement Negotiations. *Journal of Common Market Studies*, Vol. 56, Issue 3: 576–593.

Whitfield, Lindsay and Fraser, Alastair. 2008. Negotiating Aid: The Structural Conditions Shaping the Negotiating Strategies of African Governments. *International Negotiation*, Vol. 15, Issue 3: 341–366.

Wig, Tore and Rød, Espen. 2014. Cues to Coup Plotters: Elections as Coup Triggers in Dictatorships. *Journal of Conflict Resolution*. Vol. 60, Issue 5: 787–812.

Wolfe, Rebecca and McGinn, Kathleen. 2005. Perceived Relative Power and Its Influence on Negotiations. *Group Decision and Negotiation*, Vol. 14: 3–20.

World Bank. 2012. Devolution without Disruption: Pathways to aSuccessful New Kenya. Main report (English). Working Paper. 72297. Vol. 2.

World Bank. 2019. Kenya's Devolution. (Retrieved November 5, 2020: https://www.worldbank.org/en/country/kenya/brief/kenyas-devolution).

XinhuaNet. 2020. Chinese Investment Boosts Kenya's Manufacturing Competitiveness. (Retrieved November 4, 2020: http://www.xinhuanet.com/english/2020-08/14/c_139291257.htm)

Yao, Yang. 2010. The Encompassing State—A Contribution of the East Asian Model. *Procedia - Social and Behavioral Sciences*, Vol. 2, Issue 5: 7422–7427.

Yasin, Mesghena. 2005. Official Development Assistance and Foreign Direct Investment Flows to Sub-Saharan Africa. *African Development Review*, Vol. 17, Issue 1: 23–40.

Yin, Jason and Vaschetto, Sofia. 2013. China's Business Engagement in Africa. *The Chinese Economy*, Vol. 44, Issue 2: 43–57.

Zeng, Douglas. 2016. Global Experiences of Special Economic Zones with Focus on China and Africa: Policy Insights. *Journal of International Commerce, Economics and Policy*, Vol. 7, Issue 3: 1650018.

Zhao, Dingxin and Yang, Hongxing. 2013. Performance Legitimacy, State Autonomy and China's Economic Miracle. CDDRL Working Papers. Stanford University.

Zitelmann, Rainer. 2019. China's Economic Success Proves the Power of Capitalism. *Forbes* (Retrieved June 22, 2020: https://www.forbes.com/sites/rainerzitelmann/2019/07/08/chinas-economic-success-proves-the-power-of-capitalism/#619fcbd83b9d)

Index

Note: Pages followed by "n" refer to notes.

accountability, lack of 79
advantage of backwardness 11
Africa: Chinese investment stocks in (2017) 45; experimental evidence from Nigeria 75–119; foreign direct investments in 6–8; historical relationships between China and 139–141; weak economics in 15–18
Africa Opening Up 142–143
Africa-China studies *see* China-Africa studies
African bargaining power 1–6; background characteristics 122–123; case selection logic 121–125; experimental evidence from Nigeria 75–119; governments acting as price setters 186–200; new theory on 27–38; perceptions across selected cases 125–132; perceptions of 120–133
African National Congress (ANC) 128, 138
agricultural land 42
Algeria: Chinese investment stocks in 3; U.S. investment stocks in 3
All Progressives Congress (APC) 139
Amahara Region, Ethiopia 160
American Chemistry Council (ACC) 192
Ang, Yueng 27
Angola 2–3, 195–196; Chinese investment stocks in 4; U.S. investment stocks in 4
appendix: Chinese company survey 211–217; government survey 201–211
authoritarian regimes, survival of 194–195
authoritarian/one-party dominant systems *versus* competitive democracies 138–139
Average Component Interaction Effect (ACIE) 86
Average Marginal Component Effect (AMCE) 86

Babangida, Ibrahim 141
background characteristics 99–119
background variables 82
Bahir Dar 176
Baldwin, Katharine 181
Bandung Conference of Non-Aligned Nations 26n1
bargaining power: actual 16; assessing relationship with deal quality 39–74; definition 11–12; importance of perceptions of 36–38; information-sharing incentives around 160–185; information/historical frames around 134–159; measuring 41–44; perceived 16; question of relative benefits/costs 30–31; as variable affecting deal quality 80–81
bargaining power-deal quality relationship: appendices 53–57; experimental evidence from Nigeria 75–119; methodology 58–74; overall assessment: distribution patterns 46–48; LASSO predictions 48–51; private Chinese investment stocks 51
bargaining power-deal quality relationship, assessing 39–40; measuring bargaining power 41–44; measuring outcomes 40–41; overall assessment 44–46
Barrick Gold Corp 193
Bates, Robert 9
BATNA of private Chinese investors, determining: benefits 31–32; costs 32–35
Berge, Tarald 76
Best Alternatives to a Negotiated Agreement (BATNA) 30–31
bilateral investment treaty (BIT) 76
Black Economic Empowerment (B-EE) 128
Blair, Robert A. 81

Boko Haram 32
Brandenburger, Adam 30
Bräutigam, Deborah 32, 131, 145, 189
Broad-Based Black Economic Empowerment (B-BBEE) 6, 10, 128, 144
Buhari, Muhammadu 139

catch-up growth 14
central government-sub-regional unit communication 174–178
centralization 161, 162
centralized *versus* de-centralized systems: central government-sub-regional unit communication 174–177; inter-ministerial competition 167–174
Chama Cha Mapinduzi (CCM) 137, 138
Chanaka, Teshome Toga 193
Chapman, Steven 189–190
Chen, Yunnan 40
China: correlations between investment stocks and deal quality 47; determining BATNA of private Chinese investors 31–35; foreign direct investments of 6–8; hidden village Chinese industrial parks 178–183; historical relationships between African parties and 139–141; investments in Africa 1–6; long-term learning about bargaining power/policy options 143–151; in Nigeria and Kenya 126–128; and outward-focused strategies 143–151; and quality of investment deals 8–15
China African Investment Company (CAIC) 179
China Harbour Engineering Company (CHEC) 193
China Merchants Holdings 136
China-Africa Research Initiative (CARI) 39, 46
China-Africa studies: assessing bargaining power-deal quality relationship 39–74; experimental evidence from Nigeria 75–119; new theory on African bargaining power 27–38
Chinese Communist Party (CCP) 140
Chinese company survey 211–217
Chinese model 156–158
Chinese Polytech School 198
Cold War 9, 139–140, 152, 196
Companies Act 151
conventional wisdom, challenges to 18–20
Corporate Income Tax 98
corruption 42
corruption, lack of 79

COVID-19 94–95, 157, 192–193, 197
Cummins 27, 189–190

Dar es Salaam 174
Dar es Salaam Stock Exchange 144
de-centralization 163–166
deal quality: assessing relationship with bargaining power 39–74; existing explanations for quality of 11–15; experimental evidence from Nigerian on 75–119; quality of 8–11; variables influencing 78–81
Deal Quality Index 130
Deal Quality Index 2020 10, 41
deal quality *see* investment deals
debt, deal quality and 47
Democratic Republic of Congo 195
Department for International Development (DFID), UK 158
Department of Trade, Industry, and Competition (DTIC), South Africa 172–173
dependency theory 1
Dickovick, Tyler 163, 176
distribution patterns 46–48
diversification 191–194

Ease of Doing Business (EDB) Index 37, 40, 157–158
East Asia, light manufacturing business in 29
Easterly, William 13
economic and technological cooperation, agreement 141
Economic Development and Poverty Reduction Strategy II 197
Economic Partnership Agreement 76
Edo State, Nigeria 175–176
educational sphere 156–158
Egypt 196
electricity 42
endogenous forces, economic growth as result of 28
Enlai, Zhou 140, 148
Enterprise Limited (LPLEL) 193
environmental regulations 99
Equatorial Guinea 8
Ethio-China Polytechnic College 147
Ethiopia: actual/perceived bargaining power 125–132; authoritarian/one-party dominant systems *versus* competitive democracies 138–139; background characteristics 122–123; central government-sub-regional unit communication 174–178; and

centralization 162; Chinese investment stocks in 3; governments acting as price setters 186–200; historical relationships to West 152–158; historical relationships with China 139–141; information-sharing incentives 160–185; inter-ministerial competition 167–174; long-term learning about bargaining power/policy options 143–151; outward-focused strategies 142–143; Strong Perceived Bargaining Power in 129–132; U.S. investment stocks in 3
Ethiopian Investment Commission 171
Ethiopian People's Revolutionary Democratic Front (EPRDF) 138
experimentalism 1
experimental economics 13
Export Processing Zone Authority 174
exports 42
external shock 94–95
external validity 96–97

facilitation payments 98
FDI Regulations Index 2012 41
Financial Times Nigeria Summit 2018 157
foreign direct investments 6–8
foreign employment 97
foreign ownership 97
Forums on China-Africa Cooperation (FOCAC) 7, 140, 198
Françafrique 196
Francophone West Africa 196–197
Fraser, Lindsey 198

Gauteng 172
GDP 42
Gerschenkron, Alexander 11
Ghana 196
Global Competitiveness Index (GCI) 40
Gonder 176
Goodwill Ceramics 32
government assistance with investment procedure and settlements 99
government indicators 43–44
government survey 201–211
government–government model 128
Green, Eliott 164
growth 191–194
Growth and Transformation Plan 143, 176

Hall, Peter 9
Harrod–Domar model 28
He, Canfei 7, 161

hidden village Chinese industrial parks 178–183
Highly Indebted Poor Countries (HIPC) 142, 146, 153
hypotheses 84–85

ideological sphere 156–158
import-substitution industrialization (ISI) 137
imports 42
Indigenization and Economic Empowerment Act 2, 14
Industrial Development Cooperation (IDC), South Africa, 1990
Industrial Policy Strategy (IPS) 9, 130, 143
inflation 42
information flows 134–136; authoritarian/one-party dominant systems *versus* competitive democracies 138–139; historical relationships between African parties and China 139–141; long-term learning 136–151; long-term learning about bargaining power/policy options 143–151; outward-focused strategies 142–143
information-sharing incentives 160–162; centralization and 162; centralized *versus* de-centralized systems 166–178; de-centralization experiments 163–166; hidden village Chinese industrial parks 178–183
intellectual sphere 156–158
inter-ministerial competition 167–174
International Finance Corporation (IFC) 41
International Monetary Fund (IMF) 12
investment deal rating 82–84
investors, Chinese 2–7, 16–17, 22–23, 39–40, 52, 186, 198; distribution patterns 46–47; determining BATNA of 31–35; experimental evidence from Nigeria 78, 80, 81, 96, 100; and importance of perceptions in power bargaining 36–38; information and historical frames 135–138, 145, 147, 150–152, 155–158; information-sharing incentives 173, 177; and LASSO predictions 48–51; and measuring bargaining power 41, 43–44; and perceptions of bargaining power 120–132
InvestSA 173

Jimma 176
Jingping, Xi 33

Joint-Venture (JV) 29
Jonathan, Goodluck 139

Kagame, Paul 198
Kaplinsky, Raphael 7
kebeles (localities) 163
KenInvest 169, 174, 175
Kenya: actual/perceived bargaining power 125–132; authoritarian/one-party dominant systems *versus* competitive democracies 138–139; background characteristics 122–123; central government-sub-regional unit communication 174–178; governments acting as price setters 186–200; historical relationships to West 152–158; historical relationships with China 139–141; information-sharing incentives 160–185; inter-ministerial competition 167–174; long-term learning about bargaining power/policy options 143–151; outward-focused strategies 142–143; Weak Bargaining Power Narrative in 126–128
Kenya African National Union (KANU) 138, 140
Kenyan Ministry of Industry 174
Kenyatta, Uhuru 141
Kibaki, Mwai 139, 170
Korea Trade-Investment Promotion Agency 161
KwaZulu Natal 172

Lagos 174–175
Laikipa County, Kenya 160
LASSO predictions 48–51
Lekki Free Trade Zone Port 193
license fees 98
Local Content Regulations 130
long-term learning 95–96; about bargaining power/policy options 143–151

Madagascar 3; Chinese investment stocks in 4; U.S. investment stocks in 4
Magufuli, John 130
majimbo 165
Malawi 148
Mankiw, Romer and Weil Model 28
manufacturing 42
market-seeking motivations 43
Mauritius 8, 196
Maxter Group 176
McGinn, Kathleen 75
McKinsey 4, 7, 33–34, 40, 51–52, 126, 128, 130

Medium Perceived Bargaining Power: in South Africa 128–129
Medium-Term Expenditure Framework (MTEF) 164
Mekele 176
Memorandum of Understanding (MOU) 160
Ministry of Budget and National Planning (MBNP) 167–174
Ministry of Commerce (MOFCOM) (China) 48
Ministry of Foreign Affairs (MFA) 167–174
Ministry of Industry, Trade and Investment (MITI) 167–174
Mkapa, Benjamin 146
Moerland, Anke 75
Moi, Daniel arap 141
Morris, Mike 7
Mozambique Liberation Front (FRELIMO) 196
Mugabe, Robert 2, 13–14

Nalebuff, Barry 30
Nasser, Gamal Abdel 196
National Council of Provinces 164
National Liberation Front of Angola (FNLA) 141
National Planning Commission 150
National Rainbow Coalition (NARC) 138–139
natural resource rents 42
neoclassical economics 1
new theory, African bargaining power 27–30; determining BATNA of private Chinese investors 31–35; importance of perceptions 36–38; question of relative benefits/costs 30–31
Nigeria: actual/perceived bargaining power 125–132; authoritarian/one-party dominant systems *versus* competitive democracies 138–139; background characteristics 122–123; central government-sub-regional unit communication 174–178; and centralization 162; governments acting as price setters 186–200; and hidden village Chinese industrial parks 178–183; historical relationships to West 152–158; historical relationships with China 139–141; information-sharing incentives 160–185; inter-ministerial competition 167–174; long-term learning about bargaining power/policy options 143–151;

outward-focused strategies 142–143; Weak Bargaining Power Narrative in 126–128
Nigeria, experimental evidence from 75–78; case selection 78; conjoint analysis 81–85; external validity 96–97; implementation 85–86; long-term learning 95–96; results 86–95; COVID-19 as external shock 94–95; government perceptions 87–93; subgroups 93–94; sampling 85–86; variables influencing deal quality 78–81
Nigerian Civil War 141
Nigerian Investment Promotion Commission (NIPC) 126, 160, 167–174
Nigerian Ministry of Industry, Trade and Investment 174
NIPC Act of 1995 155
Non-Aligned Movement 124
Non-Citizens (Employment Regulation) Act 130

Obasanjo, Olusegun 139
Odinga, Jaramogi Oginga 140–141, 152
Odinga, Ralia 138–139
Ogun Guangdong Free Trade Zone (OFTFZ) 179
Ogun State 179–183
Ogun State, Nigeria 34
One China, policy 139
Ordinary Least Squares (OLS) 86
Organization for Economic Cooperation and Development (OECD) 6
Osinbajo, Yemi 167–175
outcome variables 84
Oyo State 32–33
Oyo State, Nigeria 160

participatory democracy 164
People's Movement for the Liberation of Angola 195–196
People's Democratic Party (PDP) 139
People's Movement for the Liberation of Angola (MPLA) 141
perception, importance of 36–38
Pitcher, Anne 142–143, 150
policy attributes 97–99
policy uncertainty 99
political stability and absence of violence and terrorism 42
population 42
poverty trap 1
price setters, governments acting as: future of economic/political development 190–195; future research areas 198–200; implications for other African recipients 195–198; main findings 186–188; policy implications 188–190
price takers 8
property rights 98–99
Prosperity Party 195
Public Private Partnership (PPP) 176
Putnam, Robert D 75

Ramamurti, Ravi 26n8, 151–152
Ramaphosa, Cyril 172
Rapid Deployment Joint Task Force 152
Reagan, Ronald 152
research design 20–22
resource-seeking motivations 43
Riker, W. 161
Rodrik, Dani 13, 191
Roessler, Philip 81
Romer, Paul 28
rule of law 42
Rwanda 197

Sachs, Jeffrey 12–13, 27, 157
Seko, Mobutu Sese 195
Senegal 196
Seychelles 8
Singapore Economic Development Board 161
socialism 144–145
Solow model 28
Soskice, David 9
South Africa 6; actual/perceived bargaining power 125–132; authoritarian/one-party dominant systems *versus* competitive democracies 138–139; background characteristics 122–123; central government-sub-regional unit communication 174–178; and centralization 162; governments acting as price setters 186–200; historical relationships to West 152–158; historical relationships with China 139–141; information-sharing incentives 160–185; inter-ministerial competition 167–174; long-term learning about bargaining power/policy options 143–151; Medium Perceived Bargaining Power in 128–129; outward-focused strategies 142–143
South African Native National Congress (SANNC) 138
Soviet Union 152
Special Economic Zones Advisory Board 176–177

spheres, permeation of 156–158
Standard Gauge Railway 141
State General Reserve Fund, Oman 136
state-owned enterprises (SOEs) 7; determining BATNA of private Chinese investors 33
Stiansen, Øyvind 76
Strong Perceived Bargaining Power 129–132
Studwell, Joe 157
sub-regional unit-central government communication 174–178
sub-Saharan Africa 7
Sustainable Development and Poverty Reduction Program 143
Swedlund, Haley 198

Tanganyika African National Union (TANU) 138
Tanzania 3; actual/perceived bargaining power 125–132; authoritarian/ one-party dominant systems *versus* competitive democracies 138–139; background characteristics 122–123; central government-sub-regional unit communication 174–178; Chinese investment stocks 4; governments acting as price setters 186–200; historical relationships to West 152–158; historical relationships with China 139–141; information-sharing incentives 160–185; inter-ministerial competition 167–174; long-term learning about bargaining power/policy options 143–151; long-term learning in 136–138; outward-focused strategies 142–143; Strong Perceived Bargaining Power in 129–132; U.S. investment stocks in 4
Tanzania Investment Centre 170–171

Tanzansino United Pharmaceuticals (T) Ltd 145–146
TAZARA Railway 140
Tecno 34–35
Tshisekedi, Félix 195
Tukur, Bamanga 141
Two Chinas, policy 140

Uganda 148, 197
UNCTAD 155

Weak Bargaining Power Narrative 5, 13–14, 30, 75, 78–79, 151, 182; in Kenya 126–128; in Nigeria 126–128
weak economics 15–18
Weinhardt, Clara 75
West Africa 196–197
West, historical relationships to 151–152; perceptions of bargaining power and deal flexibility 155–156; permeation of Western spheres 156–158; promise of investments in 1990s 153–154; since independence 152–153
Western Cape 172
Wolfe, Rebecca 75
woredas (districts) 163
World Bank 12, 37, 153

Xiaoping, Deng 157

Yar'Adua 139
Yerima, Ahmad Sani 165

Zambia 196
Zhu, Shengjun 7, 161
Zimbabwe 196; Chinese investment stocks in 3; U.S. investment stocks in 3
Zimbabwe African National Union (ZANU) 196
Zuma, Jacob 172

Taylor & Francis eBooks

www.taylorfrancis.com

A single destination for eBooks from Taylor & Francis with increased functionality and an improved user experience to meet the needs of our customers.

90,000+ eBooks of award-winning academic content in Humanities, Social Science, Science, Technology, Engineering, and Medical written by a global network of editors and authors.

TAYLOR & FRANCIS EBOOKS OFFERS:

A streamlined experience for our library customers

A single point of discovery for all of our eBook content

Improved search and discovery of content at both book and chapter level

REQUEST A FREE TRIAL
support@taylorfrancis.com

Routledge
Taylor & Francis Group

CRC Press
Taylor & Francis Group

9781032312507